Preaching the Atonement

Preaching the Atonement

PETER K. STEVENSON
AND
STEPHEN I. WRIGHT

t&t clark

T&T Clark International
A Continuum imprint

The Tower Building, 11 York Road, London SE1 7NX
15 East 26th Street, New York, NY 10010

British Library Cataloguing-in-Publication Data
A catalogue record for this book is available from the British Library.

ISBN 0 567 08989 4 (Hardback)
ISBN 0 567 08999 1 (Paperback)

Library of Congress Cataloging-in-Publication Data
Stevenson, Peter K.
    Preaching the atonement / by Peter K. Stevenson and Stephen I. Wright.
        p. cm.
    Includes bibliographical references and index.
    ISBN 0-567-08989-4 – ISBN 0-567-08999-1 (pbk.)
        1. Atonement–Sermons. I. Wright, Stephen I. II. Title.

BT268.S74 2005
232'.–dc22

                                                    2005048559

Typeset by Free Range Book Design & Production Ltd
Printed and bound in Great Britain by MPG Books Ltd, Cornwall

Contents

Preface

The idea for this book emerged from our shared experience teaching homiletics at Spurgeon's College, London. Both of us are ordained ministers who preach regularly (Peter a Baptist, Stephen an Anglican). We have each come to homiletics via another theological discipline (Peter systematic theology, Stephen New Testament studies). We felt it could be creative and helpful to bring these various areas of experience together in an exploration of preaching the central Christian doctrine of atonement.

Peter has taken overall responsibility for Chapters 2, 4, 6, 9 and 10; Stephen for Chapters 1, 3, 5, 7 and 8. We are glad to have four 'guest preachers' contributing sermons in Chapters 1, 3, 7 and 8. It was not originally planned that these would all come in Stephen's chapters, but Stephen has partly made up for having contributed only one sermon himself by writing the commentaries for Peter's sermons in Chapters 6 and 9 in addition to those in his 'own' chapters.

We have not attempted a rigid consistency of format or approach. In particular, it seemed best in some chapters to write a commentary on the sermon that was interwoven with the sermon itself, allowing attention to be drawn to features of specific sections, but in other chapters to present the sermon as a whole before the commentary, highlighting its overall flow.

We are glad to put our joint signature to the whole.

Peter Stevenson
Stephen Wright

Acknowledgements
and Abbreviations

The authors acknowledge with gratitude the stimulus and insight they have received through discussion with colleagues and students at Spurgeon's College and within the College of Preachers; as well as through the experience of 'preaching atonement' and conversing with congregations in various settings. They are particularly grateful to the colleagues from the UK, Canada and the USA who have contributed sermons for Chapters 1, 3, 7 and 8: David Southall, Kent Anderson, Kathy Grieb and David Schlafer.

'Love the Wild Swan', copyright © 1935 and renewed 1963 by Donnan Jeffers and Garth Jeffers, from *Selected Poetry of Robinson Jeffers* by Robinson Jeffers. Used with permission of Random House, Inc.

Extracts from Afua Kuma, *Jesus of the Deep Forest: Prayers and Praises of Afua Kuma*, copyright © 1981, reproduced with permission of Asempa Publishers, Christian Council of Ghana, Box GP 919, Accra.

Extract from *Hard Work* by Polly Toynbee. Copyright © 2003 Polly Toynbee. Reproduced by permission of the author c/o Rogers, Coleridge & White Ltd, 20 Powis Mews, London W11 1JN.

Abbreviations

BDAG	Walter Bauer, William F. Arndt, F. William Gingrich and Frederick W. Danker, *A Greek–English Lexicon of the New Testament and Other Early Christian Literature* (Chicago: University of Chicago Press, 3rd edn, 2000)
BNTC	Black's New Testament Commentaries

Int	*Interpretation: A Journal of Bible and Theology*
JSNT	*Journal for the Study of the New Testament*
LCC	Library of Christian Classics
LXX	Henry Barclay Swete (ed.), *The Old Testament in Greek according to the Septuagint* (3 vols.; Cambridge: Cambridge University Press, 1887, 1891, 1894)
NIBC	The New International Bible Commentary
NICNT	The New International Commentary on the New Testament
NIV	New International Version
NRSV	New Revised Standard Version
RSV	Revised Standard Version
WBC	Word Biblical Commentary

Introduction

This book explores a variety of ways in which the Christian doctrine of the atonement, God's act of making humanity one with himself in Christ, may be presented in preaching today. It issues from three basic convictions.

First, *Scripture remains the primary source and resource for preaching*. Each chapter in this book is based on a passage of Scripture which points, directly or indirectly, to the truth of the atonement. Both Testaments provide us with a range of stories and images that represent the truth, in partial but complementary ways.

Attention in theology and homiletics has increasingly focused on the *form* in which the biblical revelation comes to us. This, by and large, is a *narrative* form, and that fact has considerable implications for preaching. Briefly stated, it means that to treat Scripture as if it were a systematic handbook of doctrine is to mistreat it. This is not only the case with the obviously 'narrative' books such as the Gospels. It is becoming more apparent that even those parts of the Bible traditionally thought of as summaries of particular doctrines, notably the Pauline epistles, depend on a rich narrative substructure and indeed possess some of the overt characteristics of narrative too. To preach the atonement in a scriptural way – like preaching any other aspect of Christian truth – entails telling a story.

More basic even than narrative form is the evident reality that biblical truth comes to us in words which carry metaphorical as well as literal freight. If all our language is bound, in some way, to be metaphorical, nowhere is this more true than in our language about God. That is why to insist on the 'literal truth' of Scripture can be a contradiction in terms, if much of its truth is mediated to us through metaphor. A metaphor may be a single image – such as the familiar terms related to the atonement, 'redemption', 'justification' and so on – or it may be an entire narrative: a story such as the testing of Abraham in Genesis 22 is metaphorical when it is taken, as it frequently has been, as pointing somehow to the sacrifice of Christ. Thus special attention is paid in the following chapters to the metaphorical resonance of texts, both within their own historical and literary contexts and within Scripture as a whole.

Second, *preaching takes place as a part of the ongoing dialogue between Christian tradition and Scripture.* We are deluding ourselves if we think that we can read Scripture without the mediation of centuries of interpretation. This fact does not preclude fresh insights into biblical truth arising in each generation. But it does call for gratitude for the real insights of the past, honesty about the spectacles which we ourselves are wearing, and a readiness to submit the particular stream of Christian tradition in which we ourselves stand to scrutiny. If we believe in the providence of God, then we must not only see Scripture as his gift for the Church in every age, but also see the potential of every age to achieve faithful and fruitful interpretations of it.

The atonement in fact provides an especially clear case both of the need for the Church's interpretative role in respect of Scripture, and of the influence of particular traditions on the way that Scripture is read. From earliest times the narratives and metaphors of Scripture were reflected upon and wrestled with in an attempt to grasp the enormity of what had happened in Christ. Different models appealed to different groups and eras.[1] Each model in different ways naturally, and inevitably, reflected not only the content of Scripture but also the factors in the culture of the interpreters concerned that made a particular way of expressing the doctrine comprehensible and potentially insightful for their time.

Those who (like the present authors) stand broadly in the Reformation tradition, which has exalted both Scripture and the doctrine of the atonement, need particularly to be aware of how that particular tradition has shaped our understanding of this doctrine. For instance, there has been lively debate in recent years about the extent to which the notion of 'imputed righteousness' really owes as much to Luther as it does to Paul. Whatever tradition we stand in, there is a perpetual temptation to equate 'our' way of seeing a particular doctrine with 'the biblical' way. Hence the necessity of listening to biblical scholarship (which may or may not be shaped by any particular Christian tradition) as a constant check on interpretations which may be ultimately misleading and prohibitive of fresh insight.

Thus we shall refer in these chapters to various formulations of the doctrine of the atonement, but not in order to offer any definitive adjudication or ranking between them. Rather, we want to bring these expressions of doctrine into creative tension with the Scriptural texts which originally gave rise to them, so that Scripture may be allowed to speak with a fresh voice and that what is of lasting usefulness in that particular understanding of the atonement may emerge.

Third, *preaching is a communicative act which is rightly addressed to a specific congregation against a specific cultural backcloth.* This does not imply that the core content of a sermon should never under any circumstances be repeated, or that 'cultural backcloths' are monochrome. It is, rather, a way of stressing the 'occasional' nature of the sermon.

Preaching represents living theology. Drawing on Scripture and the tradition of its interpretation, we seek to bring 'the grace and truth of Christ to this generation'.[2] That suggests that we use language, including narratives and metaphors, which is fresh and appropriate to our hearers, as well as faithful to the gospel. This freshness is more than a matter of finding suitable up-to-date 'illustrations' of 'timeless truths'. It means discerning the contemporary applicability of particular doctrines, seeing the points at which *these* people at *this* time especially need to hear the message of (say) the atonement, and embodying that message in words which truly touch those points.

Not only the language, but also the structure of preaching is 'occasional'. The *form* of the sermon has been a major theme in recent homiletics, and a variety of forms of preaching is represented in this book. The significance of this is that the ways in which the atonement may be preached are in principle as numerous as those who preach it, multiplied by the occasions on which it is preached. The existence of revealed truth should not lead us to think that narrow limits are set on the ways in which it is set forth. Indeed, the awesome nature of the subject matter should call forth all the imaginative capacities of the preacher, and inspire us to shape its presentation in such a way that the particular congregation will be able to receive it.

This means, of course, that guidance on preaching from beyond the immediate situation can only take the preacher thus far, and no further: the really crucial moments in the forging and delivery of sermons, those moments in which something living comes to birth, happen always and only in the specific context of the occasion itself and preparation for it. It means, too, that printed sermons in books can only ever be pointers beyond themselves, saying 'this is how it was done once, or might be done – but you will have to do it a fresh way yourself'. The example may inspire; it enters, indeed, into the Christian tradition with which, as we have seen, each preacher is called to wrestle. But a printed sermon cannot dictate others' preaching, still less substitute for it. We hope, at least, it will be clear in the sermons presented towards the end of each chapter with the comments upon them that they constitute genuine attempts to relate atonement teaching to the twenty-first century, in a range of settings that are quite diverse both ecclesiastically and socially.

The occasional character of preaching should be stressed in another way too. Every sermon is incomplete, an act of partial interpretation of Scripture and tradition cut off at an essentially arbitrary point (the moment of delivery), constrained and hemmed in by countless human contingencies: not least the background of the preacher, their state of mind, the extent and limitation of their reading, their spiritual integrity, their knowledge of the congregation whom they address. It is with such raw material that, marvellously, God works. But it is vital to disabuse ourselves of any notion that preaching is simply about the offloading of complete, neatly packaged exegeses of texts, or 'correct' formulations of doctrine. The biblical commentaries and handbooks of doctrine which are precious resources for us as preachers should themselves remind us, constantly, of the vastness of the subject-matter with which we deal, the huge areas of uncertainty surrounding the historical contingencies of revelation, and the ludicrousness of any idea that we could adequately *comprehend* the truth it is nonetheless our business to proclaim.

For the one who preaches the atonement, this means that each time we do it we shall be taking soundings in different parts of the doctrine, and finding fresh ways to bring it home to our hearers. We shall be sharing our discoveries with them, not pontificating from on high. The implications for the contents of this book are that we make no claim or attempt to provide a complete, 'state-of-the-art' summary of scholarship concerning the relevant texts or the relevant doctrines. It is not our aim to replicate the plentiful commentaries on the biblical books concerned or the considerable literature on the atonement, still less to trump them with another offering claiming to be the last word. We wish, rather, to explore ways in which Scripture, doctrine and particular preaching occasions may be fused to yield fertile and faithful interpretations of the atonement today. We hope that through the following discussions of individual texts and doctrinal formulations, the printed sermons and comments upon them, readers may be encouraged to lay this book aside and preach the atonement themselves with renewed commitment and joy.

1

The cost of a father's commitment: Genesis 22.1–19

1. The story

The disturbing story of God's test of Abraham, known in Jewish tradition as the *Akedah*,[1] prompts reflection on a wide range of themes, not all immediately connected with that of atonement: for instance the nature of God's 'testing' of human beings, the meaning of faith, and ancient (or modern) attitudes to child sacrifice. Yet with its motifs of costly offering, obedience and the father-son relationship, it has resonated especially deeply with Christians through the ages as they have meditated on the meaning of the Cross.[2] Following the example of great interpreters such as Augustine, however, before we turn to this 'spiritual' or 'sacramental' import of the story, we will trace the contours of its 'plain' or surface meaning.[3]

The narrator tells us the inner meaning of the event at the outset: God is testing Abraham (v. 1). There is therefore a similarity with the story of Job (though in Job the word 'test' is not used).[4] Another difference from Job's story is that there is no 'Satan' here in Genesis. Job 1 and 2 probably reflect a later worldview in which there was greater reluctance to ascribe 'testing' or evil occurrences to God. The problem a modern reader has with Genesis 22 derives precisely from the strong conviction, evident through most of the Old Testament, that God's sovereignty implies his direct responsibility for all that happens;[5] the story is one of the sharpest and (for us) most uncomfortable evidences of this conviction.

Thus God, starkly and without intermediary, tests Abraham by telling him to go and offer his son as a burnt offering. Abraham is offered no reason (like Job, he is not privy to the information possessed by the reader about the test). God allows himself no alibi, no disguise. Indeed Abraham learns at the end that it is his simple obedience to the 'voice' of God which has won him the fresh assurance of God's

1

blessing on him, his descendants, and the nations through them (vv. 17, 18). It is a shame to flatten 'my voice' into 'me' as in the NIV translation of v. 18: the NIV reflects the fact that reference simply to the person (of God or of a human) is often represented in Hebrew by a locution involving a part of the body, but that should not imply that nothing is ever lost by removing the idiom in translation. In this case, 'my voice' reminds us of Abraham's extraordinary risk of faith. All he had to go on was a voice that had spoken to him in the past and that, he believed, was speaking to him again now. Similarly, it is simply the voice of the LORD's messenger (nothing is said of his appearance) which addresses him when he is about to kill Isaac (v. 11) and subsequently reiterates the promise (v. 16). It was this readiness to stake all on the call of a voice, in violation of universal ethical principle, which Søren Kierkegaard saw as the very epitome of the difficulty and paradox of faith.[6]

The special pathos of the story lies, of course, in the fact that the son Abraham was being asked to sacrifice was the long-awaited son whom God had promised (Gen. 17.19), through whom God's pledges of blessing would be fulfilled. The pathos is felt with mounting intensity as the story proceeds.[7] The motif of the journey allows us to feel the anticipation of the dread event, though nothing is said explicitly about Abraham's psychological state. This sickening anticipation is heightened when the point comes for the servants to be left behind with the donkey and Abraham and Isaac to go on alone (v. 5).

This final stage of the journey is recounted with methodical slowness. Nothing is said of the thoughts of either father or son, but when Isaac speaks up in v. 7 it seems natural to assume that he is breaking a long silence. He says 'Father' and waits for Abraham's reply before asking the question which the reader has known all along is inevitable: 'The fire and wood are here, but where is the lamb for the burnt offering?' (v. 7). Abraham's laconic, tortured answer reveals a faith that is not shaken, and simultaneously a dread of telling the whole truth: 'God himself will provide the lamb for the burnt offering, my son' (v. 8).[8]

The suspense continues to the very end. Even when they reach the place for the sacrifice, the narrator gets us to watch Abraham building the altar, arranging the wood, binding Isaac and laying him on the wood before we come to the terrible moment where he reaches out his hand and takes the knife to kill him (vv. 9, 10). At this last moment the LORD's angel calls out from heaven to prevent the sacrifice from taking place (vv. 11, 12).

Verses 13 and 14 are interesting from the point of view of the mindset they reveal in the narrator and in Abraham. The response to this wonderful reprieve is not to sing, dance and set off for home. A profound sense remains that a sacrifice must still be offered. The ram in the thicket is seen as God's provision for this purpose. After the angel's reassurance to Abraham of God's purpose for him and his descendants, the story ends in the same terse manner in which it has proceeded, laden with unexpressed emotion: 'Then Abraham returned to his servants, and they set off together for Beersheba' (v. 19). What might possibly have been said by father, son and servants? Can we even begin to imagine it? But even as we ask the question, we are confronted with the almost brutal restraint of human emotion that the narrator seeks to impose upon the reader: the sense that however profound and full of pathos the human feeling involved, the real issue at stake here is infinitely deeper and more majestic.[9]

The story raises the fundamental question: what kind of God is this who puts a person through such a test? Can the fact that, apparently, he never intended Abraham to sacrifice Isaac, but led him through this torment as a 'test', really exonerate him from the charge of inflicting profound emotional damage on his two protégés?[10]

From a Christian perspective, it is natural to ask if the God of whom this passage in its 'plain sense' speaks can be reconciled at all with the God who was to be revealed as the Father of Jesus Christ, and if there is therefore not an intolerable disjunction between the 'plain sense' and a 'spiritual' interpretation of the story as somehow referring to the atonement. A God who directly commands a man, already the object of his favour, to sacrifice his beloved son, only to relent at the last moment because the test of obedience has been passed, may seem shockingly capricious and cruel. By contrast, the New Testament picture of God's action is not of incomprehensible commands to be met by blind obedience, but of Father and Son working together in close intimacy and mutual knowledge (Jn 5.19–20), and of the Son sharing all this with his friends (Jn 15.15). Is this not, in other words, a classic case of 'progressive revelation', in which the experience of God recounted in Genesis 22 is of a very limited and partial kind by comparison with the experience of God recounted in the New Testament? On the other side of this argument, it has been pointed out that the climax of the story shows conclusively that God does *not* require child sacrifice; indeed, the story has sometimes been read precisely as a polemic against the practice. Yet this does not deal with the apparently perverse cruelty of the test itself. Why should Abraham be put through this in order to learn this lesson, and bequeath it to future generations? And is the consequence of this perversity that Genesis 22 should be consigned to the archives, rather than used to preach any gospel of atonement?

We must let this looming question stay in the background for the moment, while we move on to consider in more detail a New Testament perspective on the narrative.

2. Genesis 22 in New Testament perspective

Comparatively little use is made of Genesis 22 in the New Testament. Abraham is clearly an important figure in Paul's thinking, but in the key passages (Rom. 4.1–25; Gal. 3.6–18) it is God's promises and Abraham's faith (as the background for the Christian gospel and faith) that are the issue, not the meaning of the near-sacrifice. The incident in Genesis 22 is not even used, explicitly, to illustrate the strength of Abraham's faith in Rom. 4.16–25. We may certainly see an echo of Genesis 22 in Paul's words about Abraham believing in 'the God who gives life to the dead' (v. 17), but it is Abraham's faith that he would have a child at all, despite his and Sarah's age, which Paul uses for his explicit example (vv. 18–21). Heb. 11.17–19. sees Abraham's action as an example of faith in God's power to raise the dead.[11] Jas 2.21 cites Genesis 22 to illustrate the need for faith to be expressed in works.

The one place where the New Testament appears to draw a clear link between Genesis 22 and the atonement is Rom. 8.32: 'He who did not spare his own Son, but delivered him up for us all, how shall he not also with him freely give us all things?' Douglas A. Campbell has recently mounted a strong argument, on the basis of this verse, for seeing the story of Abraham's near-sacrifice of Isaac as the key narrative underlying the whole 'story' Paul tells in Romans 8 of God's sending and giving of his Son.[12] But while it is plausible to see a direct allusion here – not only because of the Father-Son motif, but also because of the use of the same verb 'spare' in both Rom. 8.32 and the LXX of Gen. 22.12[13] – this does not take us very far in trying to answer the question of how to use *the story itself* to speak of the atonement, for Paul's allusion (in Campbell's persuasive account) entails a radical re-reading of the story, transferring Abraham's readiness to give up his son to God himself.[14] This raises the fundamental issue of how far Christian preaching should be dependent on the sometimes radically revisionist readings of the Old Testament in the New Testament. To anticipate my main argument, I suggest that while we will clearly wish to respect such New Testament usages as canonical Scripture, we should not take them as exhausting – or being intended to exhaust – the allusive potential of the Old Testament narratives.

Furthermore, Paul's allusion to Genesis 22 in this verse may be seen as *heightening* the theological difficulty of the original narrative: instead of overcoming its moral ambiguities, it raises them to a new plane of seriousness. Whereas Abraham *did* spare his son, in the end – by the express will of God – God '*did not spare*' his. As Anthony Clarke has recently pointed out, Rom. 8.32 is one of a number of key New Testament texts in which direct responsibility for the death of Jesus is ascribed to God.[15] For a contemporary reader this prompts the question whether the gospel entails the announcement of a God who is violent – violent, moreover, in a way from which our culture recoils in peculiar horror: the torture and killing of one's own child.[16] Clarke suggests helpfully that the way through this difficulty is to note that this language of divine responsibility in no way diminishes, for the New Testament, human responsibility (including that of Jesus himself) for the death of Jesus. The point is focused in the observation that the verb παραδίδωμι, 'give up', 'hand over', used with God as subject in Rom. 8.32, is used of Jesus' own self-giving in Gal. 2.20 and Eph. 5.2, 25 (suggesting that Jesus was no mere *victim*, but a willing agent) and frequently in the gospels for the 'handing-over' of Jesus by the Jewish authorities, Pilate and especially Judas Iscariot (suggesting that insofar as he *is* a victim, he is a victim of human beings).[17] But as soon as we return from these texts to Genesis 22, our difficulty returns, for what is highlighted here is precisely the emphasis of Rom. 8.32: *God* was behind the plan to sacrifice Isaac; Isaac does indeed appear as a victim, remaining utterly submissive throughout the narrative, but nowhere expressly joining his own will to the project; and the human being whose victim he is appears not in the guise of the 'wicked men' who conspired to do away with Jesus (Acts 2.23), but that of his own loving father obeying the voice of his God.

Thus far, therefore, it might appear safer simply to let Genesis 22 stand behind Rom. 8.32 as the story from which Paul quarried his language, rather than to use the story itself as a vehicle for preaching the truth of the atonement. Paul's words could then be set in the context of the other New Testament usages of παραδίδωμι with the aim of giving a balanced picture of the divine and human agencies involved in the death of Jesus.

Moreover, we should underline the point that Genesis 22 in its plain sense does not directly concern the estrangement of the human race from God and his remedy for it. Certainly it reinforces the sense that God takes the initiative in dealing with human beings; and in the restatement of God's promise it points to his great plan for humanity. But the heart of Christian atonement teaching, in which God and humanity are reconciled through the removal of a barrier or the overcoming of an enemy, is not present here. Notwithstanding later Jewish interpretations,[18] it is nowhere stated that the anticipated sacrifice of Isaac, or the actual sacrifice of the ram, is a sacrifice of atonement. Indeed the meaning of the sacrifices is not stated at all. They appear to be seen as simple responses to God of obedience and worship.

This means that any 'atonement' meaning must be found via a symbolic, metaphorical or allegorical reading of some kind. But another obstacle in our way here is precisely that the story cannot be neatly turned into an allegory of salvation. Paul's apparent use in Rom. 8.32 of Abraham's readiness to sacrifice Isaac as a picture of God the Father's readiness to 'sacrifice' God the Son – entailing, of course, the potent contrast between the readiness in the first case and the actual deed in the second – screens out the fact that God himself is a key player in the story of Genesis 22, as well as Abraham. The story simply does not fit into a tidy trinitarian or soteriological shape.[19] We may see this clearly by asking 'where is Jesus?' in the story. We might find *traces* of Jesus in several places. We can see something of him in Abraham, in his faithful obedience to God's call and his readiness to make the most painful and paradoxical of sacrifices. We can see something of him in Isaac, in his obedient accompaniment of his father and his becoming at the end a helpless victim. And we can, of course, see something of him in the ram provided by God for the offering. If we wish, we can see traces of him in all three figures simultaneously. But what we cannot do is read off the story a clear pattern in which Jesus as Son is related to God as Father, or fulfils the Father's purpose of atonement as Christian teaching proclaims it.

These are weighty considerations. They should give us pause before using this chapter in preaching,[20] and they act as boundary markers, reminding us of danger zones beyond. Yet despite all this, I believe that the Christian instinct to connect this story with the atonement has been profoundly authentic. For undoubtedly, there are powerful *resonances* between the *Akedah* and the story of Christ. It is these resonances that we will explore now, and it is the mode of 'resonance' which, I believe, gives us the clue to a fitting way of preaching the atonement from this chapter.

3. The power of resonance

To speak of 'resonance' or 'echo' in the study of literature is to speak of the way in which one text may evoke another. Without explicit quotation – maybe even without direct verbal parallels – themes, phrases, moods can suddenly or gradually strike a reader or hearer as uncannily similar, in a way that can set off potent lines of interpretation.[21] The power of such connections often lies precisely in their obliqueness and understated quality. Further, such echoes may heighten a sense of contrast between texts or stories, as much as a sense of similarity. The study of 'intertextuality' may be extremely fruitful for Christians wrestling with the issue of the Old Testament's relationship to the New.

It is neither wise nor profitable to build great edifices of doctrine upon resonances or to make strong claims that the connections were 'intended' by human authors. Thus in drawing attention to resonances between Genesis 22 and the New Testament I am not claiming that the author(s) of Genesis had extraordinary insight, or that the New Testament authors were fully aware of these resonances. I am simply suggesting that within this diverse body of literature that we call Scripture there are links between different parts which can be pursued for our insight and instruction, which may be channels of God's revelation and give depth to our preaching. Here I will trace four points at which this small story of Abraham and Isaac seems to evoke and foreshadow, in a haunting fashion, the larger story of Christ which looms above and ahead.

a. The obedience of Abraham and Jesus

First, the implicit obedience of Abraham to the command of God, even though what was asked must have seemed up to that point utterly unthinkable, resonates deeply with the implicit obedience of Jesus, even though he understandably shrank from what was asked of *him*.[22] The accounts of his temptation in the wilderness (Mt. 4.1–11; Lk. 4.1–13) and his prayer in the garden of Gethsemane (Mt. 26.36–46; Mk 14.32–42; Lk. 22.39–46) reveal his intense struggle. The writer of Genesis shows us almost nothing of the inner struggles of Abraham, but that is a matter of his restrained style of writing: it does not mean that he is insensitive (or means his readers to be insensitive) to the terrible turmoil that a command like that of 22.2 must have caused. In the case of both Abraham and Jesus, it is a matter on the one hand of the anticipation of excruciating pain – emotional with the former, emotional and physical with the latter – but on the other hand (surely) of the sheer darkness of perplexity as to why it has to be.

Linking this resonance with the doctrine of the incarnation, we may suggest that, in Jesus, God experienced for himself the utter horror of Abraham's calling in Genesis 22. How are we to expand this in a way that is faithful to classic atonement teaching yet also illuminates it freshly? One might say that God's experience in Jesus is his final and only answer to the torment of those perverse inner compulsions for which humanity has no other explanation but him. One might say, in other words, that this Old Testament story offers the profound problem to which the story of Jesus offers the profound solution: and that for us the Old Testament story is necessary to highlight the nature of the New Testament one. The charge that this implies a historical change in the character of God might be answered by saying that in Jesus, what human beings have experienced as a tension in the very being of God, between fatherly love and dangerous mystery, comes to historical resolution.[23] The sting of the danger is drawn even as the cost of the love is revealed. Having seen God (as it were) put himself through Abraham's test, we have no more reason to doubt his love.

b. The unity of father and son

Second, the closeness of Abraham and Isaac in the story has awakened in Christian readers, from the New Testament writers onwards, the thought of the closeness of Father and Son in the life and mission of God the Holy Trinity. Isaac is Abraham's only son, whom he loves (Gen. 22.2). Jesus is revealed by God at his baptism and transfiguration as 'my son, whom I love' (Mt. 3.17; 17.5 and parallels[24]). He is described in John as 'God the only Son' (1.18) whom the Father loves (5.20). The Johannine picture of Father and Son acting in concert (e.g. 5.17) can be seen as imaged in the repeated portrayal of Abraham and Isaac 'going on together' (Gen. 22.6, 8). In addition, the departure of Abraham and Isaac from the servants while they go to 'worship' (Gen. 22.5) foreshadows the moment in Gethsemane when Jesus goes 'a little farther' than his disciples to pray (Mt. 26.39; Mk 14.35; Lk. 22.41). In those moments of prayer, Jesus calls on the Father, and Luke makes it especially clear that the Father has not departed from him (22.43). The Father and the Son are going together into the heart of darkness. Isaac carries the wood (Gen. 22.6) as Jesus was to do, according to John (19.17), though the

Synoptics describe that burden being borne by Simon of Cyrene (Mt. 27.32; Mk 15.21; Lk. 23.26).

This picture of the close harmony between father and son may help us set the context for Abraham's readiness to 'give' Isaac, and prevents a Christian reading of the story from driving a crude wedge between Father and Son. Here we return to Rom. 8.32, which describes God as not 'sparing' his own Son, but 'giving him up' for us all. Colin Gunton suggests that it is a serious mistake to see such a verse as implying (crudely) a God who indulges in a kind of divine child sacrifice (as if the nightmare the reader fears from the start of Genesis 22 has come true after all!) – whether this idea is (perhaps unwittingly) something advocated, or implied by hymnody, or something recoiled at. This would tear a hole in the New Testament's implicit Trinitarianism. It is precisely through the willing *self-offering of Jesus* that the New Testament sees the *'gift' of God* clearly being given.[25] It is this self-offering, fully expounded in Hebrews, which is evident in the life of Jesus, not least as told by John: Jesus lays down his life of his own accord (Jn 10.18). But, as Gunton points out,[26] this human gift is interpreted as being simultaneously the gift of God: 'God so loved the world, that he gave his only son' (Jn 3.16). Gunton further makes the vital point that this double gift turns the Old Testament notion of sacrifice on its head. *God* is now the one who sacrifices, not Israel or her priests. So, returning to Genesis 22, we may say that Abraham and Isaac *together* truly foreshadow the readiness of God, Father and incarnate Son, to give himself up.[27]

c. The ram and the lamb

Third, however, we note the further richness (and complication!) of resonance that enters in when we consider the ram provided by God in the place of Isaac. For here we face the *contrast* between Abraham and Isaac on the one hand, and the action of God in Christ on the other. Abraham and Isaac were both spared, and the ram was provided to take Isaac's place. The *parallelism* now shifts from 'Isaac ~ Christ' to 'ram ~ Christ'. By the same token, Isaac can be seen as representative of the humanity now spared because of the intervention and provision of God.

Irresistibly, it seems, Christians from New Testament times onwards have seen in this image of the ram mercifully provided by God a picture of his ultimate act of merciful provision in Christ. God, through the ram, averts a terrible fate for Isaac (and Abraham): God,

through Christ, averts a terrible fate for humanity and the world, and
so for us there is endless pathos in the promise of Abraham to Isaac:
'God himself will provide the lamb for the burnt offering, my son'
(Gen. 22.8). Here indeed is a graphic picture of substitution, which
evokes for us John the Baptist's words: 'Behold, the lamb of God, who
takes away the sin of the world' (Jn 1.29).[28] We receive this lamb with
open arms as, we imagine, Abraham did the ram in the thicket.

The substitution of the ram for Isaac in Genesis is not in any
way *penal* substitution. There is nothing in the text to suggest that
the sacrifice of Isaac was initially required as a punishment for his
(or Abraham's) misdeeds – or that an animal could in any way be
'punished' instead. Sacrifices were offered for a variety of purposes
in antiquity generally, including within Yahwistic religion.[29] No clear
indication of how the sacrifice of Isaac was to be conceived is offered
to us; we learn only that Abraham intended to go and 'worship' (Gen.
22.5). This is a substitution which simply functions as sheer relief to
Abraham, Isaac and the reader. It is not even as if we feel the magna-
nimity of God here: we are just glad that God 'did not want that after
all'. We are relieved that 'there was another way'.

To glimpse Christ in this ram, and the ram in Christ, is to sense this
relief in a profound and cosmic way. The upshot of the story is indeed
that God did *not* require human sacrifice. The New Testament takes
this further, showing that he does not now require animal sacrifice
either. But relief is succeeded by bracing challenge. These kinds of
sacrifice are replaced by a greater. The ultimate cost of this cosmic
relief was infinitely more than the blood of a single ram. It was the
conscious, obedient self-offering of God's Son (Heb. 10.5–7). And that
unique sacrifice sets in train the true human sacrifice which transcends
all ritual (Rom. 12.1). God came most painfully to sacrifice *himself*
for his people, and the upshot is that they themselves are caught up
into his cosmic purposes, the vanguard of his legions in the ultimate
battle.[30]

d. The promised child as victim

The fourth intertextual echo worth listening to between Genesis 22
and the New Testament is the theme of the promised one becoming the
victim – apparently by the ordinance of God. Isaac, in the narrative
of Genesis, was not just any 'beloved son', but the child of promise,
the one through whom Abraham had been pledged a multitude of
descendants, through whom the nations would be blessed (Gen. 12.2,

3; 15.5). So Jesus, too, was heralded as the long-awaited deliverer. Just how early in his life this perception arose, and what precisely various individuals thought they meant by the titles they gave him, and how exactly he understood his own vocation, will no doubt remain matters of dispute among historians. For our purposes, however, it is sufficient to note that the central subject of the New Testament witness is a paradox. The New Testament does not simply say that God came to fulfil his promises; nor does it simply say that a charismatic figure died a shameful (though transformative) death. It says that *it was precisely through the death of the promised Messiah that the arrival of the time of fulfilment was confirmed.*[31]

Reading the Isaac story in the light of this paradox, we may start to be able to glimpse the strange purpose even in this apparently perverse 'test' of Abraham. If in God's ultimate plan even Jesus Christ, the supreme 'child of promise', must die, there is a sense in which all the lesser 'children of promise', before and after, must die too. Or rather, the heirs of the promises must 'die' to every temporary manifestation of the promises' fulfilment, in order that their hope and joy may rest in the ultimate gift, not in its temporary foreshadowings or reflections. And of course in Genesis 22 it is really Abraham, not Isaac, who is called to die: Abraham who is called to put an end to cherished dreams on a cruel altar.[32] That calling can only begin to make sense as a part of the grand narrative at whose climax God himself discovers what it is to die, as the awful prelude to realizing his glorious dream of cosmic atonement.

It should be apparent that no one perspective on this story can possibly do justice to the wealth of echoes that it awakens. There can be no single, all-encompassing Christian reading of the passage. Indeed this text illustrates, as well as any other, what Augustine called the *mira profunditas* or 'wondrous depth' of Scripture, which we can scarcely begin to fathom.

Christian preaching that is faithful to such a text will surely seek to awaken this sense of awe at mysterious truth, always beyond our reach yet visible in flashes, audible in echoes, which transform our understanding and move our hearts and wills. It will not pretend to have mastered a text which has perplexed scholars and theologians for centuries; nor will it shirk the hard questions it elicits from readers and hearers. The following sermon seems to fulfil these requirements.

Sermon[33]

Some time later God tested Abraham
And what a test: 'sacrifice your son, your only son'.
Take him to a mountain and bind him and sacrifice him.

Human sacrifice wasn't uncommon
Abraham had answered the call to obey god in the past
And now he realized that this god was just like all the other gods
For some reason needing human sacrifice
And so he took his son and set out on the fateful journey.

Can you imagine it?
Early the next morning, when he got up, the sinking feeling that he felt
Right in his guts, in the pit of his stomach
He was going to obey this god and kill his son

This is unthinkable to us
And to him, well he could hardly move with grief

As he saddled the donkey, he thought of the past
All the good times they had had
He had seen him grow from a baby
Heard his first words
Seen him walk
And grow and grow
This was part of him and today it was going to die

And think of his mother
How would she cope?
Hearing that her son had been sacrificed by her husband

Imagine him cutting the wood for the burnt offering
Each stroke of the axe bringing pain
This was his son who was going to die

And each step of the journey to the mountain
Did he think of turning back?
Did he think of throwing it all in and going his own way?
But he was constrained
Trapped in the will of god

Unable to depart from him
Even with this horrible thing hanging over him

And then, as his son spoke the words he had feared all along
It was too much for him
'Dad, where's the sacrifice?
We've got everything but not the lamb for the sacrifice
Fire. Wood. The knife but...'
I wonder if Isaac suspected
Even if he didn't the pain in Abraham's voice
The look on his face must have given it away
His words stuck in his throat
'God will provide it' he said.

I wonder, as Abraham arranged the wood, if Isaac was looking around for the sacrifice.
I wonder if Abraham was able to look into the face of his son as he tied him to the altar.
Could he look into his eyes?
As he reached for the knife
As he lifted it up in the air
As he paused, ready to strike...

Stop
You have passed the test
You fear God. You did not withhold your only son from me

One day God tested Abraham.
God did indeed provide
And because of it, all nations have been blessed
One day God tested Abraham.

One day God tested himself.
And what a test: 'sacrifice your Son, your only son'
Take him to the hill and bind him and sacrifice him.

Human sacrifice wasn't uncommon
The Romans were doing it all the time
Would he pass the test?
It seems a barbaric thing to ask
But committed to righteousness and justice
He took his son and set out on the fateful journey

Can you imagine it?
That last morning when he got up, the sinking feeling that he felt
Right in his guts, in the pit of his stomach
He was going to do this and kill his son

This is unthinkable to us
And to him, well the grief welled up in his mind
He watched it all from a high vantage point
As he appeared before Pilate and the chief priests
As he went from soldier to soldier
As he was struck and spat upon
Maybe he thought of all the things he had seen and planned

All the good times they had had
He had seen him grow from a baby
Heard his first words
Seen him walk
And grow in the wisdom and stature of God
This Jesus was part of him and today it was going to die

And think of his mother
How would she cope?
Hearing that her son had been sacrificed by his own Father

Imagine him
He had made the very tree
Created it from his own hands
He had seen it cut down
And fashioned into a rough cross
And all the time he thought about his son

And as he saw each step his son took
On the way to the hill
Did he think of calling it all off
Did he think of throwing it all in and letting these people go their own way

But he was constrained
Trapped by his own love
Unable to depart from his own plan.
He had sworn by himself
Right back in Abraham's day, that all people would be blessed
And now was the time to bless the nations

And he never broke a promise
Even with this horrible thing hanging over him

And then, as his son spoke the words he had feared all along
It was too much for him
'Dad, where's the sacrifice?
We've got everything but not the sacrifice
The cross and the nails but...'

We know that the son suspected
We know that the son knew all
But even then it stuck in the father's throat
'I will provide the sacrifice' he said

I wonder if the Father could look, as the crosses were laid on the ground, ready for their victims
I wonder if Abraham was able to look into the face of his son as he was nailed to this altar
Could he look into his eyes?
As the hammer blows rained down
As the cross was about to be lifted up into the air
As he paused,

Stop
BUT NO ONE WAS THERE TO SAY STOP
No one was there
And the cross was lifted up
And this son
And this father
Experienced the agony of separation
No one to say stop as they mocked him as he died
No one to say stop as they gave him wine vinegar
No one to say stop as those being crucified with him hurled insults at him
No one to say stop as he cried out
Oh and how those words rang in the father's ears
My God my God why have you forsaken me?
Why? Why?
What sort of God are you?
What sort of dad are you?
But there was no one to say stop
And he died

You have passed the test, God

You kept your promise.
You did not withhold your only son from me
You passed the test

One day God tested himself
He did what he had never asked anyone else to do
God did indeed provide the sacrifice
And because of it, all nations have been blessed

God loved the world so much that he gave his one and only son so that everyone who believes in him might not perish but have eternal life.

God, who did not spare his own son but gave him up for us all – how will he not also, along with him, graciously give us all things?

Commentary

In what respects does this sermon illustrate our preceding discussion?

First, we note the simple two-part structure: the story of Abraham and Isaac, then the story of Jesus. God tests Abraham: God tests himself. One story is 'laid alongside' the other, in a way suggestive of the idea of 'parable'.[34] This conjunction of stories stays close to the form of Scripture, which presents a variety of discrete narratives alongside each other, offering many possibilities for the reader to make mutual interconnections, but which often draws few explicit conclusions from those links. On a grand scale this is true of the conjunction of Old and New Testaments. The New Testament does of course make a number of explicit connections with its predecessor narrative, but these function as tokens or hints, pointers to the reader to make their own explorations – for which the possibilities are almost endless. This sermon takes the hint supplied by Paul in Rom. 8.32 and sensitively draws out some of the possibilities of intertextual echo between Genesis 22 and the story of Jesus' passion.

The structural device of simply following one story with another – with just enough echoes of the first in the second to spark the imagination, but not so many as to suggest that wooden point-by-point typologizing or allegorizing is being attempted – invites a profound mutual illumination between them and allows the hearer to ponder the mystery of the overarching narrative of God's purposes which holds the two together. For many hearers, this might well shed startling fresh light upon the meaning of the passion: not so that 'it all makes sense', or becomes easy, but on the contrary so that it is broken open from the safe tameness of 'standard' explanations in which it can easily become enclosed, and be glimpsed as the unfathomable cosmic drama it really is.[35]

Second, we note the focus of the intertextual echoes which are awakened here. It centres upon the second of the four broad possibilities outlined above, viz. the close relationship between father and son, augmented by aspects of the fourth, viz. the promised child becoming a victim – especially in relation to the cost paid by both fathers. The other possibilities lurk in the shadows – the obedience of Jesus, the substitution of the ram – but neither of these receives direct attention. It was surely a wise decision not to overload the sermon with these (or other) further dimensions. The preacher needs to tread a path between (on the one hand) opening up the wealth of Scripture's possibilities and (on the other hand) offering to the hearers a single clear trajectory for them to pursue on this one occasion. There is rich fare here for ongoing meditation, without any implication that this exhausts the story(-ies) or constitutes the final word upon them.

In focusing upon the father–son relationship, the preacher alludes to the language of Rom. 8.32, not shrinking from some shocking expressions (*He was going to do this and kill his son... And think of his mother / How would she cope? / Hearing that her son had been sacrificed by his own Father*). But he guards against the danger, outlined above, of isolating Paul's words in such a way as to drive a wedge between the persons of the Trinity. He succeeds in this fundamentally because, in the second story, the pain being communicated is clearly that of the Father as well as that of the Son; indeed even before it is that of the Son. In presenting the attitude of Jesus, the emphasis is very much on the traditions of his agony and despair (*What sort of God are you? / What sort of dad are you?*), rather than those of his humble obedience, but this is balanced by the vivid and moving expression of the essential unity between Father and Son (*This Jesus was part of him and today it was going to die*).

Third, see the way in which the preacher helps the hearer to enter into the emotion of both stories (and therefore the overarching story), without shirking the pain, yet without sentimentality. Scripture's restraint in *describing* emotion is not, as Erich Auerbach showed with respect to Genesis 22,[36] equivalent to a lack of interest in *suggesting* it. Indeed its very restraint makes the emotion more powerful, and this is surely as true for the passion narratives as for Genesis 22. The preacher stands between the text and contemporary hearers. Simply to replicate the text(s) in all respects would be to abjure the calling to preach: mere repetition is not our business. We are called, surely, to help people to enter into the moods of the various stories, and that means to draw out, without mawkishness, some of their suppressed and implied emotion. This entails an act of imaginative empathy both with the stories and with our hearers.

Thus the preacher speaks of 'the sinking feeling that he felt / Right in his guts, in the pit of his stomach'; the fathers' memories of 'All the good times they had had'; the mothers' feelings; the fathers' sense of being constrained and trapped; the appalling moments as the climax looms ('Could he look into his eyes?'); the utter bewilderment of the son (apparent more in the presentation of the second story, but clearly echoing back from it into that of the first). Note too the preacher's respect for the congregation in not seeking to impose emotion upon them or imply that his own reading is 'canonical', seen in the repeated phrase 'I wonder...'. In all of this, not just overt messages but a subliminal one are being conveyed: that the drama of atonement is played out not just on a distant and alien heavenly stage, but on earth, among men and women very like us. The human embrace of the sermon reflects – *contributes to!* – the atoning God's own embrace of humanity.

Thus like all productive sermons, and Scripture itself, this one suggests far more than can be captured in words, yet tells the gospel story with striking simplicity.

2

Taking away their iniquities: Leviticus 16.15–22

1. The holiness of God

Reading the Bible can be an uncomfortable experience for preachers. One of those painful passages occurs in Leviticus 10, where Nadab and Abihu offer 'unholy fire before the Lord', with the result that 'fire came out from the presence of the LORD and consumed them, and they died before the LORD' (Lev. 10.2). Reflecting on this situation leads Walter Kaiser to say that 'those who, by virtue of their office and ordination, are privileged constantly to approach God's presence are also exposed to danger when God is not honoured through their ministries'.[1]

The exact nature of Nadab and Abihu's sin is not entirely clear; but what their story takes for granted is the mysterious holiness of God. This God is not the cosy, cuddly God depicted in some contemporary worship songs, who is forever at our beck and call; but a holy God who deserves to be treated with care and respect, because 'our God is a consuming fire'.

The death of Aaron's sons in ch. 10 provides the backdrop for the opening verses of ch. 16 where God speaks to Moses, telling him to advise Aaron not to turn up in the tent of meeting at any old time. Rather than presuming upon God, he should observe the guidelines for purifying the sanctuary, and for taking away the sins and iniquities of the people.

In Lev. 16.11–14 Aaron is advised about various things he will need to do if he wants to remain alive. Gordon Wenham explains that 'entry into the Holy of Holies is fraught with danger. To protect himself from the wrath of God, the high priest has to prepare a censer full of hot charcoal taken from the altar of burnt offering in the outer court and put in it fine incense. The smoke of the incense was to *cover the mercy seat*, so that the high priest would not be killed (vv. 12–13)'.[2] Rather than a cloud of incense preventing God from 'seeing' the sinful high priest, Wenham argues that the emphasis lies on the incense clouds protecting the high priest by making it impossible for him to gaze directly on the Holy One of Israel.

2. Sacrifices and offerings

The Old Testament describes a range of sacrifices and offerings which God had provided to deal with sin and keep it under control. John E. Hartley separates the various sacrifices under three main headings. First, various sacrifices involved presenting *a Gift to God*; and 'a sacrifice was a gift to Yahweh in recognition of his sovereign lordship. A citizen would not presume to enter the presence of a king without a gift; neither would a worshiper approach Yahweh, the King of Israel, without a gift... The cost of sacrificing an animal, which for an ancient family was the basis of its livelihood, certainly bears witness to that family's recognition of Yahweh's lordship.' Secondly there were sacrifices which functioned as *a Means of Expiation*, which 'were the primary means by which a person or the community as a whole overcame the wrong produced by a sin'. Finally, some sacrifices were seen as *a Means of Communion between Yahweh and Members of the Community*. Such sacrifices involved a meal at which Yahweh was the unseen guest of honour, for it was 'believed that Yahweh was a personal God who sought the fellowship of his people. The primary sacrifice for a shared meal between Yahweh and a family was an offering of well-being, for the majority of the meat was returned to the offerer. The meal from that sacrifice strengthened the spiritual bond between Yahweh and that family.'[3]

3. Purifying the sanctuary

The sacrifices in Leviticus 16 are a means of expiation; and detailed instructions are provided for the sacrifices that are needed to cleanse and purify the tabernacle. Wenham explains that 'the main purpose of the day of atonement ceremonies is to cleanse the sanctuary from the pollutions introduced into it by the unclean worshippers (cf. 16.16,19)'.[4] On this special day the high priest wears a simple garment in keeping with the solemnity of this occasion. On other occasions the high priest could wear 'beautiful coloured materials, intricate embroidery, gold and jewelry'...which made 'him look like a king. On the day of atonement he looked more like a slave.'[5]

The significance of these actions arises from the spiritual significance of the tabernacle itself. For the people of Israel the tabernacle was a sacred space where God had freely chosen to dwell. Samuel Balentine explains how in obedience to Yahweh, Israel had constructed the tabernacle and thereby brought 'into existence a cultic order centered in the tabernacle, which provides God's holy residence in the midst of a fragile world...In sum, the ritual order, like the cosmic order, establishes the boundaries and categories that enable a holy God to dwell in the midst of a world vulnerable to sin and defilement.'[6]

What begins to emerge is the sense that the Holy of Holies was the spiritual nerve centre for the whole of creation, because it was the dwelling place of the only one who could keep chaos at bay. As a result of this, 'the sanctuary is a barometer that measures not only the *spiritual health of the community of faith*, but also, more important, *the stability of the world God has created*'.[7] Danger exists because sin is an unholy contagion which is mysteriously attracted to the sanctuary. Over time these impurities defile the tabernacle, rendering it unfit for divine habitation; thus putting at risk not only the life of the nation, but also the stability of creation. If the sanctuary becomes contaminated by sin to such an extent that God departs, this threatens to fray 'the fabric that swaddles the entire universe in God's protective plan. The rituals on the Day of Purification, therefore, engage the community of faith in an active restoration of the sanctuary, *not for its own sake alone but for the sake of the world*. When the sanctuary is holy, God is present, and the world is secure.'[8]

Such an understanding of the purification offerings on the Day of Atonement implies that atonement involves not only cleansing the sins of individuals, but also restoring a fallen world that is in danger of self-destruction. While the language and concepts are very different, the idea of God intervening to save creation from destruction reappears centuries later in Anselm's *Cur Deus Homo*.[9]

The idea of satisfaction, which is a prominent part of Anselm's theology of atonement, is open to the criticism that it relies too heavily on the assumptions of a feudal society, and that it does not take the Bible sufficiently into account. This may tempt some to conclude that Anselm offers a culturally-dated package of ideas that can be safely left behind; but that would mean overlooking some helpful perspectives. For example, Anselm argues that sin must be dealt with not because God is offended, but because it disturbs the order and beauty of the universe. In this scenario it is not God, but sinners, who suffer as a result of the cosmic disruption caused by sin. God does not intervene to defend his injured pride, but acts in love in order to restore harmony to a universe thrown out of joint by human sinfulness. Gunton asks, 'What, then, is *satisfaction*? In large measure it has to do with the divine action in setting right that which has been thrown out of kilter by human sin... *Satisfaction* is therefore Anselm's way of speaking of what took place as a result of the good God's being unwilling to allow his creatures to destroy themselves. It is the act of the triune God in the unity of his personal being.'[10]

4. Purifying the people

The purification theme continues as the focus of attention turns from the sanctuary to the people. It is significant that Aaron is instructed to 'take from the congregation of the people of Israel two male goats for a sin offering, and one ram for a burnt offering' (Lev. 16.5). The two goats combine to form one offering to deal with the sins of the people. One goat is sacrificed as a sin offering, with its blood being sprinkled inside the tabernacle (16.15–19), whereas the other takes the people's iniquities away (16.20–22).

Kaiser says that 'when the two goats are seen as one sin offering, only one conclusion can be reached with regard to their connection with each other. The one goat makes possible the expiation of the sins laid on it, and thus is the *means* of expiating and propitiating Israel's sins, while the other goat exhibits the *effects* of that expiation.'[11]

Some writers, such as Kaiser, are sure that the idea of substitution is at work here and see these rituals as pointers towards notions of penal substitution. At this point, however, Leviticus does not offer an unambiguous explanation about how sacrifice manages to remove sin, but it affirms that these sacrifices are effective because they are gifts from a gracious God, who provides them to free people from the deadly consequences of sin.[12]

At this dramatic moment the high priest acts in a representative fashion, by laying both hands on the second goat and confessing over it the sins of the people. The scapegoat is then driven out to take away all their sins and iniquities. Whereas the rites performed in the Holy of Holies could not be seen by the general public, the scapegoat ritual provided 'a visual representation to the assembly of the reality that on this day their sins had been completely wiped out and the power of these sins was terminated forever'.[13]

5. The goat for Azazel

The commentators enjoy exploring the enigmatic references to Azazel (Lev. 16.8–10, 20–22, 26). One possibility is that this term arises from the combination of the words '*goat*' and '*go away*', creating the idea of 'the goat which departs'. Balentine notes that 'this rendering has been highly influential in English translations, which frequently adopt the term *scapegoat*, coined by William Tyndale in the sixteenth century, to describe the function of the animal that is sent away bearing the blame of others'.[14] Another approach is to see the word as a geographical term pointing to 'a rocky precipice' in the distant wilderness to which the goat is banished (vv. 10, 22). Different vistas open up when Azazel is understood to refer to some demon living in the desert. Although this interpretation is not without its own difficulties, Hartley suggests that 'if Azazel was a demon, this rite means that the sins carried by the goat were returned to this demon for the purpose of removing them from the community and leaving them at their source in order that their power or effect in the community might be completely broken'.[15]

At this point Hartley makes a bold connection between this aspect of the scapegoat's work and the saving work of Christ. 'Jesus' descent into hell as confessed in the Apostles' Creed is explicable in the light of the ritual with the scapegoat. Just as the goat's departure to the wilderness was a rite of riddance, leaving the people's sins with Azazel, the prince of evil, so Jesus took all sin to hell, the center of sin, to leave it there in order to free humans from the bondage of their sins.'[16]

6. The people's response

Alongside details about the rituals which were needed to purify the sanctuary, and take away the people's sins and iniquities, there is a strong call for self-examination and prayer (Lev. 16.29–31). Although these sacrifices and rituals were given by God to provide forgiveness and set people free from sin, they do not work automatically. For the Holy One, who has graciously made it possible for people to know him, longs for people who will respond in penitence and faith.

7. The fulfilment of the Day of Atonement

Although the New Testament does not explicitly describe Jesus as the scapegoat, it is difficult not to hear echoes of the Day of Atonement in the way that the saving work of Christ is portrayed. This is particularly the case in Hebrews, which portrays Christ as the great high priest who has offered the perfect sacrifice once and for all. Just as the scapegoat was driven out into the wilderness to take away people's iniquities, so Christ bore our sins as he was crucified 'outside the city gate' (Heb. 13.12–13). The sermon at the end of this chapter highlights some of the other ways in which that scapegoat theme emerges in the New Testament.

8. Scapegoats and scapegoating

The rituals in Leviticus 16 are given a different twist in René Girard's exploration of the scapegoating mechanism which he describes as mimetic desire or mimesis.[17] At the heart of this process Girard sees a triangular field of relationships involving the subject, an object of desire and the model or mediator, from whom desire is learned or imitated. Conflict emerges, as subject and model both compete for the same object of desire.

This process of mimesis is acted out on a larger canvas within groups and societies. As conflict grows and a crisis looms, 'the community satisfies its rage against an arbitrary victim in the unshakeable conviction that it has found the one and only cause of its trouble'.[18] The transference of this communal anger on to an innocent scapegoat somehow defuses the crisis and calm is restored. William Placher points to an example of this process when he notes:

> Classical Athens even maintained a number of folks called *pharmakoi* – often prisoners of war – in case of crisis. They could be paraded around town to soak up the ritual impurities, and then either murdered or driven away. *Pharmakos* means either a poison or its antidote, and the *pharmakoi* were thought to be a social poison whose expulsion provided the antidote for the social crisis.[19]

With the passage of time the murder of an innocent victim is reinterpreted in ways which imply that the innocent victim actually deserved their fate; and so a sacred myth begins to emerge. In these sorts of ways the demonic idea of redemptive violence becomes the founding myth which holds groups and societies together. In contrast to this, Girard believes that the Bible begins to undermine this demonic system, in part by refusing to believe the lie that these innocent victims were in some way guilty and so deserving of such violent treatment.

In relation to Leviticus 16 Girard notes that

> the ritual consisted of driving into the wilderness a goat on which all the sins of Israel had been laid. The high priest laid his hands on the head of the goat, and this act was supposed to transfer onto the animal everything likely to poison relations between members of the community. The effectiveness of the ritual was the idea that the sins were expelled with the goat and then the community was rid of them.

Such a ritual was less sinister because an animal rather than a human being was the victim. However, Girard seems to suggest that there was a subconscious sense that the goat somehow deserved such a fate because of 'its nauseating odor and its aggressive sexual drive'.[20]

The greatest undermining of this scapegoating process, which perpetuates demonic ideas about the value of redemptive violence, is what Girard calls the 'non-sacrificial death of Christ'[21] who dies 'in order that there may be no more sacrifices'.[22] Girard is hesitant to talk about Christ's death in sacrificial terms, because he fears that this may legitimize ideas about punishment being transferred on to the Son, in order to appease an angry Father. Instead he speaks of Jesus as 'an unsuccessful scapegoat whose heroic willingness to die for the truth will ultimately make the entire cycle of satanic violence visible to all people and therefore inoperative.'[23]

In spite of these hesitations, Girard has come around to using the term scapegoat in relation to Christ in a cautious way. In an interview he explains:

> I had avoided the word 'scapegoat' for Jesus, but now I agree with Raymond Schwager that he is the scapegoat for all – except now in reverse fashion, for theologically considered the initiative comes from God rather than simply from the human beings with their scapegoat mechanism. I think the Gospels understand Jesus basically that way, and also Paul, when he speaks of God making Christ to be sin, but also our wisdom and righteousness. He is the scapegoat for all.[24]

In comparison with the goat for Azazel, mentioned in Leviticus 16, Girard's scapegoat appears to carry different burdens on its shoulders. The scapegoat in Leviticus 16 is not, as Girard suggests, presented as a method for transferring human anger and 'everything likely to poison relations between members of the community'.[25] The expulsion of the scapegoat is viewed rather as a vehicle for the effective removal of the sins and iniquities which separated people from God. Girard also appears to overlook the way that two goats were involved in one comprehensive sin offering which atoned for sin and removed it from sight.

Placher welcomes the way in which 'Girard powerfully recovers a biblical vision of the need to break out of cycles of violence and forgive one another if society is to have hope'. However, he suspects that while 'Girard says we must stop scapegoating the innocent', he 'then seems to claim that if we only see the truth the problems of guilt will go away. The gospel, however, offers not just a revelation but a redeemer, whose love enables those who are guilty to know themselves to be forgiven.'[26] Experiencing this forgiveness is the thing which can enable people to break free from cycles of blame and violence, and to begin the painful process of forgiving others.

Girard's profound reflections on the scapegoat process provide neither a comprehensive model of atonement, nor a detailed exposition of the range of things that are taking place within Leviticus 16. However, he does provide the preacher with a useful dialogue partner, who can stimulate fresh thinking about a range of issues relating to atonement.

Sermon[27]

The chief executive of a Birmingham hospital has left amid claims he was made a 'scapegoat' over waiting list figures. Good Hope Hospital in Sutton Coldfield suspended Jeff Chandra in August (2002) while an inquiry into the management of waiting list figures was carried out. Mr Chandra says he was made a scapegoat for highlighting irregularities in the figures… 'I believe I was a scapegoat because as chief executive I sought to highlight and address these problems in an open and determined way.'[28]

[In Scotland] a social worker has alleged that he was made a scapegoat over a case in which a woman with learning difficulties was tortured. Three men have been jailed for torturing and sexually abusing a 30 year old woman with learning difficulties who was known to social services at Scottish Borders Council. [The social worker] was suspended by the local authority when the abuse of the woman, known as Miss X, came to light. An independent inquiry into the role of the Scottish Borders Council social work department in the affair blamed flaws in management procedure and heavy workloads among staff. [The social worker's lawyer has said that his client] has been made a scapegoat and managers in the social work department should be disciplined.[29]

Damned if they do and damned if they don't. For the best part of 20 years, social workers have been blamed by the media for every child protection case that went wrong. When parents were found innocent of allegations of abuse, the social workers were castigated as anti-family meddlers who intervened too zealously, ignoring the real interests of the child. When parents or stepparents were found guilty of cruelty, it was usually the social workers who were accused of failing to remove the child to a place of safety due to a misplaced obsession with supporting the family. Of course, the inconsistency in these twin lines of attack was stupendous. But the tabloids did not let that stand in the way of a good story. Their repeated search for scapegoats has probably done more than anything else to discourage entry into what is often a rewarding career [as a social worker].[30]

You don't have to be a big cheese in business or politics to suffer the humiliation of being made a scapegoat. Psychotherapist Simon Crosby says it goes on every day. 'The basic urge to scapegoat seems to be innate in all of us. We start to pick it up in the school playground'…In a society where blame is increasingly sought, often in law, it would seem that scapegoating is becoming more common. To counter that Mr Crosby has started the Scapegoat Society, in a bid to raise awareness of this unjustness.[31]

The word 'scapegoat' pops up regularly in all sorts of news stories. Maybe we've had first-hand experience of being treated as a scapegoat and being blamed for something we didn't do? Maybe when we look back we can also realize that there have been times when we've treated others as scapegoats and transferred our fears and anger on to them? This familiar word 'scapegoat' was brought into the English language about 500 years ago by the Bible translator, William Tyndale, who used it as he translated the account of the great Day of Atonement which is recorded in Leviticus ch. 16.

The Day of Atonement was the biggest High Day and Holy Day in the Jewish calendar. It was the day of great sorrow and repentance as the children of Israel remembered all the sins they'd committed during the year and confessed them to God; and the meaning of the various sacrifices and rituals is explained in Leviticus ch. 16.

But the first thing we notice when we turn into this chapter is its strangeness.
I don't know about you but I've never sacrificed a bull, or a ram or a goat.
I don't know about you but I'm glad that when we come to worship I don't have to walk around cleansing and decontaminating the church by sprinkling blood on the pews or on the people.
I don't know about you but for me the phrase 'burnt offerings' brings to mind those overcooked sausages and burgers that are on the menu at many summer BBQs.

When we read about the high priest putting on special garments and offering all sorts of sacrifices, maybe we feel that it's a bit of strange religious history; a story from a very old religious museum; not something that's relevant to people worshipping in South London on what might turn out to be the hottest day on record. But, in spite of its strangeness, it's worth reflecting on this passage because it has some important things to reveal.

It's often said that we live in a blame culture. Nothing's ever anybody's fault, and it seems that when things go wrong, people's first instinct is to deny all responsibility and find someone else to blame. But when we look at what happened on the Day of Atonement, we find a very different dynamic, because, far from denying responsibility for their actions, these sacrifices and sin offerings served as *Annual Reminders* of people's sinfulness. And as this chapter unfolds several words are used to describe the complex nature of human sinfulness.

Sometimes it's described as uncleanness (v. 16); a kind of pollution which drives God away from the people.

Sometimes it's described as outright rebellion or transgression (vv. 16, 21); the rebellion that happens when 'men and women know what they're doing and deliberately, brazenly, fly in the face of God's law'.[32]

Sometimes it's described as wickedness or iniquities (vv. 21, 22) which implies deliberate wrongdoing.

Sometimes the problem's described simply as 'sins'; which is probably a 'catch-all word for wrongdoing, serious or trivial, deliberate or uninten-tional, conscious or unconscious'.[33]

And these various elements of human sinfulness are bundled up together as the high priest lays his hands upon one of the goats, and confesses over it all the wickedness and rebellion of the Israelites – all their sins – and puts them on the goat's head. One writer notices how all these words for 'sin' are used in the plural to indicate 'the frequency and totality of humans' sinning'.[34] Another preacher argues that when you put all these perspectives on sin together you see the complex and serious nature of sin. For 'sin is spiritual pollution that needs cleansing; wilful disobedience that needs putting right; explicit wrong that needs pardoning, and manifold failure that needs forgiveness'.[35]

Once a year on the Day of Atonement, the high priest offered sacrifice and confessed the sins of the people; and by these solemn acts the people were reminded of their sinfulness; and they were reminded of how much they need God's mercy and forgiveness. Now if these actions and ceremonies had only served to *Reveal* their sinfulness, they would have been totally demoralizing affairs. But as we look closely we see that the events on the Day of Atonement not only *Revealed the people's sin*, but they also *Removed the people's sin*.

> But the goat chosen by lot as the scapegoat shall be presented alive before the LORD to be used for making atonement by sending it into the desert as a scapegoat. (Lev. 16.10)

> When Aaron has finished making atonement for the Most Holy Place, the Tent of Meeting and the altar, he shall bring forward the live goat. He is to lay both hands on the head of the live goat and confess over it all the wickedness and rebellion of the Israelites – all their sins – and put them on the goat's head. He shall send the goat away into the desert in the care of a man appointed for the task. The goat will carry on itself all their sins to a solitary place; and the man shall release it in the desert. (Lev. 16.20–22)

On the Day of Atonement people were reminded about the destructive nature of sin; and that sin was dealt with in two ways. On the one hand sacrifices were offered to atone for sin. Costly sacrifices were the God-given way to deal with the problem of sin. On the other hand the sins of the people were confessed in public by the High Priest, over the goat, the scapegoat, which was then driven out into the wilderness.

Whereas the sacrificial rites and ceremonies which took place in the Holy of Holies could not be seen by the general public, everyone could see the scapegoat ceremony; everyone could see the scapegoat being driven away into the wilderness. And that probably means that the ceremonies surrounding the scapegoat acted as a dramatic, visual aid to help people understand that their sins really had been dealt with. So if at any time the people wondered whether or not their sins had been truly forgiven, then they could remember how the scapegoat had carried their sins away, never to return. The scapegoat's permanent disappearance was a powerful sign which announced loud and clear the good news that,

> as high as the heavens are above the earth,
> so great is his love for those who fear him;
> as far as the east is from the west,
> so far has he removed our transgressions from us.[36]

And maybe this scapegoat ceremony would have carried other echoes and meanings as well.

Now, where the NIV translation talks about the 'scapegoat', some other translations try to make sense of things in a different way by talking about the goat for 'Azazel' (e.g. NRSV). And this goat for 'Azazel' may mean the 'goat that takes away' or the 'goat for total destruction' (which would imply that the sins were being totally destroyed). But it's also possible that 'Azazel' was the name of some kind of demon or devil that people believed lived in the god-forsaken wilderness. And if that's the idea, then we get the picture of the goat laden with all the sins and wickedness of the people, being sent back to where those sins came from. All the sins which the power of evil had engineered were being sent back to their source, never to return.

So this dramatic scapegoat ceremony not only *revealed* sin, but it was also a powerful and dramatic visual aid which declared, for all to see, that their sins had been *removed* and that the power of evil had been overcome. Year by year, as this day came, it was a day for confessing their sins and for celebrating that their sins had been removed.

Over the last couple of days the Government of South Africa changed its policy and decided to make available anti-retroviral drugs to help treat people struggling with HIV and AIDS. This decision is good news which will prolong the lives of some people. The drugs are not a cure for HIV/AIDS, but they do provide a treatment which will manage the condition and help people to live with it. In some ways it is an interim measure to help people while everyone waits for scientists to discover a full solution to the problems posed by this disease.

When we read in Leviticus about the Day of Atonement, it was a God-given way of managing the problem of sin. The sacrifices and the scapegoat were God-given treatments controlling the damage caused by sin. But to some extent they were interim measures, temporary measures; and their temporary nature is revealed in the way that these rites and ceremonies had to be repeated year after year. These sacrifices were not the full and complete solution to the complex problem of human sinfulness. But they pointed forward to the day when God would provide the ultimate, perfect sacrifice which would deal with the root causes of sinfulness.

And we celebrate the good news that in Jesus the great high priest, the full and final sacrifice for sin has been offered once and for all. And the letter to the Hebrews stresses over and over again how Christ the great high priest has fulfilled all that the Day of Atonement represented.

When Christ came as high priest of the good things that are already here, he went through the greater and more perfect tabernacle that is not man-made, that is to say, not a part of this creation. He did not enter by means of the blood of goats and calves; but he entered the Most

Holy Place once for all by his own blood, having obtained eternal redemption. The blood of goats and bulls and the ashes of a heifer sprinkled on those who are ceremonially unclean sanctify them so that they are outwardly clean. How much more, then, will the blood of Christ, who through the eternal Spirit offered himself unblemished to God, cleanse our consciences from acts that lead to death, so that we may serve the living God! (Heb. 9.11–14)

Now the New Testament doesn't specifically describe Jesus as the 'scapegoat', but as we read his story we can see parallels and similarities. We can see Jesus being treated as a scapegoat by the religious and political authorities. For after Jesus raised Lazarus from the dead, the authorities realized that they had a crisis on their hands and 'Caiaphas, who was high priest that year, spoke up, "You know nothing at all! You do not realise that it is better for you that one man die for the people than that the whole nation perish."'[37] And so this innocent man Jesus is treated as a scapegoat, and thrust out on to a cruel cross to die. He's driven out like a scapegoat to suffer 'outside the camp'; and is crucified 'outside the city walls'.[38]

We can also see Jesus willingly acting as a scapegoat in the sense that he takes our sin upon himself.

The Son of God identified with sinful human beings from the moment 'the Word became flesh'.

The Son of God identified with sinful humanity as he stood alongside the penitent in the River Jordan waiting to be baptized by John the Baptist.

The Son of God identified with sinners as he preached good news to the poor.

The Son of God identified with sinful people like us as he shared in the death which is the wages of sin.

All of which can be summed up in the words of the apostle Paul: 'God made him who had no sin to be sin for us, so that in him we might become the righteousness of God.'[39]

The scapegoat on the Day of Atonement had no choice in the matter; it was simply conscripted to the task of bearing the sins of the people. In contrast, Christ is not some reluctant victim, but a volunteer who offers to take upon himself the sin of the world, so that he might remove and destroy it. And his death and burial are the things which convince us that,

as far as the east is from the west,
so far has he removed our transgressions from us.[40]

As we look at Jesus through the lenses provided by the Day of Atonement, and by the dramatic ritual of sending the scapegoat out into the wilderness, it challenges the way in which our blame culture talks about scapegoats, and it offers fresh insights into the miracle of the atoning work of Christ.

And, finally, it's clear from all of this that the Day of Atonement wasn't an automatic process, because the people are advised to make this special day a time for self-denial, fasting and prayer. 'On the tenth day of the seventh month you must deny yourselves (or you must fast) and not do any work – whether native-born or an alien living among you – because on this day atonement will be made for you, to cleanse you. Then, before the LORD, you will be clean from all your sins. It is a sabbath of rest, and you must deny yourselves; it is a lasting ordinance.'[41] For 'however impressive the ceremonies enacted by the High Priest to atone for sin may be, they were insufficient. The law insists that if they are to be effective, the whole nation, Israelites and foreigners alike, must demonstrate true penitence.'[42]

In a similar way we can say that the sacrifice of Christ removes the barriers which separate us from God. It's his once and for all, perfect sacrifice which enables us – but does not force us – to respond to God.

Commentary

A sermon based on Leviticus 17 is included in Donald Gowan's *Reclaiming the Old Testament for the Christian Pulpit*.[43] Reflecting on the sermon Gowan suspects that 'the subject chosen proved to be a bit heavy for its *Sitz im Leben*, a warm July morning'.[44] A similar caveat might be entered for this sermon which was preached on what turned out to be the hottest day in London since records began. In exploring an unfamiliar piece of biblical territory, the sermon probably falls into the trap of including too much detail and ending up rather longer than necessary.

In some reflections on the sermon process, Barbara Brown Taylor mentions an idea which she thinks she has adapted from the work of Fred Craddock. When the time comes to design the shape of the sermon she thinks 'in terms of orientation, disorientation and reorientation'. From this perspective 'orientation has to do with what we all know, or think we know, about this text. That is my first goal: to start with some shared perspective on the passage at hand. That will give people a chance to settle down with me as I try to establish my trustworthiness with them.'[45]

To some extent this sermon follows that *Orientation, Disorientation* and *Reorientation* sequence. The opening stages of the sermon seek to find some common ground between the text and the experience of the hearers, by using some news reports about various experiences of scapegoats and scapegoating. To make the material more accessible, two people took turns to read out these reports, in the style of a television news broadcast. The hope was to *orient* people towards the text by drawing upon their own knowledge and experiences of the scapegoating process.

Having hopefully established something of a shared perspective on the passage in this way, the sermon then seeks to *disorient* the hearers by briefly making explicit the strangeness of this text. (This is somewhat in tension with what Taylor describes as the disorienting point, which for her is whatever shifts *her* 'perspective on the text'.[46])

In terms of *reorientation* she looks for some fresh perspective on the text, and notes that 'if there is no sense of discovery for me, then there won't be one for them either. So it is important that I hold out for some kind of revelation and then report it as best I can.'[47] Within this sermon the ideas that began to emerge had to do with the notion that these rituals were not just annual reminders of human sinfulness but were God-given ways of removing sin and reassuring people of that forgiveness.

This sermon is the work of a Christian preacher who reads the Hebrew Bible through Christian lenses. Balentine notes how most commentaries make strong connections at this point between the Day of Atonement, and the exposition of Christ's high priestly ministry in Hebrews 9–10. However, he expresses some concern that Christians may mark the contrast between Aaron and Jesus in too stark a fashion. 'Must we opt either for Hebrews 9–10 or Leviticus 16? Must we "dejudaize" our faith in order to be Christian? If Christ is our high priest, are Aaron and his children no longer our partners in the journey toward realizing the "very good" world that God has created?'[48]

Such comments raise big issues about relationships between Christianity and Judaism and about the ways in which Christians interpret the Hebrew Bible which cannot be addressed at any length here.[49] In a small way this sermon seeks to do justice to this Old Testament passage within its own context, but also sees the necessity to make explicit its fulfilment in the person and work of Christ.[50]

The senior minister who watched over the early years of my ministry once said that he wanted to 'teach me how to end a sermon'. If he had been listening to this particular offering I suspect that he might have made the same comment. The sermon concludes by referring to the need for a personal response to the forgiveness which Christ's sacrificial death makes possible. Within the context of worship it was possible to create space for members of the congregation to respond in a prayerful fashion to this invitation.

However, it might also have been useful to have found some way of returning to the scapegoating theme highlighted in the opening sections of the sermon. If Christ's innocent suffering has broken the cycle of blame and violence, then what are the implications for the way we live in a society where it is all too easy to load the blame on to someone else? Might an experience of this divine forgiveness set us free to acknowledge our own failings, and help us to resist the temptation always to blame problems on someone else?

3

The suffering of a servant: Isaiah 52.13–53.12

1. The servant in Christian theology

The fourth of the so-called 'servant songs' in Isaiah[1] has always been seen by Christians as an astonishingly vivid foreshadowing of the redemptive suffering of Jesus Christ. Indeed, as a summary of the gospel of atonement it has often featured more prominently than any New Testament passage. Its striking phrases and images have lent themselves to iconography, evangelistic preaching and hymnody. An air, three choruses and an *accompagnato* at the centre of Handel's *Messiah* use words from Isaiah 53 to declare the message and significance of Jesus' death.[2] And in the development of doctrine, the song has provided one of the main Scriptural groundings for theories concerning the vicarious nature of the crucifixion.[3]

This popularity of the song in Christian proclamation, art, devotion and teaching raises the important issue of the basis on which we should let the New Testament act as 'control' in our interpretation of the Old Testament. So attractive has it been as a vehicle for preaching Christ that Christians have often been inclined to treat it as if it *were* a New Testament passage, without thinking hermeneutically about what they are doing.

Brevard S. Childs describes the polarity in modern scholarship between those who see Isaiah 53 as central to Jesus' own self-understanding and hence to the early Church's view of his work, and those who see the links between this chapter and the Gospels as much more tenuous.[4] But Childs rightly points out that whatever the historical verdict about the influence of this text on Jesus, the link between Jesus and the figure of the servant is undeniably part of the 'kerygmatic witness' of the New Testament.[5] It is this witness, of course – rather than any putative historical reconstruction – which is determinative for preaching. But this does not entail that we can ignore the setting of the 'song' in the Hebrew Bible. As Childs shows, a sensitive reading of the 'song' suggests that the figure of the servant both had an original historical referent, and as a part of the canonical process was 'assigned a central and continuing theological role in relation to the life of the redeemed community of Israel'.[6] This implies that our preaching, in turn, should maintain a creative tension between reading the text through New Testament eyes and respecting its place in the development of Israel's self-awareness. This will involve underlining the continuity between Israel and the Church as well as avoiding the crude anti-Jewish uses of Isaiah of which the Church has often, sadly, been guilty.[7]

A qualification should be made to Childs' comment about the centrality of the New Testament's 'kerygmatic witness' for Christian theology. An understandable reluctance to try to penetrate behind the 'canonical' Jesus to the 'real' Jesus should not lead (as, perhaps inadvertently, it might) to a downplaying of the purposiveness of Jesus which the canon itself displays. The New Testament picture of him – not only in the Gospels and Acts, but also in the Epistles, notably Hebrews – is not one of a merely passive figure, whose own intentionality played little part in the events whose meaning was subsequently to be discerned, with the help of the Scriptures and the Spirit, by others. By contrast, we see here a Jesus who *actively* offered himself (Jn 10.18). Though the meaning of this offering is made much more explicit in the Epistles, above all Hebrews, the Jesus of the Gospels is clearly a dynamic figure who repeatedly takes the initiative in his movements and dealings with others. He is conscious of a divine 'must' (e.g. Lk. 13.32–33) but also of being a free agent not a puppet.[8] The Gospels, in other words, invite us not *simply* to speak of echoes of Isaiah which are heard by the community of faith, but of Jesus' self-giving drive. We may wish to remain agnostic about the nature and extent of Jesus' consciousness of 'fulfilling' particular texts, expectations or roles, but this agnosticism should not lure us into preaching a merely passive Jesus whose 'significance' is determined and discerned purely by those who come after.

Nor should we speak of the song's remarkable foreshadowing of Christ merely in terms of the marvel of prediction ('to think that someone could have seen all this so many years before!'). The greater, more subtle marvel, surely, is the continuity revealed here in the character and purposes of God.[9] The events of the gospel thus appear not as neat fulfilments of proof-texts, but as profoundly continuous with God's earlier self-revelation: bringing it to new clarity and focus, to be sure, but no mere bolts from the blue. The self-offering of Jesus will be seen not as some strange new element in God's plan, but as the focus and fulfilment of the calling of Israel, and through Israel, that of humanity as a whole.[10] Thus is preserved the aspect of atonement rightly highlighted by Gunton: the work of Jesus is no sudden 'intervention' of a previously inactive God in the midst of history, an unfortunately necessary salvage operation, but rather the bringing to completion of a plan made in eternity and patiently worked out throughout history.[11] Such a view has equally important consequences for the way in which we conceive of the present role of the Church. If Jesus' coming was not a desperate expedient, but the climax of a plan already in operation in history, through human beings, nor should his ascension be taken to mean that that plan is now being worked out on a plane purely above history, with humans perhaps as beneficiaries, but not as essential players. The continuation of the work of atonement through the body of Christ will be one of the key themes to emerge when we turn to the New Testament in later chapters.

We will now consider aspects of the structure and language of the poem before drawing together the central threads of its significance for our understanding of Christ.

2. The poem: perspective and parallelism[12]

Even in an English translation, the poetic quality of this song is evident. This fact should both condition what we can say about the truth envisioned here, and inspire a genuinely envisioning presentation of it. Walter Brueggemann comments that this poem offers no 'theory' of atonement, but instead 'a confession, an admission, a dazzlement, and an acknowledgement'.[13] It contains vivid imagery, notably the similes in vv. 2, 6, 7: 'like a young plant, and a root out of dry ground' (v. 2); 'all we like sheep' (v. 6); 'like a lamb that is led to the slaughter, and like a sheep that before its shearers is silent' (v. 7). If we read the song as a portrayal of Christ, there are ways in which much more of its language is seen as figurative, and to this I will return in the next section. But here I wish to approach the poem through two other striking literary features: the perspective(s) assumed, and the parallelisms used.[14]

a. Perspective

As a poem, recognizable as such within its literary co-text (though not divorced from it), the song presses its reader to ask: who is saying this? What 'voice' (or 'voices') do I hear? Since few poems give direct and unambiguous answers to such questions, it is clear that part of the poetry's very *raison d'être* is to entice the reader into the process of engaging with them. For the preacher (or biblical critic) to move too quickly to the supposed 'answers' is to rob the poetry of an important part of its magic.[15] We may track the way in which it invites us into a 'perspective' through its use of names, personal pronouns and adjectives, and through its sense of time.

It begins with a reference to 'my' servant (v. 13). As readers (especially if we are Jewish or Christian, and if we are familiar with Isaiah 40–55 as a whole) we are likely to assume that the voice we are hearing is that of God himself. But this 'I' soon disappears. Throughout the central part of the song, the singular voice is replaced by a plural one: 'our message' (v. 1), 'no beauty or majesty to attract us to him, nothing in his appearance that we should desire him' (v. 2), 'we esteemed him not' (v. 3); and notice especially the concentration of first-person plural designations in vv. 4–6: '*our* infirmities...sorrows...transgressions...iniquities'; '*we* considered...have gone astray'; 'the punishment that brought *us* peace...each of *us* has turned to his own way...the iniquity of *us* all'. Again, the Jewish or Christian reader will assume that this is a human grouping, on account of the references to their weaknesses and sins. Childs argues that this 'we' is the same as the 'they' of v. 15b, referring to 'a group within Israel to which has been revealed the "new things", hitherto hidden'.[16] In this section, this human perspective is confirmed by the appearance of 'the LORD' or 'God' in the third person (vv. 1, 4, 6). Vv. 7–9 appear to be transitional, for the sole first-person reference is an ambiguous one: 'my people' (v. 8) could be the utterance either of God or of a (single, this time) human figure. In the final section, v. 10 contains a further two third-person references to 'the LORD,'[17] but then we return to the perspective of the LORD himself in vv. 11, 12: 'by his knowledge my righteous servant will justify many', 'Therefore I will give him a portion among the great...' The song thus seems like an oracular divine pronouncement encasing a record of human witness.

If these are the points of view we are invited to share, on whom (or what) are we invited to fix our gaze? The focus on the single figure of the servant, the 'he' or 'him' repeated time after time, is striking, not least because (as we have seen) we come to this passage from its co-text with the notion that the 'servant' is Israel as a whole. The singu-

larity of the figure depicted here in such concentrated fashion may
be interpreted as both uniqueness and loneliness. It also lends itself
irresistibly to the Christian reading which sees Jesus as the supreme
embodiment of the figure here envisioned.

A final note about the designating pronouns is of interest. In two
places, the Hebrew uses 'you': in both cases the NIV changes a second
person into a third; this only happens in the NRSV in the first case.[18]
In v. 14, this 'you' is clearly the servant – 'Just as there were many
who were appalled at you' (NIV, NRSV 'him'). In v. 10, it is the
LORD – 'though you make his life a guilt offering' (NIV 'the LORD
makes'). We may ponder the effect of this shift from 'you' to 'him'.
It makes a logically plausible identification of the person referred to,
but removes the point of view expressed in the text (which is admittedly angular, in the context of so many third-person designations).
For by the introduction of 'you', another kind of posture enters the
song: in addition to oracle and witness, we have a direct address to
both the servant and the LORD. 'Prayer' is not quite the word; it is
rather a simple acknowledgment by the one speaking of the presence
of these figures. The 'you' of v. 14 (the servant) is especially interesting
for a Christian reader, for whom it is as natural to address Jesus the
servant as God the LORD. (In light of Christian convictions, an even
more striking reading of v. 14 – which would probably depart from
an 'original Jewish' sense, but in a canonically Christian way – would
be to read 'you' as 'the LORD' – an abrupt response to the oracle of v.
13: i.e. the LORD himself is identified with the servant at whom many
were appalled, etc.) Preachers, therefore, who wish to stay close to the
form of the text in the form of the sermon may appropriately reflect its
perspectives in three ways: by echoing its oracular framework, sharing
in its human witness and doing so with explicit, awed acknowledgment of the presence of both the servant and the LORD.

The song invites us not only into the perspectives of certain human
or divine persons, but also into a certain perspective of *time*. Granted
that the two Hebrew 'tenses' of perfect and imperfect between them
must cover the wider range of tenses distinguishable in modern
English and many other languages, there seems to be fair agreement
among modern translators as to how to read the tenses of the song.
The exaltation of the servant is seen as a future event whereas his
suffering is seen as being in the past. This makes a pressing question
for any reader: where are the readers invited to see themselves, and
what is happening, *now*?

For the Christian reader, of course, it means that the time perspective
of the song can be adopted smoothly into our own perspective (and

preaching): we have seen the suffering of the servant, but we do not yet see his glory – though this must be refracted through the lens of Heb. 2.8, 9: we do not yet see *everything subject* to the son of man, but, by faith, we *do* see him crowned with glory and honour because of the suffering of death.

However, the depth of perspective offered to us here is yet richer and subtler. What is the significance for us of the fact that this is a *pre-Christian* vision which yet seems to speak of the servant's suffering in the *past*? To be sensitive to this tense-perspective will lead to closer integration in our preaching of the story of Jesus with the larger story of Israel. It is not just that Jesus' story is illustrated in interesting ways by Israel's story. It is the continuation and climax of Israel's story. Jesus is not the first 'suffering servant', even though for us he is undoubtedly the greatest. The utter strangeness of this conviction about the redemptive achievement of a particular figure was painfully obvious to the poet-prophet in his own time: 'Who has believed our message?' (v. 1).

b. Parallelism

The parallelism characteristic of Hebrew poetry is no mere ornamental device, but has important consequences for interpretation. Balancing pairs of lines or phrases invite us to read one term of the parallel in light of the other. A build-up of multiple parallels or, conversely, the absence of any parallelism at all can yield a striking emphasis.

In this poem, it is worth noting first the emphasis created by the fourfold parallelism of v. 13: through the use of four different expressions, the poet points at the outset to the end of the story, the sure exaltation of the servant: 'See, my servant will prosper, he will be raised and lifted up and highly exalted'.

Second, we observe how the parallelism builds up a picture of the despised servant in which just a few key elements are emphasized, but in a rich variety of ways. Thus vv. 2, 3 present a cluster of images and phrases which paint the servant as unprepossessing, apparently weak, eliciting only scorn and dismissal. In v. 4 we start to approach the climax in v. 6, as the servant's suffering is interpreted. The antithetical parallelism of the verse underlines the paradox: in the first half the poet's conviction about the true meaning of the servant's pathetic state is declared in two similar phrases – 'Surely he has borne *our* infirmities and carried *our* diseases'[19] – and in the second half the previous, and more natural reading of affairs is given, the three phrases 'outdoing', as it were, the previous two, showing how extraordinary it all is: 'Yet we counted him stricken, struck down by God, and afflicted'. Verse 5 then 'caps' this by a *fourfold* underlining of the vicarious nature of the servant's suffering (compare v. 13), amplifying v. 4a.

Third, we note v. 6b. While almost every line in the poem (and some phrases within a line) has a balancing parallel, in which the thought is either repeated, or contrasted,[20] here at the centre is a line with no parallel: 'And the LORD has laid on him the iniquity of us all'. After the repetitions of vv. 3–5, and the two parallel clauses of v. 6a ('We all, like sheep, have gone astray, each of us has turned to his own way') this comes as a sombre and striking statement, falling with lapidary heaviness, and surely indicating the heart of the message which the song announces.[21]

Fourth, there are some interesting 'parallels' between words or ideas that are clearly perceived as being closely related, though not identical, and these have resonances with New Testament themes. We mention two instances. There is the close proximity of the 'wicked' and the 'rich' in v. 9 – reflecting no doubt the standard identification of the obedient faithful with the LORD's 'poor', and the prophetic polemics against the oppressive wealthy (e.g., in this book, Isa. 3.13–26).[22] This is a subversive picture, for it undercuts any smug self-identification of Israel as 'the poor' who have a right to God's favour: in his death, it was *the wicked rich* with whom this servant was identified. The stories of Jesus' association with 'sinners' continue this subversive thrust – for though he did indeed bring good news to the 'poor' (Lk. 4.18), few seemed to be prepared for how he would interpret this category: it certainly included those who were materially wealthy (indeed part of an oppressive system), but socially ostracized (Lk. 19.1–10). In the process, of course, Jesus found *himself* stigmatized. Then there is v. 11b, where it is instructive to see how the statement that the servant will 'make many righteous' appears in parallel to 'and he will bear their iniquities': the two are inextricably related, as in 2 Cor. 5.21. Similarly in v. 12, 'he bore the sin of many' is closely linked with the parallel statement 'and made intercession for the transgressors', evoking for Christians the close link between Christ's self-offering for the sins of humankind and his continued intercession for us (Heb. 7.23–28).

There is no doubt much more to be gained from a close study of the way parallelism works in this song; the foregoing is offered as a suggestive sample. It further underlines, however, the poetic nature of the passage, and invites us to read and preach it not as flat wooden prose, but with an ear to the rhythms and stresses of verse.

3. The servant as Christ

It is time to focus directly on the portrait of the servant and note certain aspects which demand our attention as preachers of Christ, and the issues which they raise.

a. A human figure

First, it is clear that the servant is a human figure. His rootedness in earth is memorably expressed in v. 2: 'He grew up before him like a tender shoot, and like a root out of dry ground'. As a human, he is rejected, suffers and dies: 'a man of sorrows, and familiar with suffering' (v. 3). But his exaltation is also conceived humanly, in the classic Hebrew terms of long life and seeing one's descendants (v. 10: compare the end of Job's story – Job 42.16). It entails 'a portion among the great' and dividing 'the spoils with the strong' (v. 12) – a very down-to-earth glimpse of one human victor among others. Even in its original context the latter pictures are probably to be construed metaphorically: these are very human ways of depicting a success which, in this case, seems to go far beyond anything normally known in human experience. The beginning of the song hints at this uniqueness, through the fourfold announcement of the servant's lifting-up (v. 13) followed by the statement that his appearance was disfigured 'beyond that of any man' and his form marred 'beyond human likeness' (v. 15). In any case, a Christian reader will certainly see these portrayals of the servant's victory as metaphorical with respect to Christ, who had no physical offspring, did not 'prolong his days' in any normal sense, was not given a status among the 'great' of the earth, and certainly did not consort with conquerors to 'divide out spoils'.[23] Almost automatically, schooled by long tradition of the 'spiritual' reading of such passages, we read these portrayals as pointing to the spiritual 'children' begotten through Christ, his eternal resurrection life, and his real and ultimate victory, of a very different kind from those recognized by the world's 'victors' generally.

But such readings should not screen out the humanity we see in the servant, which lights up for us the human Jesus, and reminds us of the essential human dimension of the sacrifice through which atonement was won. At the same time, however, as Christian readers we recognize this as only half the picture, for if *God* was not indeed in Christ 'reconciling the world to himself' (2 Cor. 5.19) then there is no true atonement, for God and humanity – even the greatest representative of humanity – are operating independently. In light of this, we need to look carefully at the ways in which the LORD's relationship to the servant is described in the song, in order that we may highlight the way in which a fully Christian view of atonement fills out the picture given here. We shall see that in fact this Old Testament vision of a human servant comes closer to the New Testament vision of a divine–human Christ than might at first glance be supposed, for in both the language of divine sovereignty is prominent.

The LORD is here seen as the sovereign one, in the manner attested throughout the Old Testament. This visionary equates his message with a revelation of the 'arm' or 'power' of the LORD (v. 1): *that* is the ultimate source and cause of the servant's exaltation-through-humiliation. Verse 4 poses the paradox of the servant in terms of *what God was really doing* in him. That God is at work in human life is taken for granted: the question for the biblical writers is how we *interpret* that activity when we observe events. Thus the second half of the verse speaks of the immediate conclusion one would be likely to draw from the servant's sufferings ('yet we considered him stricken by God'), while the first half, though not mentioning God, implies that it is offering the alternative, strange yet *true* interpretation of God's activity in the servant: 'Surely he took up our infirmities and carried our sorrows'.

That 'taking up' and 'carrying', though obviously on one level something which the servant 'does', is therefore more profoundly a statement of the meaning and purpose which God *invests* in his suffering. This is consonant with the overall picture of the servant here: as a human being, he appears entirely passive.[24] He is the butt of others' scorn (v. 3). The number of passive verbs through vv. 4–5, 7–9 underscores the picture: he is on the receiving end of others' cruelty and wickedness. But when the redemptive *purpose* of that suffering is mentioned, it is clear that there is a divine grounding to these passives. It was through the 'arm of the LORD' that the servant was pierced *for our transgressions*, crushed *for our iniquities* (v. 5). This, indeed, casts a helpful light on the next clause in this verse: 'the punishment that brought us peace was upon him'. This clause has been seen as a cornerstone for a 'penal' view of the atonement and its interpretation is thus crucial for both advocates and opponents of such a view. The 'piercing', 'crushing', 'wounding' of the parallel clauses are human activities through which a divine purpose is at work. This surely is the case with the 'punishing' also. There is no doubt that on a human, judicial plane the death of Jesus *was* a punishment. The implication of the song is that it was a punishment caught up into a divine purpose. This saves us from the unhelpful way in which 'penal' language when used of the atonement can drive a wedge between Father and Son, implying (whether intentionally or not) the direct 'punishment' by the former of the latter. Thus the song, rather than introducing language about God at this point concerning which the Christian might be embarrassed when speaking of Christ, in fact helps us with its stress on divine sovereignty *through* human cruelty and judicial process (cf. v. 8, which points to this process whether one opts for the NIV translation 'by oppression and judgement, he was taken away' or the NRSV's 'by a perversion of justice he was taken away').

What, though, of those verses in the song which speak more directly of the LORD's activity in respect of the servant? The climactic statement in v. 6b can and should be interpreted in light of what we have just said: 'the LORD has laid on him the iniquity of us all' is not a denial of human agency in the servant's suffering: it is rather a statement of what the LORD was doing through that human event. It is the same with the second clause of v. 10, 'though you [the LORD, NIV] make[s] his life a guilt offering,'[25] and the penultimate clause of v. 12, 'he bore the sin of many': these are statements of what the LORD achieves through the servant's suffering. It does not of course imply that his attackers know the deeper meaning of what they are doing; nor need it imply that the servant himself was fully aware of it. The one statement, however, which can seem very difficult is the *first* clause of v. 10: 'Yet it was the LORD's will to crush him and cause him to suffer'. Surely this seems to utter (from a Christian point of view) the very sentiment which we have described above as objectionable, driving a wedge between Father and Son, and effectively creating a breach in the economy of atonement?

The first observation to make on this is that even if this were the case, a Christian theology of the atonement cannot allow itself to be *controlled* by any Old Testament passage. There are many ways in which the New Testament fills out or transcends Old Testament teaching. Thus a preacher might simply avoid such a verse, or at least interpret its stark presentation of God's agency in the light of the more indirect 'divine passives' found in vv. 4, 5. But perhaps this is not necessary. The real problem we have[26] concerns not just the activity of God in relation to the servant or to Christ himself, but the sovereignty of God *per se*. Thus it makes little difference whether this sovereignty is presented in 'passive' or 'active' terms. That is the nature of the God of the Old Testament and, indeed, the New Testament, and somehow we need to come to terms with it.

Statements about God's direct causation of human suffering in Scripture, rather than giving embarrassment, can and should be seen as part of a coherent biblical matrix which holds together three elements: God's ultimate (but also intimate), and beneficent, direction of human affairs; the temporary intrusion of mysterious, Satanic influence; and continuing human responsibility. This has all sorts of practical consequences. To name but two: we can and should continue to pray fervently for God to exercise his victory over evil in the affairs of the world, *at the same time* as we work in all practical ways for the right exercise of human responsibility in the world; and we can and should cry out to God directly from under the weight of suffering, as the Psalmists did, *at the same time* as we and others work in all practical ways to deal with the human causes of that suffering. Let us then note how this digression on divine sovereignty helps us make sense of Isa. 53.10.

To say 'it was the LORD's will to crush him and cause him to suffer' is to present a 'hands-on' God to whom the servant could cry (as the human Jesus did indeed cry: Mk 15.34). It is not to deny the agency of other humans in the event – clearly portrayed in this song, as we have seen. Nor is it to deny that such an event can also be construed in terms of the 'power of darkness' having its 'hour' (Lk. 22.53). Above all, it is to assert that though it might seem terrible at the time, and is beyond our rational explanation even in retrospect, the suffering is taken by the God whom we know to be good as his responsibility. The song as a whole shows it to be purposeful, the necessary prelude to glory for the servant and for many.

How does this help us further to relate the song's picture of the human servant to the New Testament picture of Christ and his work? In New Testament terms, v. 10 offers an incomplete picture of Christ: it shows us a human sufferer on whom the sovereign God is acting. For the New Testament, Christ is *more* than this: a divine–human person in whom God himself is suffering. The point is that he is not *less* than this: from a human perspective, this is indeed how he may be seen.

One further point must be made relating to the humanity of the servant. Notwithstanding what was said above concerning his passivity, there are glimpses in the song of a more active posture. He is called 'my righteous servant' (v. 11). Interestingly, this 'righteousness' is construed first in negatives, underlining the moral force of the servant's passivity: he did not open his mouth in the face of torment (v. 7); he was neither violent nor deceitful (v. 9). But at the end of the song two verbs are used which reveal an *active* propulsion for the servant's suffering: he 'poured out his life unto death' and 'made intercession for the transgressors' (v. 12). This self-giving movement, for the sake of others, is discerned by the New Testament writers, above all the writer of Hebrews, at the heart of the story of Jesus, and must be held alongside his passivity, human wickedness, the devil's mischief and God's sovereignty in any account of his atoning work.

b. Vicarious suffering

At the heart of this 'servant song' is the picture of the servant's *vicarious* suffering. 'The LORD has laid on him the iniquity *of us all*' (v. 6), and that image gives the New Testament its key terminology for describing the significance of Jesus' death: Christ 'died for our sins according to the Scriptures' (1 Cor. 15.3). How is this vicarious suffering to be understood?[27]

It is easy for those who are the heirs to particular conceptions of this suffering to assume either that it 'obviously is' or 'definitely is not' 'substitutionary'. While recognizing that the mode of such vicarious suffering is bound to be beyond definition, and indeed was not defined in the creeds, it is worth trying to clear up some misunderstandings.

First, to say that this chapter does not necessarily imply a 'substitutionary' view of the servant's atoning work does *not* entail a denial either of God's grace in that work or of the profound human need for it. It is simply to assert that these truths are expressed in the more general language of a 'vicarious' suffering. The sheer gift of what the servant does is beautifully encapsulated in v. 5. In the first half of the verse we see the servant bearing the negative consequences of sin: he was pierced for our transgressions, he was crushed for our iniquities. In the second half of the verse we see the positive outcome he achieves for us: the punishment *that brought us peace* was upon him, and by his wounds *we are healed*. There can be no doubting either the dire need of humanity expressed here, or the wonder of the gift bestowed through the servant. What seems lacking is any sense of what the consequences would have been for humanity *had the servant not been thus 'pierced' and 'crushed'*. Undoubtedly he is seen here drawing on to himself the weight of human estrangement from God; but any alternative scenario is kept from view. Those who for good reasons drawn from elsewhere in Scripture, and Christian tradition, are unwilling to use the language of 'substitution' in speaking of the atonement can thus point to the emphasis of this verse to support their reticence.[28]

Conversely, however, we should recognize that interpreting this chapter in terms of 'substitution' is not necessarily to run counter to its thrust. Certainly there is no sense here of a strictly mathematical equivalence between the suffering of the servant and the sin of humankind,[29] or, indeed, of 'penal' substitution.[30] But the word 'substitution' does capture something that seems inherent in the portrayal of the servant's sufferings: the sense that *without* them, we would be – in unspecified but presumably terrible ways – in a parlous state. The servant's experience works, as it were, to fill the breach, to ensure that we do not remain in a state of brokenness. In that way he acts to substitute himself for the dire but unnamed results of human sin.

So it may not be so much a question of whether it is right to use 'substitutionary' language in using this 'song' to speak about the atonement; the more important question is *how* we use it, if we do. The text neither necessitates nor excludes it; but undoubtedly it is more reticent than many preachers who have offered graphic portrayals not only of the servant's saving work but also of the supposed destiny of those who do not avail themselves of it. It would be foolish to oppose such portrayals purely on the grounds that they 'go beyond Scripture' at points like this; theology and preaching must always, in some sense, 'go beyond Scripture' in their relating of God's truth to contemporary hearers. Equally, however, it can be salutary to return to Scripture and realize afresh what it does not say as well as what it does.

It is important also to note the implications of the song for the idea that Christ in his death is a 'representative' figure. The LORD's servant is identified as *Israel* several times in the co-text of Isaiah 40–55 (most explicitly in 41.7; 44.1, 21; 45.3; implicitly in 42.19 and 43.10).[31] In this identification there is already a sense that the nation is being personified as an individual. In the so-called servant songs (42.1–6; 49.1–7; 50.4–11; 52.13–53.12) it is as if this personification is expanded so as to depict the outlines of this single figure – humble, rejected, yet called to be a light and a witness not only for Israel herself, but for the world. The servant's sufferings in some sense bring to a head those of the nation as a whole.[32] As we recognize in Jesus the embodiment of the servant's vocation, we see him as the supremely representative figure, taking up into himself not only historical Israel but the entire human race. This is what can make his vicarious suffering truly effective. But it also means that his experience sets the pattern for the experience of the race. As a meaning is discerned in the servant's suffering through the 'will of the LORD' (v. 10), so meaning can be discerned in the suffering of all God's servants. As he was victorious through and beyond suffering, so all those he represents may share in that victory. Thus it is to victory, finally, that we turn.

c. Victory

This is, above all, a victory song. The servant's exaltation is announced at the outset (v. 13) and reiterated at the end in terms of honour and power (v. 12a). Moreover, we are shown this victory not just from the perspective of the God who raises up, but from that of the servant himself, who will 'see his offspring and prolong his days', and 'see the light of life and be satisfied' (vv. 10, 11). Undoubtedly this glorification is the work of God – just as, we saw, the meaning of the sufferings is the work of God through human wickedness. But just as the picture of the suffering servant is not one of total passivity, but of a righteous one who 'poured out his life unto death' and 'made intercession for the transgressors' (v. 12), so too the picture of the glorified servant shows us not only his receipt of glory, but also his *achievement* and *enjoyment* of it. This further underlines the humanity of the servant as well as the power of his story of reversal.

It is important to see that, as with the great narrative of the New Testament, this is not just a story of victory coming *after* defeat, of suffering *succeeded* by happiness in a merely chronological reversal.[33] It is, precisely, a story of victory coming *through* defeat, of suffering *achieving* something. Thus the victory is not seen at all in terms (for instance) of a turning of the tables in which the servant takes vengeance on his persecutors.[34] Apart from the phrase 'he will divide the spoils with the strong' (probably metaphorical even in original intention, v. 12) there is no hint of this being a victory over human enemies (or even spiritual ones). It is, rather, about the turning of the whole surging tide of human life. The one who by an unjust judgement was taken away (v. 8) will 'justify many' (v. 11). The servant through his meek bearing of injustice and oppression sets humanity to rights. This, the Church recognizes, was the historical achievement of Jesus Christ. The sermon which follows takes up the theme of the servant's victory, as it explores but also subverts the idea of the narrative with a 'happy ending'.

Sermon[35] and commentary

We all love happy endings. A little creative tension is all right. You can make us sweat and make us scream. Fill us full of fear and trembling, if you like, but when the final credits roll, we want to have a smile on our face. We want to see the good guys win. We want a happy Hollywood ending.

I spent some time last night with my nose in a book of old fairy tales – stories of beasts and beanstalks and sleeping beauties – stories of ugly ducklings that turn into beautiful swans and henpecked scullery maids who end up going to the ball. And every one of them has a happy ending.

Not much like life really, but maybe that's why we like them. Real-life endings can be hard and unforgiving. In real life the bad guys win far more than what seems fitting. Real life hurts and keeps on hurting. There is no certainty. Real life endings feel unpredictable, as if there is no scriptwriter to ensure that everyone lives happily ever after.

The sermon begins by evoking our experience both of the urge for a 'happy ending' in fiction or fantasy, and of the lack of happy endings in real life. A tension is set up which awaits resolution.

Well, I've got a story for you today – a story you won't believe about a nation long ago and far away. It is a story about a people who have lost their hope because they have lost their way. There is no army, no power, no hope. Of course, there is God – not that he has lifted a finger to help in recent memory. But now here is this strange prophet, with his stories of help and hope and a 'suffering servant' who would come to win the day.

This one is a good story if we could believe it. Like all good stories, it has a surprise ending. Deliverance will come from an unlikely source. The last one any of us would have expected, the most unlikely candidate, will end up playing the hero. Sure, it will take time, but these people will get their happy ending. And so will we.

Jesus provides happy endings. It is his business. It is what he does. It is why he came. Jesus is in the business of bringing peace and bringing healing. He came to solve our sin and crush our iniquities. He provides happy endings.

A temporary resolution is achieved with the introduction of a story that is not fiction or fantasy, but that truly does lead to happy endings on a universal scale. However, the hearers sense that the resolution is incomplete: for the preacher acknowledges that this is a 'story you won't believe', 'a good story if we could believe it'. This is no glib gospel being proclaimed, but one which has the measure of the intractability of human unbelief. Note too that without labouring the complex hermeneutical issues, the preacher pays due attention to the original setting of the song before applying it to Jesus. Its message was good news for Israel first.

The prophet knew it would be hard to believe. Jesus was not your classic leading man. He is all wrong for the part. Weak profile, low approval ratings – the people are tired of him. It's the classic story. He grew up young and tender, the camera loved him, but now he's dried up and past his prime. He doesn't have the look we need. I mean, this guy is no Charlton Heston. You look at him and you just don't think 'majestic deliverer'.

Not this guy. People have had enough of him. Despised, rejected, yesterday's news. The man is too sorrowful. He's taken too many hits. He's the kind of guy that you cross over to the other side of the street when you see him coming because it would be too painful to have a conversation with him.

We didn't see it coming. It didn't occur to us that he would be the one who would take up our infirmities and carry our sorrows. We looked at him as if he were some grotesque mistake by God, and yet all the time he was serving us. He was pierced for our transgressions. He was crushed for our iniquities. The punishment that brought *us* peace was upon *him*, and because he was wounded, we were healed.

It's quite a story and we don't know the half of it. That is, we don't want to know the half of it – how Jesus died, why Jesus died – the horror. Jesus went to the cross that first Good Friday and accepted the sin of all humanity. Time and space converged in this one man and this one moment. Jesus by deliberate intent of will hangs in the epicentre of human ugliness so that we could have our happy ending.

The mood darkens as the reason why the story is hard to believe is probed further. The hero is so far from answering to the specification of 'hero' that human beings are accustomed to, now just as much as in the sixth century BCE or the first century AD. The 'we' of the song becomes the 'we' of congregation and preacher: 'we' are drawn deeper into recognition of our natural aversion to this figure – 'We didn't see it coming…we looked at him as if he were some grotesque mistake…we don't know the half of it…we don't want to know the half of it…' The preacher reminds us that it was all 'so that we could have our happy ending', but at this point in the sermon we have perhaps started to wonder whether we really want it after all.

Arrogant Assyrians gloating over the captives they skinned alive… SS troops machine-gunning women and children… Child molesters making sure their victims would never testify against them… Pharaohs sacrificing thousands of faceless labourers to build themselves a tomb. Jesus took on all this and more. It fell on him with unspeakable violence. Enraged fathers beating toddlers to death, pimps seducing teen runaways into lives of drugs and prostitution, Canaanites burning their children as a sacrifice to Moloch, nice church ladies cannibalizing other nice church ladies over coffee, grand inquisitors piously binding conscience to the rack and demanding right doctrine at a stake, impoverished parents in China selling their daughters into slavery, Bible-believing elders praying long and loud while their wives sit in the back pews hoping heavy makeup covers the bruises. On and on it goes… Jesus amid embezzlers, gangsters, bullies, rapists, liars, the indifferent, the sadistic, the self-righteous.

It's a scene of unbearable horror and unspeakable madness…Wasted lives, heartache, monstrous atrocity, petty transgression – humanity dumps its wreckage on this one spot.

We all are like sheep, Isaiah says. We've gone our own way and the Lord has dumped on him (on Jesus) the iniquity of us all.

He takes it. He doesn't say a word. It is surprising. We didn't expect it would be like this. He refuses the narcotic they offered him. He wants to have his wits about him as he does battle with the darkness. Oppressed and afflicted, he doesn't open his mouth. Led like a lamb to the slaughter, like a sheep to be sheared, he refuses to fight back. He doesn't cry out the injustice. He doesn't raise his fist to fight.

Good thing for us. Because it was by this very act that Jesus won our forgiveness. It was this very sacrifice that provides our happy ending.

With a catena of instances from human history, pre-exilic Israel jostling alongside the modern western world and Church, the preacher faces us with the full force of the 'iniquities' that were laid on the servant. We need to have such graphic reminders of the specific meaning of concepts like 'sin' which otherwise easily become remote and unapplied. Note too the way in which the words of the text are incorporated in the sermon: not pedantically explained, but enacted, brought to life, put to work.

We don't deserve a happy ending. I suppose it should be obvious by this point. There is nothing that merits this. No way to pay it back. We don't deserve the thing he's done for us.

They did an updated movie of Cinderella a year or two ago. My wife liked it so much she bought her own copy. It is interesting to me that whenever I have watched the movie with my wife or read the story to my daughters, I've identified with Cinderella. It's the same with you, I'm sure. The poor damsel, despised and rejected who nobody loves and nobody cares for and who never gets to have any fun. We love to watch the tables turn, sharing Cinderella's triumph as the slipper fits and the prince smiles and the wicked stepsisters get their just deserts. We all imagine our foot would fit that slipper.

We'd better read the story again because I'm afraid we've been reading the wrong part. I think we may have heard the wrong casting call. Read the text. We're not playing Cinderella. We're the wicked stepsisters!

Look at what it says… We're the ones who despised and rejected him. We're the ones who turned our backs. We're the ones who caused his pain. There is always a wicked stepsister, it seems – the embittered outsider, unsure of her place in the family tree, compensating with an aggressive kind of viciousness, embracing a forced and unnatural kind of happiness. It's an ugly role played by ugly people – not a very happy ending.

Yet we live happily ever after. We find what we're looking for. We find forgiveness. We receive grace. We live happily ever after.

By the start of this section the sermon has reached a turning point. We have descended to the depths, and still there is another jolt to come. The happy ending has remained in view throughout, but we needed to come on this journey to be able to feel what is at stake in anticipating it. We needed to face the reality of our sin. Now the preacher stresses, from a different angle, how easily we evade playing the appropriate role in the drama. Just as we more readily identify with Cinderella than with the ugly sisters, so we easily forget that before we can identify with Christ in his victory, we must see ourselves as 'those who caused his pain'. Yet the upshot of this, in the mood of the sermon and the wonderful drama of grace, is not guilt, but forgiveness. Forgiveness must be a much more powerful reality for the ugly sisters than for Cinderella, as the final section will show.

Cinderella and the prince ride off into the sunset, the screen darkens and the credits roll. It leaves you feeling a little flat when you're playing the part of the wicked stepsister, imagining the sequel – Cinderella 2 – where she has kids and gets fat and loses her beauty – old age, divorce even? Bitter people can only hope.

Maybe we could write a different ending. Cinderella has pity on us wicked stepsisters – yeah, that's it. Despite all our derision and despite all our sin, Cinderella takes pity on us and welcomes us into the royal family – full forgiveness and a rich welcome.

That is how the real story ends, you know. I was surprised to read the original text last night.

Her two sisters threw themselves at her feet to beg pardon for all the ill treatment they had made her undergo. Cinderella embraced them and cried that she forgave them with her whole heart and desired them always to love her. Cinderella, who was no less good than she was beautiful, gave her two sisters lodging in the palace and, that very same day, matched them with two great lords of the court.

So the stepsisters find love, the ugly duckling becomes a swan, the sinner finds grace – in Jesus who suffered for us, we find the truest of happy endings.

We know our own ugliness. We don't always want to own it. Yet deep inside we feel the insecurity of the stepsister. We've learned how to elevate ourselves by diminishing other people. We've learned how to get what we want by pushing other people back.

It's not necessary. We just need to quit being hard on people. Quit messing with people and start loving people. Start giving grace to people. We don't need to live an ugly life. It's not necessary. Not when we've been forgiven. Not when we've been given grace.

We know our own ugliness. Now we know grace. Now we can truly live happily ever after.

The original ending of the Cinderella story becomes a pointer to the true marvel of the 'happy ending' achieved for us by Jesus. The tension set up at the beginning has been resolved: fond dreams and harsh reality have been reconciled through the strange story of the servant. But in keeping with the thrust of the sermon, and the gospel, we are made aware that our task now is not simply to sit back and enjoy this happy ending, but to allow the process of transformation through which the sermon has led us to continue, as we find ourselves not just recipients of grace, but sharers of it.

4

The crucified God:
Mark 15.25–39

1. The way of the cross

For the last 15 years, each Good Friday has involved following the cross as it has been paraded through the streets of our part of south London. Walking behind the cross, alongside Christians from various churches, has become a helpful way of entering into that story which not only shapes the life of the Church, but also moulds our understanding of God.

The walk of witness ends with an open-air service with local ministers taking it in turns to preach. Good Friday sermons come in all shapes and sizes; but sometimes the preacher yields to the temptation to jump too quickly from the pain of the cross to the joy of the empty tomb.

However, when we tune into Mark's account of the death of Jesus, there is no escaping the pain and brutality of what took place. For, as Larry Hurtado puts it, 'Mark's intent in presenting Jesus' execution in such stark terms is to confront the reader with the brutal reality of Jesus' humiliation'. But there is no masochistic wallowing in the pain, because 'in the context of Mark's theology the reader is to see that precisely in this brutal humiliation of Jesus the redeeming purpose of God comes to expression'.[1]

As we reflect on this passage, various features emerge which shed light on the redeeming purposes of God, and which offer rich resources to the preacher.

2. Rejection and mockery

The outlook is bleak for Jesus, who has been betrayed by Judas, denied by Peter and abandoned by his friends. Things become even bleaker as he is rejected by the religious leaders and condemned to death by Pilate. Jesus is flogged and ridiculed by the soldiers (Mk 15.15, 17–20). He is beaten so badly that Simon of Cyrene has to be press-ganged to help carry the cross beam (v. 21). The condemned man's clothes become prizes in a lottery and, in another act of mockery, a placard proclaiming the dying Jesus as the King of the Jews is nailed to the cross. Not to be left out, those crucified alongside Jesus join in taunting him (v. 32).

This note of rejection is also sounded on both occasions when Jesus is offered something to drink. Craig Evans sees the soldiers' offer of wine mixed with myrrh as another act of mockery (v. 23), an interpretation supported by Luke's account (Lk. 23.36–37). Hence, Jesus' refusal to drink is not so much that he wants to keep a clear head for the testing time ahead, but that 'he refuses to participate in the mockery'.[2] Hurtado similarly suggests that the intention of those who offered Jesus sour wine (v. 36) 'was to keep him alive for a while longer, but simply for cruel sport'.[3] Far from letting him die in peace, Jesus' opponents appear to take every opportunity to add insult to injury.

3. The day of judgement

The sombreness of the occasion is further underlined as Mark narrates that 'at the sixth hour darkness came over the whole land until the ninth hour' (v. 33). Such darkness is best read in the light of passages such as Exod. 10.22; Jer. 15.9; Joel 2.10; and Amos 8.9, where the darkness clearly symbolizes divine judgement. Morna Hooker thus concludes that 'the darkness at midday symbolizes the judgement that comes upon the land of Israel with the rejection of Israel's king'.[4] The NRSV margin offers 'the whole earth' as an alternative translation of ὅλην τὴν γῆν in v. 33. Noting this, James Edwards uses a wide-angle lens to show that 'the emphasis on darkness covering "the whole land" has universal connotations: the whole earth…is implicated in Jesus' death, not just the Jews'.[5]

While some parts of the Church regard a robust doctrine of divine judgement as the touchstone of orthodoxy, others find the notion something of an embarrassment. One dimension of this problem may be that judgement can too easily be equated with penalty or punishment. It is worth considering whether or not it may be more appropriate to think of judgement as the inevitable consequence of human sinfulness rather than a penalty imposed upon sinners.

Whatever conclusions may be reached about the nature of judgement, it is clear that Mark portrays Jesus as the one who endures divine judgement on our behalf.

Well aware of the ways in which the word 'substitute' can be misused, Gunton argued that

> we have to say that Jesus is our substitute because he does for us what we cannot do for ourselves. That includes undergoing the judgement of God, because were we to undergo it without him, it would mean our destruction…Moreover the centre of the doctrine of the atonement is that Christ is not only our substitute – 'instead of' – but that by the substitution he frees us to be ourselves. Substitution is *grace*. He goes, as man, where we cannot go, under the judgement, and so comes perfected into the presence of God. But it is grace because he does so as God and as our representative, so that he enables us to go there after him.[6]

4. Abandonment

The release of *The Passion of the Christ* generated heated debates about the level of violence in Mel Gibson's portrayal of the death of Christ. As Mark pictures the scene for us, however, it is not the intensity of the physical violence which catches our attention, but rather the inner agony of the one who cries out 'My God, my God, why have you forsaken me?' (v. 34).

Throughout this chapter there are many allusions to Psalm 22, which begins with the righteous Psalmist crying out to God. Not surprisingly some suggest that Jesus was quoting the opening line of the psalm as a way of calling to mind the big picture of a psalm which moves from pain to praise, and through tragedy to triumph.

Such a cool, calm and collected assessment of the situation was firmly rejected by John Calvin who saw the cry of dereliction as part of Christ's descent into hell. He argues that when 'we see that Christ was so cast down as to be compelled to cry out in deep anguish: "My God, my God, why hast thou forsaken me?"', there can be little doubt that 'his words were clearly drawn forth from anguish deep within his heart'.[7]

Within the context of a gospel which describes Jesus repeatedly encountering misunderstanding and rejection, the cry of dereliction is best understood as pointing to the profound sense of abandonment experienced by Jesus on the cross. If that is the case, however, it forces us to ask some important theological questions as to why this Jesus should experience such godforsakenness.

Reflection on this cry of dereliction leads Jürgen Moltmann to assert that the distinguishing feature about the death of Jesus is that historical investigations indicate that 'Jesus died with the signs and expressions of a profound abandonment by God'.[8] He did not die with the calm detachment of Socrates, but with an overwhelming sense of desolation expressed in the cry 'My God, my God, why have you forsaken me?' For Moltmann, the possibility that these words might reflect the interpretation of the early church does not significantly affect his conviction that they bring us as near as possible to the historical reality of the death of Jesus.

Throughout his life Jesus had experienced an intimate relationship with the God who was loving, gracious and near. For Jesus to be abandoned by such a God was nothing less than the torment of hell.

As a 'blasphemer', Jesus was rejected by the guardians of his people's law. As a 'rebel' he was crucified by the Romans. But finally, and most profoundly, he died as one rejected by his God and Father. In the theological context of his life this is the most important dimension. It is this alone which distinguishes his cross from the many crosses of forgotten and nameless persons in world history.[9]

Theologically, the mystery as to why Jesus should suffer such godforsakenness is intensified for Moltmann when this cry of dereliction is viewed from the eschatological perspective. If, as the resurrection demonstrates, Jesus is the Christ, the Son of the living God, then how could he possibly have died in such a state of godforsakenness? Why should the perfect Son have to endure that state of desolation which is the divine judgement upon the sinfulness of godless people? The answer for Moltmann lies in the recognition that 'godlessness and godforsakenness are two sides of the same event. The heathen turn the glory of the invisible God into a picture like corruptible being – "and God surrenders them to the lusts of their heart" (Rom. 1.24; par. 1.26 and 1.28). Judgement lies in the fact that God delivers men up to the corruption which they themselves have chosen and abandons them in their forsakenness'.[10] From this perspective the godforsakenness of the dying Jesus is no mistake or accident, but is the occasion when the Son of God stands in the place of godless people and willingly accepts the godforsakenness which is God's judgement upon sin.

While aspects of Moltmann's view of the cross are open to debate, *The Crucified God* helps the preacher by underlining the significance of the cry of dereliction. The stakes are high here because 'to deny the absolute loneliness of Christ's experience on the cross is, implicitly, to suggest that Christ cannot really be with us in our moments of absolute loneliness. For only a Christ who has experienced the darkest valley of the shadow of death can truly walk with us through our dark and forsaken valleys.'[11]

Preachers hearing this cry of dereliction should not pass by on the other side, as they hurry on their way to proclaim the glad news of resurrection. William Placher helpfully sums up this dimension of the cross as *solidarity*, for it reveals how Christ stands in 'solidarity with us even in the worst of our suffering and sins'. For

> the cross represents the culmination of the incarnation: divinity fully united with humanity... Therefore nothing that can happen to us – no pain, no humiliation, no journey into a far country or even into the valley of the shadow of death – can 'separate us from the love of God in Christ Jesus our Lord' (Rom. 8.39). The Incarnation shows us that in Christ God is with us. The cross shows that in Christ God is with us, no matter what. Even when we doubt or disbelieve or think ourselves completely cut off from God, Christ has been there before us.[12]

Anthony Clarke develops this idea of the cross as a unique act of solidarity with creation that awakens our response. He asks

> what then is changed by Jesus' Godforsakenness? Firstly God is changed by this divine experience of human suffering, enabling God to have a greater depth of solidarity with us. Secondly, as God stands in solidarity with me, calling forth and creating a response, I am changed. Thirdly, then, my relationship with God is changed. God's seeking act of solidarity draws my response of repentance and I am reconciled to God. There is atonement. What is more, with this image of solidarity there is a clear link between Jesus' Godforsaken death and our atonement with God.[13]

What is being suggested here is not some subjective view of atonement whereby the cross atones by exerting its moral influence over us. Something definitive and objective happened when the God-Man entered into solidarity with sinful humanity through incarnation and crucifixion. It is God's gracious initiative which transforms the human situation and makes human response possible.

5. Access to the Holy of Holies

After Jesus breathes his last, an apocalyptic event takes place, because 'the curtain of the temple was torn in two, from top to bottom' (Mk

15.38). The curtain referred to is probably the important inner curtain, at the entrance to the Holy of Holies, which the high priest was allowed to pass through only once a year. This dramatic event is seen by some in negative terms as a prophetic act announcing the future destruction of the temple as a place of worship. More positively it can be seen as Jesus, the great high priest, entering into the Holy of Holies once and for all and opening the way for others to follow. Hooker expresses it well by saying that 'Mark does not spell out the symbolism in terms of the ritual of the Day of Atonement, but he may well have in mind the idea of the removal of a barrier which kept men out of God's presence.'[14]

6. Truly this man was God's Son (Mark 15.39)

Grammatically it is possible to translate the anarthrous phrase υἱὸς Θεοῦ as 'a son of God'. However, when those words are used at the beginning of Mark's Gospel (1.1), the interpretation 'the son of God' is generally preferred. During his ministry unclean spirits had acknowledged that Jesus was the 'Son of God' (Mk 3.11; 5.7; 1.24). On two occasions a divine voice had clearly stated that this Jesus was God's Son (1.11 and 9.7). After a careful examination of the evidence, Clarke says that

> the facts that Mark uses this title so precisely, that on other occasions in the Gospel it clearly means 'the son of God', and that the centurion's confession is the climactic ending so carefully prepared for, lead to the conclusion that this confession, despite being on the lips of a Gentile before the resurrection, is meant to carry full Christological weight. There is certainly the sense in which the acclamation is pregnant with meaning beyond the centurion's own comprehension. Mark's readers, then, are clearly intended to hear the centurion speak of *the* Son of God.[15]

Our familiarity with the story can easily lead us to overlook the shocking fact that the first human being to confess that Jesus was the Son of God was the Gentile centurion on duty at the foot of the cross. As the story of the cross concludes, 'the centurion stands at this point as the representative of those who acknowledge Jesus as God's son. His words form the climax of Mark's gospel, for they are the words used in the confession of Christian faith, and they are found in the mouth of a Gentile at the moment of Jesus' death.'[16]

The centurion stands clearly as the first fruits of a mighty harvest which will result from the preaching of Christ crucified; but that is not the whole of the story. For the centurion's cry suggests that the cross is surprisingly the place where the truth about the nature of God is revealed.

This idea was explored centuries ago by Martin Luther, whose distinctive theology of the cross surfaced first in the Heidelberg Disputation of 1518. There he asserted that the true theologian does not speculate upon the divine nature on the basis of human reason, but acknowledges instead that the truth about God is revealed in the shame and suffering of the cross. 'But he is worth calling a theologian who understands the visible and hinder parts of God to mean the passion and the cross.'[17]

Human wisdom would never dream of looking for God in the sad spectacle of the cross, but surprisingly the truth about God can only be found at the foot of the cross where God reveals himself to faith in the midst of suffering and disgrace. At the cross human beings encounter the crucified and hidden God (*Deus crucifixus et absconditus*) because, like Moses of old, believers are given only a glimpse of God from the rear (Exod. 33.23). The God who remains hidden in the midst of all that would appear to contradict him (*abscondita sub contrario*) reveals himself while still retaining the essential mystery of his divine nature. The cross thus provides a genuine revelation of God which at the same time maintains the unique qualitative difference between creature and creator. Assuming that the hidden God is consistent with the revealed God, the cross can serve as the essential criterion for all statements about God. Hence we can say with Luther that *crux probat omnia* (the cross tests everything).

Presenting the cross in this way, as the key which unlocks the truth about God, is one of Luther's most significant insights. The decision to develop our understanding of God from the foot of the cross paves the way for a biblical, and a distinctively Christian, understanding of God. Perhaps in the past this vital insight did not attract the attention it deserved, but the revival of interest in Luther's work in the twentieth century has meant that this aspect of the *theologia crucis* has played a creative role in contemporary theology.

However, it has to be conceded that Luther himself did not always work on the basis of the cross testing everything. In his debate with Erasmus about free will and salvation he amended his understanding of the hiddenness of God in a way that tended to sever God from his revelation in the word of the cross. For there he claimed that 'God does many things that he does not disclose to us in his word; he also wills many things which he does not disclose himself as willing in his word. Thus he does not will the death of a sinner, according to his word; but he wills it according to that inscrutable will of his.'[18]

Such language creates the unhelpful impression that God is not so much revealed, as hidden at some inaccessible distance behind his revelation. If this is the case then a chilling contrast arises between the God who is preached and the God who is hidden. Not unreasonably Alister McGrath concludes that 'the *Deus incarnatus* must find himself reduced to tears as he sees the *Deus absconditus* consigning men to perdition. Not only do such statements suggest that Luther has abandoned his earlier principle of deriving theology solely from the basis of the cross: they also suggest that the cross is not the final word of God on anything.'[19]

In *The Crucified God*, Moltmann offers a creative development of Luther's ideas about the *Deus crucifixus*. His focus upon the godforsaken dimension of Jesus' death leaves him feeling dissatisfied with the traditional theism which assumed an impassible God whose innermost being is, by definition, immune to any forms of suffering and death. Nothing less than a revolution in the concept of God is called for, he believes, because 'if this concept of God is applied to Christ's death on the cross, the cross *must* be "evacuated" of deity, for by definition God cannot suffer and die'.[20]

Moltmann adopts a dialectic principle of knowledge which asserts that God is only revealed as 'God' in his opposite; in the context of the godlessness and godforsakenness of the cross. Rather than assuming that human beings naturally know what God is like in himself, he argues that we must build our understanding of God's nature from that event at the cross where God reveals the truth about himself. If, like the Roman centurion, on duty at the cross, we discover the truth about the Son of God in his dereliction and death, then we are forced to change our preconceived ideas. The event of Golgotha forces us to speak about a crucified God who exposes himself to tragedy and suffering, and it constrains us to understand God in trinitarian terms.

The cross reveals the vulnerability of God because it displays the divine Son suffering and dying in the darkness of godforsakenness. For Moltmann believes that Golgotha reveals that the Father is directly affected by suffering. While he does not suffer in identically the same way as the Son, nevertheless he suggests that the Father truly suffers pain, enduring grief at the death of his beloved Son. The event of the cross, which lays bare the innermost being of God, does not therefore reveal an immovable, impassible deity, but rather exposes the passionate, vulnerable heart of the crucified God. This discovery is confirmed, for Moltmann, by the reflection that a God who was unable to suffer would likewise be incapable of the love which the Bible ascribes to him.

For some, Moltmann's approach brings serious theological dangers. Does the inclusion of the whole uproar of history within God help resolve the problems of suffering and injustice, or does it serve only to perpetuate the problem? Does his picture of a God who is so vulnerable to suffering remove the traditional distinctions between the economic Trinity and the immanent Trinity and have the undesired effect of eternalizing evil? Might the logic of his proposals imply that evil is perpetuated into the future as a permanent and essential part of God's own being?

Sensitive to such concerns, Anthony Clarke talks helpfully about God's willing vulnerability. He argues that such divine

> vulnerability does not imply that suffering is in any way forced upon God...but that it is God's nature to always choose the path of love in which the possibility of suffering befalling God is a real, and even likely, possibility... Vulnerability actively places God on the side of the victims, sharing in their suffering, in a morally acceptable way, so that God genuinely suffers yet always as the result of divine freedom.[21]

Moltmann also asserts that the cross causes a further revolution in the metaphysical concept of God by forcing Christians to think and speak in trinitarian terms, because Father, Son and Spirit are all involved in the crisis of the cross. The Father 'delivered up' his Son to suffer the death of the godforsaken (Rom. 8.32). This is not the case of a vindictive Father imposing his will upon a reluctant Son, because the Son willingly offered himself on the cross (Gal. 2.20). The cross created a radical rift within the nature of God, but the unity of the Trinity was preserved by the power of the Spirit of love. The Father and Son were united in the Spirit of surrender because Christ offered himself unblemished to God 'through the eternal Spirit' (Heb. 9.14). The life-giving Spirit thus flows from the event that takes place between the Father and the Son. Consequently the doctrine of the Trinity is not some far-fetched piece of speculation, but is in fact 'a shorter version of the passion narrative of Christ'.[22]

Sermon[23]

A few days ago I received an email from a military chaplain explaining that he was leaving on a government-sponsored trip to the Middle East and that he didn't know precisely when the return trip would be.

Day by day the news is full of the build-up to war in Iraq.
But as we think about the many innocent people who'll die in such a war...
As we ponder the explosive ramifications of such a war...we ask...

Why does God allow such things to happen?
Why doesn't God do something about it?

As you're probably aware, today, something like 20,000 children will die because of poverty and malnutrition.

20,000 yesterday
20,000 tomorrow...

And if we can bear to open our eyes to catch a glimpse of the injustices and suffering in our world...a little voice within us asks...

Why does God allow such things to happen?
Why doesn't God do something about it?

And as we've listened to the story of a young preacher who was

100% obedient to God
  100% loving and compassionate towards others;
    but who ends up being mocked and insulted
      who ends up hanging from a cross
        who's put to death in a most barbaric fashion...

...As we hear about Jesus being executed slowly, painfully and cruelly

...As we see love and goodness being rejected and snuffed out...we wonder

Why does God allow this to happen?
Why doesn't God so something about it?

I wonder what helps you when you're feeling down...when you're feeling blue?
  Maybe different personality types find different things helpful?
  For me it's often a piece of music which

Touches a nerve
  Changes a mood,
    Pours oil on troubled waters.

Now I don't know where Jesus would fit in the Myers Briggs Personality Type Indicator… I don't know what he would've found helpful…

But some suggest that when Jesus cried out *My God, my God, why have you forsaken me?*

He was using some familiar words

> To reassure himself
> > To encourage and help him through the trauma of the cross.

And the familiar words he used – words from Psalm 22 – come from a prayer which begins in a mood of despair and ends on a note of praise.

> The Psalm is a prayer which begins with tragedy but moves through to triumph;
> It moves from doubt to renewed faith.

So, as Jesus hung on that painful cross – was he reciting those familiar words to remind himself that there would be a happy outcome? That his suffering would eventually be rewarded?

Maybe…but…

…But it seems to me more likely that when Jesus cried out *My God, my God, why have you forsaken me?* he was using familiar words, not to cheer himself up, but to express the depths of the forsakenness he was experiencing.

You see, throughout his life Jesus had enjoyed a special, close, intimate relationship with God His Father.

At his baptism God had said *You are my beloved Son…*

> On the mount of transfiguration the heavenly voice said *This is my Son. Listen to him.*

> > And that special, intimate relationship was expressed in the prayers of Jesus as he addressed God as *Abba, my dear Father.*

Throughout his life Jesus had experienced this close, intimate relationship with God his Father…with a God who was loving, gracious and near.

But now in his darkest, bleakest hour
   Not only was he abandoned by his friends,
      But he was also abandoned by this God;
         And for Jesus, such an abandonment was nothing less than the
         torment of hell.

When Jesus hung on the cross he didn't die with a *fixed evangelical grin* across his face; but he touched the depths of abandonment and godforsakenness; and that's why he cries out, *My God, my God, why have you forsaken me?*

And as we tune into the depths of pain voiced in that cry of dereliction we can't help asking:

> *Why should he be abandoned by God?*
>   *Why didn't God the Father step in and do something?*

One of the long running TV programmes I sometimes watch is *A Question of Sport* which includes that round which asks 'What happened next?'

   Will the goalie throw the ball into the back of his own net?
      Will the pole vaulter's pole snap at the wrong moment?
         Will the show jumper fall off her horse and end up in the water?

Well…we know what happened next after Jesus cried out *My God, my God, why have you forsaken me?* We're familiar with what happened next, and maybe our familiarity means that we miss something surprising?

> *And at the ninth hour Jesus cried out in a loud voice, 'Eloi, Eloi, lama sabachthani?' – which means, 'My God, my God, why have you forsaken me?' When some of those standing near heard this, they said, 'Listen, he's calling Elijah.' One man ran, filled a sponge with wine vinegar, put it on a stick, and offered it to Jesus to drink. 'Now leave him alone. Let's see if Elijah comes to take him down,' he said. With a loud cry, Jesus breathed his last.*

And surely with his death it appears that the whole Jesus experiment was over.
Surely the death of Jesus shows that all this talk about loving God, neighbours and enemies just doesn't work in the rough, tough world we live in.

But *what happened next?*

Well, faced with the death of Jesus – faced with the apparent defeat of love…something surprising happens, because, '*With a loud cry, Jesus breathed his last. The curtain of the temple was torn in two from top to bottom. And when* the centurion, who stood there in front of Jesus, heard his cry and saw how he died, he said, "Surely this man was the Son of God!" '

> It's not the miracles of Jesus
> > It's not the teaching of Jesus
> > > It's not the success of Jesus
> > > > Which impress the centurion.

It's the suffering love of Jesus which opens the centurion's eyes and leads him to say *'Surely this man was the Son of God!'*

Maybe he didn't fully understand.
But we can see that the truth about Jesus comes out at the cross.
The cross reveals the truth about Jesus…reveals the truth that this man *was and is* the Son of God.

The one who suffers and dies.
   The one who enters into all the pain and suffering and injustice that causes us to cry out *My God, my God, Why?…is none other than the Son of God.*

Why did God allow this to happen?

Well in part to reveal the truth about himself.

In part to remove the barriers of sin and error that keep people away from God. The cross was necessary so that people like the centurion, and people like us, can know and experience the truth about God.

A God who doesn't keep his distance from pain and suffering.

> But a God who loves us so much that he is willing to identify with us and take upon himself the judgement our sins deserve.

A few weeks ago I was working with a group of Masters students in Ghana, and it was exciting to see how many of them are beginning to catch a glimpse of a new theology of mission. They're moving from a very church-centred view of mission and ministry and beginning to see the need to turn the church around, and to turn the church outwards to face and serve the community in Jesus' name. Seeing things differently is leading them to do things differently.

As we stand at the cross we see God differently, and we see the world in a new light. Yes, the pain, injustice and suffering are still there, but we also see the

God who bears the scars of suffering standing with us; giving us the strength to endure, and the power to live for him in a painful unjust world.

A few days ago Colin Powell made an important speech to the UN laying out the evidence which proves that the Iraqis are baddies and the Americans are goodies. And that speech has provoked very different reactions.

The *Jerusalem Post* in Israel concluded that *'Powell's presentation to the UN Security Council was masterful and devastating. He reduced any inconceivable case for inaction in Iraq to rubble'*.

In London, however, the *Daily Mirror* suggested that Powell's presentation was a good bit of *'dramatic theatre'*, but *'there wasn't enough evidence to convict someone of shoplifting, let alone the killer facts that might condemn thousands to death, some of them British servicemen. Some smudgy old photos and blurred taped conversations are not the basis for war.'*

As we listen to the account of Jesus' death on the cross, we see that then, as now, people confronted by Jesus reached very different conclusions.

Some hurled insults in his direction:

'he's getting what he deserves';
    'he's a misguided fanatic who cried in vain to Elijah for deliverance.'

Others, like the centurion, discovered, much to their surprise, that the truth about God is revealed through the bloody and painful episode of the cross.

Faced with the cross,

Some believe, and some reject, because we're dealing with a loving God who invites, but who doesn't compel our belief.

Why does God allow bad things to happen to good people?
Why doesn't God do something about it?

Well, the cross of Jesus doesn't give us answers to all of those questions; but it does reveal a God who has done something about it.

For at the cross we see God the Son sharing in the pain and suffering which leads us to cry out *My God, my God, Why...?*

The cross doesn't give us all the answers but it reveals a God who is with us in the suffering we all must face.

And for me that's enough

Enough to encourage me to take up the cross daily and to follow Christ.

Commentary

For many people today suffering and injustice act as barriers which stand in the way of belief in a loving God. In such a context preaching the story of the cross plays its part by helping to demolish false pictures of a remote God who keeps safely away from the pain and anguish of life on earth.

Helping people to believe in the face of suffering is traditionally seen as part of theodicy rather than atonement, but is it necessary to choose between the two? The message of the God-Man who suffers in solidarity with us clearly offers vital insights for anyone wishing to justify the goodness of God in a world scarred by injustice. Perhaps that message also has the potential to atone and reconcile to God by virtue of revealing the truth about God and by removing some of the obstacles which keep people from faith?

In response to questions about contemporary preaching, Anna Carter Florence wonders if the problem might be with preachers who feel that their job is to *explain* the text rather than to *preach* the text. So she tells her homiletics students that

> their job is not to make the text understandable, or logical, or relevant, or fun. Their job is quite simple, really. It is to *preach the text*, because there isn't anything more interesting or sensible than that. Preach the text, offer it in all its thickness and inscrutability, and trust that it will speak better than we could to the competing worlds of consumerism and militarism and individualism and anxiety that plague our people.[24]

The preceding sermon represents one attempt to preach the Markan text without trying to explain every element of it. It was prepared for a group who were participating in a weekend exploring the links between preaching and personality types, shortly before the start of the war in Iraq.

In terms of structure the sermon roughly follows the stages of Lowry's *Homiletical Plot*.[25] It begins by 'upsetting the equilibrium', raising a series of questions about why God permits various kinds of suffering. The sermon then begins 'analyzing the discrepancy', by turning to the story of Jesus and wondering why someone who was 100% obedient to God should end up dying such a godforsaken death. Reflection upon the centurion's confession of Jesus as the Son of God 'discloses the clue to resolution'. The sermon then invites the congregation to 'experience the gospel' by briefly considering some of the implications of discovering God's presence in the midst of the suffering of the cross. Conscious that people react differently to many things, the final section invites hearers to 'anticipate the consequences' of the cross for their own lives.

5

Forgiveness from the cross: Luke 23.32–43[1]

1. The Gospels and the narrative of atonement

The Gospels preach no developed *theory* of the atonement. It would be a mistake to conclude from this, however, that 'atonement' was none of their concern. Rather, they tell the *story* of the one through whom human beings from every race would come to know that they were indeed 'at one' with God. Though the means by which they suggest the significance of the events they recount are more indirect than those of the epistles and later creeds – sayings, stories, images, and the whole web and movement of their narrative – their perception of that significance is clear enough.

The challenge, therefore, for those who wish to 'preach the atonement' from the Gospels is to tell the story in such a way that *our* hearers can begin to grasp its significance, but not in such a way as to ride roughshod over the Gospels' narrative manner. For example, one can profitably tap into rich veins of truth through meditation on a single verse – such as Jesus' prayer that the Father would take the 'cup' from him (Lk. 22.42) or his promise that the dying criminal beside him would be with him in paradise (Lk. 23.43). But if these verses are not set in some narrative context, the danger is that the gospel message becomes uprooted from the soil of harsh history, perhaps emasculated in the process into a formula for an individualized salvation rather than an announcement of God's mighty acts for the world.

If, then, we are to take the Gospels seriously as vehicles for the truth of the atonement, we need to consider the story they tell as a whole. Luke–Acts is specially instructive, for it takes the story well beyond the resurrection of Jesus into the spread of the good news throughout the Roman empire. It gives us the opportunity to observe the *transformation* brought about in the first disciples of Jesus through their experience with him. In short, we see atonement *happening*, not only being reflected upon.

The process as Luke portrays it is essentially simple, if stunning in its implications. The clear evidence, for Luke, of the new oneness with God enjoyed by the disciples is the gift of the Spirit. In the Gospel, God's Spirit is bestowed uniquely upon Jesus. In Acts, the Spirit is bestowed on his followers.[2] Pentecost, described by Luke as the programmatic account of the coming of the Spirit on God's people in fulfilment of prophecy (Acts 2), ushers in a new era in which the disciples enjoy the same kind of relationship to God as Jesus had, and are equipped with the same power. The giving of the Spirit is the sign that God has indeed raised and vindicated the crucified Jesus (Acts 2.22–36). It is therefore fascinating and crucial to observe the developing relationship between Jesus and his disciples, those who first experienced the atonement mediated by Jesus. In the story of Jesus with his disciples we see prefigured in many ways the continuing story of Jesus with his Church.

Attention to the Gospel narratives as vehicles for the truth of the atonement can especially help us to achieve the right balance between stressing the uniqueness of Jesus, his initiative and power to do something we could never do, and highlighting his exemplary role, the fact that we are indeed called to follow in his steps. An imbalance in either direction leads to an inadequate conception of the atonement in which the real *transformation* in human beings brought about by Christ is underplayed. If we overplay Jesus' unique power to save and give us a new status we may underplay God's *intention* to transform us and make us like him, because we stress the contrast between a holy, powerful Christ and sinful, weak humanity. If we overplay Jesus' exemplary role we may underplay God's *power* to effect this transformation, because we lay stress not on his salvation but on our efforts.[3]

The significance of this relationship between Jesus and his disciples is seen most sharply in the narratives of Jesus' suffering. There we catch sight not only of the human dynamics of those last hours of Jesus' life, but also of significant aspects of what the early Christians had come to believe about his achievement. Each Gospel has a distinctive way of telling this story. In this chapter we will reflect on the suggestiveness of Luke's portrayal of Jesus' suffering and death, in the light of Luke's overall theme and purpose, for our own preaching of the cross.[4]

2. 'Atonement' in Luke

a. Forgiveness prophesied

Jesus' birth is heralded in Luke with prophecies by Mary and Zechariah, announcing God's arrival to fulfil his promise and save his people (1.46–55, 68–79). This act of God seems at first to be conceived in purely political terms: bringing down rulers, lifting up the humble (1.52), rescuing Israel from her enemies (1.71, 74). Towards the end of Zechariah's song, however, a different note is introduced: the knowledge of salvation is to come to God's people *'through the forgiveness of their sins'* (1.77). Such forgiveness, for the Jewish people, was no mere inward gift, but would signal a decisive new era, as promised through Jeremiah: 'For I will forgive their wickedness and remember their sins no more' (Jer. 31.34).[5] This promise was bound up with the beautiful picture in the preceding verse of all God's people 'knowing' him, from the least to the greatest – a graphic image of 'atonement'. 'Forgiveness', then, is not as unrelated to the visions of national deliverance as it might at first appear to be; it has society-wide ramifications. But it is still unclear at this stage just how the great reversal in political fortunes, or the forgiveness, will come about – and how they will be related to each other.

By the time of the birth of Mary's baby, however, we are well prepared for the angels' proclamation: 'Glory to God in the highest, and on earth peace to men on whom his favour rests' (2.14). We know at least we are reading the story of an act of God to bring peace to human beings. When Jesus is presented in the temple, eight days later, we glimpse something further that will be pivotal for Luke's narrative. The salvation now made visible is 'a light for revelation to the Gentiles' as well as 'glory to [God's] people Israel' (2.32).

By what means, though, will God achieve this salvation? His purpose is to be embodied in a Messiah, an 'Anointed One' who can himself be called a Saviour – Christ the Lord (2.11). This God-given leader is already seen as tacitly challenging the rulers of the world, since Rome, the greatest power of the time, claimed for its emperor the titles 'Saviour' and 'Lord' and the achievement of 'good tidings of peace' throughout its realm.[6] But how will this Messiah fulfil his task?

b. Forgiveness announced and enacted

Gabriel's words to Mary indicate a royal child ('He...will be called the Son of the Most High [a royal title, cf. Ps. 2.7]...he will reign over the house of Jacob for ever', 1.32–33). Yet from the humble circumstances of his birth onwards, there are no signs of any trappings of royalty about Jesus. It is in Jesus' calling as a *prophet* that his 'anointedness' is especially seen in Luke.[7] In Jesus' sermon at Nazareth, which Luke clearly sees as interpreting his whole ministry, not only does Jesus declare that his 'anointing' is to preach (in prophetic fashion) good news to the poor, but he further identifies himself with the prophets in saying that the words from Isaiah were 'fulfilled' that very day in his congregation's hearing (4.16–21). In his words and actions he invited comparison with the great prophets of Israel and many recognized him in this light (7.16).[8]

The Nazareth sermon reveals Jesus' sense of calling to announce the God-given reversals already declared by his mother in 1.46–55. The same day, however, it becomes clear that he himself will pay a heavy price for following through the implications of the good news. For saying that God's care and power will not be confined within the borders of Israel, he is the victim of an attempted stoning (4.24–29). From this point, it is clear that this Messiah's vision of the nature and means of God's salvation is very different from the dominant expectations of the time. For Jesus, this rescue is not to be achieved through violent revolution, nor an intensification of law-observance. Rather, it will come about through the proclamation and enactment of God's forgiveness in the midst of ordinary life.

Luke more than any of the other Gospels highlights Jesus' coming to individuals, often the outcast or disadvantaged, with the gift of salvation and, specifically, forgiveness: the woman of ill repute in the Pharisee's house (7.48–50), 'tax collectors and sinners' (15.1–2), Zacchaeus the rich chief tax collector (19.10). To the first he declares 'Your sins are forgiven...your faith has saved you'. In the hearing of the second he tells the story of the lost son, in which Jesus' own attitude and action towards Israel's renegades is graphically reflected in the forgiveness extended by the father (15.11–32). With reference to the third he declares 'Today salvation has come to this house, because this man, too, is a son of Abraham' (19.10).

So far from overthrowing faithful Israel's enemies, then, this Messiah appears to be befriending them. Yet there *is* fierce conflict involved here – with the forces of evil which trap people in physical, social and spiritual bondage. The story of Jesus' healing of the crippled woman (13.10–17) is an excellent example: Jesus responds to the synagogue ruler's objection that he had healed her on the Sabbath with the words 'Should not this woman, a daughter of Abraham, whom Satan has kept bound for eighteen long years, be set free on the Sabbath day from what bound her?' (v. 16).

The forgiveness Jesus offers may itself be seen as an act of power. The verb regularly translated 'forgive' denotes 'to release from legal or moral obligation or consequence'.[9] The related noun, usually translated 'release', appears twice in Jesus' quotation of Isaiah at Nazareth (4.18).[10] Jesus is announcing a year of Jubilee, a time for the literal cancellation of debts and reordering of social relations, as well for the transformation of attitudes. His declarations of forgiveness and befriending of sinners are bound up with his healings and exorcisms: not that sickness is seen as an indicator of individual sin, but that the restoration he brings encompasses the entire spectrum of human disorder. Release not only from unfulfillable legal or moral obligation but from the superhuman powers to which human beings are enslaved in body, mind, spirit and society is the first step in the new creative act which God accomplishes through his Messiah. Forgiveness, therefore, is revealed to be far more than the righting of an individual's relationship with God or with another person. It is the undoing of the brokenness of the world through the setting aside of demands which stand in the way of reconciliation and communion. It comes from God and was released into the world by Jesus.[11] But there is no enjoyment of it if it is not extended to others in the same movement in which it is received. Jesus taught his disciples to pray 'Forgive us our sins, for we also forgive everyone who sins against us' (11.4).[12]

But there was a cost. Jesus' friendship with the 'sinners' meant that, in stricter eyes, he would contract their ritual uncleanness. All the Gospels give us the sense that Jesus knew very well what he was doing, and ploughed his lonely furrow with clear-eyed certainty. In Lk. 9.51 he 'set his face to go to Jerusalem' – and he continued on his way undeflected, for he knew that 'no prophet can die outside Jerusalem' (13.33).

God's promised salvation, then, is seen arriving in a Messiah who announces and enacts forgiveness. This Messiah fulfils the vocation not of a majestic king but of a lonely prophet. It is utterly clear that he, and he alone, is the 'saviour' (2.11). But what of those he called to follow him? In Luke's picture of the disciples, we may see a picture of our own participation in the salvation Christ has brought.

c. Forgiveness received and required

On one level, those with whom Jesus deals, such as the prostitute of 7.36–50, the crippled woman in 13.10–17 or Zacchaeus in 19.1–10, are simply the glad recipients of his forgiveness and healing. It is clear, however, that Jesus does not mean to leave people unchanged: he tells of God's rejoicing over the sinner *who repents* (15.1–10). We see clear evidence of such repentance in the prostitute's gesture of love and Zacchaeus's gesture of generosity and restitution. But it is also clear that Jesus called disciples not only to respond in gratitude and repentance to his forgiveness, but also to *be like him in extending and expressing that forgiveness*. The clear intent, for instance, of Jesus' parable of the father and his two sons in 15.11–32 is to offer an attractive example of reaching out to the unclean and alienated, as he was doing himself, *so that others too might be inspired to tread that path*.

Luke, indeed, is distinct from Matthew and Mark in the narrowing of the space which separates Jesus and the disciples. Their abject failure, highlighted at various points especially by Mark,[13] is played down by Luke, who presents us with disciples who still fail, certainly, but are closer to being models for the Christian communities for whom Luke writes. This becomes clearest in the 'travel narrative' of Jesus' journey to Jerusalem (9.51–19.27), which is not only the story of Jesus' own pilgrimage, but also an account of his schooling of his followers in the 'way of the cross'. Luke wants his readers to join in the journey, and presents it as a possibility, as hinted by his insertion of the word 'daily' into Jesus' saying about taking up the cross (9.23). Acts will tell the story of how the followers of Jesus are fully empowered to go the way of Jesus, enduring suffering as they speak and embody the good news of forgiveness far beyond the borders of traditional Israel. But first, Jesus must die.

3. Luke's passion narrative

As the darkness closes in on Jesus, the sense both of his lonely vocation and of the close bond with his disciples is intensified. In his account of the Last Supper (22.14–30), Luke (unlike Matthew and Mark) places special emphasis on Jesus' provision for his disciples of a way of both recalling with gratitude what he did and being renewed in their corporate calling, as Jews 'remembered' the Exodus at Passover time (22.19). The repetition of the act of sharing bread and wine will enable the disciples to 'remember' Jesus during the time of his physical separation from them, to re-enact the covenant which his blood would seal (vv. 19, 20). The supper they are sharing, just before he enters his time of darkness, is something he has longed for (v. 15). In this Passover meal he starts to accomplish his 'exodus' (9.31) as, like a new Moses, he leads his people out of their bondage.

Luke places here the argument among the disciples about who would be the greatest (22.24–29): both Matthew and Mark position their equivalent accounts earlier (Mt. 20.24–28; Mk 10.41–45). Luke's placing of the story highlights the sense that with the impending departure of Jesus, the movement he started will be leaderless, and the disciples will need guidance as to how they carry it forward. Although Jesus had spoken much of a 'kingdom', they must not think of themselves as rulers of an earthly dominion, but as servants, the posture that Jesus himself adopted among them. The striking thing about Luke's account of this episode is that after Jesus has corrected the disciples' misconception about 'greatness', he affirms their loyalty: they have stood by him in his trials (v. 28). And this loyalty, he implies, will be the gateway to a real kingdom, to feasting with him, and positions of unique authority. They will indeed take forward his Messianic victory in the world.[14]

From this point, however, there is a sharp sense that Jesus must go forward alone. In Luke's account of Jesus' last night and morning, Jesus appears as the solitary hero. What he does for his disciples – and for others far beyond their circle – provides unforgettable pictures and assurances of what he can and does do for those in every generation who place themselves beneath the shadow of the cross. Let us gather these together under the great metaphors of atonement: the battle against evil, the establishment of justice, the offering of sacrifice.[15] In each way, we see Jesus taking on the role of the suffering servant of Isaiah,[16] as he does for his people what they could never do for themselves.

a. Jesus the victor

First, Jesus here enters in earnest upon the great battle. He has had skirmishes throughout his ministry, starting with his encounter with Satan in the wilderness (4.1–12), after which the devil departed from him 'until an opportune time' (4.13). As in Matthew and Mark, Jesus is also 'tested' by his opponents (11.16; 20.23).[17] Now he warns Simon that Satan has demanded to 'sift' the disciples, i.e. to put them to a hard test (22.31). Ominously, Satan has already 'entered' Judas (22.3), but he is the exception. Jesus' assurance to Simon that he has prayed that his faith will not fail implies that he is not going to let Satan have his way: Jesus is the defending champion of his people.

The cost of this protection of the disciples, however, is soon apparent. The scene where Jesus takes his disciples to pray on the Mount of Olives (22.39–46) omits Jesus' expression of overwhelming sorrow to his disciples, and his plea that they should watch with him, which are central to the equivalent accounts in Matthew (26.36–46) and Mark (14.32–42). Instead in Luke we have a stark contrast between the simple, repeated command to the disciples, 'Pray that you will not fall into temptation' (22.40, 46) and the central picture of Jesus in the very midst of the 'temptation', surely seen as the ultimate end-time trial,[18] agonizing in prayer over what he sees ahead. Jesus recognizes that this trial is one he must face alone, and his desire is that his disciples should be spared it.[19] That surely is the implication of his words in 21.36 heralding the imminent arrival of the end-times: 'Be always on the watch, and pray that you may be able to escape all that is about to happen…' The 'temptation' is no trivial matter; it is the ultimate battle. The paradox is that the disciples, who had slept instead of praying, manage to escape (this is not seen as reprehensible desertion as in Mt. 26.56 and Mk 14.50: rather it is just what Jesus seems to have encouraged in his practical instructions for their safety, in Lk. 22.35–38). But Jesus, who prayed to be spared, is taken. It is a graphic demonstration of the vicarious nature of Jesus' suffering and victory.

At the centre of the scene is the account found only in some manuscripts of Luke (22.43–44), of Jesus being strengthened by an angel, and sweating drops of blood in the anguish induced by the path he felt bound to take. The word used for his agony (ἀγωνία) expresses the necessary mental preparation of an athlete before the contest, and contrasts with the 'sorrow' mentioned in Luke as the cause of the disciples' sleep (22.45), a word (λύπη) expressing dishonourable weakness and capitulation before the fight.[20] Thus the role of Jesus as champion in the great contest is further underlined. This continues to be seen as the story unfolds, for instance in his clear-eyed compassion for the daughters of Jerusalem, urging them to weep not for him but for themselves (23.28). All the Gospels point to Jesus' loneliness in death, but for Luke it is not dereliction which is stressed (there is no cry of godforsakenness as in Matthew and Mark) but the loneliness of the hero who achieves victory on behalf of others. Through the hours of his passion we see the travail of Jesus' soul (Isa. 53.11) and know, from our perspective, that he will 'see the light of life and be satisfied'; he will have 'a portion with the great' (Isa. 53.12). But for him, of course, in those moments, the paradox was ghastly. To every outward appearance and inward instinct, the grim truth was that victory was on the other side: 'this is your hour, and the power of darkness' (Lk. 22.53).[21] Not for another three days will he be able to show his disciples that it was necessary for the Christ to suffer these things before entering his glory (24.26).

b. Jesus the righteous one

The second metaphor of atonement enacted here is the establishment of the justice of God in the midst of human injustice, and with the intention of reversing it. In all the Gospels Jesus is seen as the obedient one in contrast to the murky machinations of the authorities and the failure of the disciples. In Luke's account, the contrast is at its starkest. Jesus is the accused not at two trials, but three: before the Sanhedrin (22.66–71), Pilate (23.1–7, 13–25) and Herod (23.8–12). Three times Pilate himself declares Jesus innocent (23.4, 14, 22) and thus testifies against his own decision to give in to the demand for Jesus' crucifixion (23.24). Luke underlines this by repeating the indictment against Barabbas, the man released instead of Jesus: 'He released the man who had been thrown into prison for insurrection and murder, the one they asked for, and surrendered Jesus to their will' (23.25). This paradoxical testimony to Jesus' innocence is continued after his death by the Roman centurion overlooking the proceedings, who 'praised God and said, "Surely this was a righteous man"' (23.47). Thus Jesus fulfils the Servant's destiny: 'taken away' by a miscarriage of justice (Isa. 53.8), he is nevertheless – to the eyes of faith – the 'righteous servant' who 'justifies many' by his 'knowledge', that is by the experience of what he goes through.[22] In him the human agents of 'justice' are revealed as unjust, while those regarded as unjust by themselves and society are revealed as acceptable to God (see, e.g., 18.9–14). The resurrection reverses the authorities' verdict on Jesus (Acts 2.23–24; 3.14–15; 13.28–31) and seals God's surprising verdict on 'sinners' (Acts 2.38–39; 3.19–20, 26; 13.38–39).

c. Jesus the sacrifice

Third, we find in this story of Jesus' last hours the theme of sacrifice. At the supper he had spoken of his body given and his blood poured out 'for you' (22.19–20). His prayer on the Mount of Olives, 'Father, if you are willing, take this cup from me; yet not my will, but yours be done' (22.42) shows his readiness to drink the 'cup' of suffering, seen in the Scriptures as containing the 'wine' of God's anger with the wicked (Ps. 75.8). Notwithstanding the agony involved, he voluntarily gives himself to the Father's will that he should 'drink' it. This commitment is seen in all four Gospels (cf. Mt. 26.42; Mk 14.36; Jn 18.11). It contrasts with the reflex of violence still seen in the disciples (Lk. 22.49–51). Luke underlines the attitude of trustful self-giving through reporting Jesus' final cry on the cross: 'Father, into your hands I commit my spirit' (23.46). Once more Isaiah is fulfilled. Jesus poured out his life unto death (cf. Isa. 53.12a) and those with eyes to see recognize that in so doing 'he bore the sin of many' (Isa. 53.12b).

d. Loneliness and solidarity

In these ways Luke invites us to gaze at the solitude of Jesus, to see him as the unique Saviour who wins a victory, achieves a justice and offers a sacrifice as no other could do, and who does so on behalf of many. Beside his victory, his disciples are seen as powerless. Beside his righteousness, his accusers are seen as perverters of justice. Beside his voluntary self-giving, no one else seems truly free. Thus Luke in his distinctive manner pictures for us the truth that salvation is won through Christ alone. Yet, as we have seen, it is also characteristic of him to accent the high calling of the disciples and their crucial role in the advancement of God's plan.

So although the central victory is won by Jesus, Luke shows us that this is no isolated achievement, but one in which we can truly share. We have already noted the reference to the disciples' having 'remained' with Jesus in his trials (22.28). But earlier in the story it has been clear that Jesus sees both 'trials' and victory as not only his, but theirs. There would be 'testing', leading some to 'fall away' (8.13). But when the seventy-two whom Jesus sends out return to him to report joyfully on the victory they have witnessed on their mission, Jesus interprets what has been happening thus: 'I saw Satan fall like lightning from heaven' (10.18). In the shadow of Peter's imminent denial, Jesus foresees a time when he will strengthen his brothers (22.32). The book of Acts is a story of triumph. Trials are faced and endured, and some – notably Stephen (6.8–7.60), James (12.2) and Paul (21–28) – closely replicate in various ways the suffering of

Jesus himself. But it is the story of how the purpose of God is being fulfilled: 'repentance and forgiveness of sins' are being 'preached in [Christ's] name to all nations, beginning at Jerusalem' (Lk. 24.47). At the conclusion of the book Paul is testifying to Christ in Rome, the heart of the known world.

Next, although Jesus is supremely 'the righteous one', Luke's story is encased in the tales of righteous people worshipping in the temple (1.5–25; 2.22–52; 24.53). It includes many vivid instances of the possibility of true righteousness or its reverse (e.g. the stories of the priest, Levite and Samaritan in 10.30–37, or the rich man and Lazarus in 16.19–31). And even here at the cross we have both a Gentile attesting Jesus' righteousness, and thereby, unwittingly, his own (23.47) and a 'righteous' Jew who demonstrates his goodness through burying Jesus (23.50–53). It is noteworthy that though the rulers sneer, the 'people' simply watch, then beat their breasts and leave (23.35, 48) while there are friends of Jesus, especially women, who apparently linger (23.49). The players in the drama are not all opponents of Jesus.

Finally, although the sacrifice offered by Jesus is presented as unique, it is clear that the destiny of the disciples is not to remain as merely passive recipients of its benefits. They are to continue the work of the Messiah's kingdom by serving in the way that he has served (22.27).

e. Forgiveness to the end

Luke's portrayal of the scene of Jesus' crucifixion (23.32–43), on which the sermon at the end of this chapter is based, gathers together all the great thrusts of his good news of atonement.[23] Here indeed, though attested only in mockery, is God's Messiah, 'the king of the Jews' (vv. 35, 38). Jesus' Kingship, announced by Gabriel (1.32–33) but then veiled through the story, has resurfaced in the acclamation of the crowds on Palm Sunday (19.38) and the accusation of the leaders (22.2–3). But the pattern of Messiahship that has become increasingly evident through the Gospel here comes to a climax. Instead of royal robes, Jesus is reduced to nakedness, while the soldiers cast lots for his clothing (v. 34). Instead of the fine wine of luxury, he is offered palliative vinegar (v. 36). Here indeed is salvation, though the rulers, the soldiers and the criminal all taunt Jesus (vv. 35, 37, 39). Had he not 'saved' many? Why could he not save himself, and his fellow-victims? Here the victory of Jesus is seen in the continuation of his ministry in the very hour of his agony (vv. 34, 43). Here the righteousness of Jesus is recognized by the criminal who clearly sees the contrast between Jesus and his two neighbours (vv. 40, 41). Here the sacrifice of Jesus comes into sharp focus: if he was truly and universally to save others, it required not the saving of himself, but the giving of himself (vv. 35, 37).

And the outcome of it all is that central reality which Luke has highlighted throughout: *forgiveness.* Jesus' prayer that the Father would forgive those crucifying him (v. 34) is a speech-act of extraordinary power, revealing the meaning of the event for all generations. Luke, and the Church down the ages, recognize that the hope of divine forgiveness and peace lie in the crucified man who in his very powerlessness has power to mediate them. It is a reminder that it is not only – perhaps not mainly – the deliberate acts of evil from which humanity needs release, but the unwitting sins, for which a (temporary) means of atonement had been provided under the old covenant,[24] and which form that dismal, clouded web of alienation, resentment and fear which Jesus once for all pierced through. This forgiveness was promised and provided personally to the very fellow-victim beside him – as it had been experienced personally throughout Jesus' ministry. That very day, Jesus told him, 'you will be with me in paradise' (v. 43), and those words, too, have provided wonderful assurance to every generation. Jesus was, indeed, 'coming into his kingdom' (v. 42), and the very worst of sinners can share in its freedoms and privileges. Then, even as the darkness descended in full, the curtain of the temple would be torn apart, symbolizing the end of distance and estrangement between God and his creatures (23.44, 45). Through his death, Jesus has achieved God's salvation: and this means not only that he has done for humanity what we could never do for ourselves; nor only that he has provided a wonderful example of forgiveness; but that he has released into the world a power of love that will, in time, renew the cosmos.

Luke also has words specifically for the preacher; for the prophetic, Spirit-inspired ministry exercised by Jesus is now exercised by his Spirit-filled followers (Acts 2.1–41). The task of proclaiming release for the captives, the forgiveness of sins, is now ours. And the words we speak in the name of Jesus, like Jesus' own, are directed not merely to the pacifying of individuals, but to the transformation of the whole created order.[25]

Sermon[26] and commentary

Some of you may have read recently the story of an elderly man who was a prisoner of war at the hands of the Japanese in the 1940s.[27] He was one of those sent to lay the so-called Railway of Death through Thailand and Burma, nearly half of whom never came home. Beaten with bamboo canes and rifle butts, kicked unconscious while lying in the dust, forced to hold a heavy drum above his head for eight hours in the blazing sun, or he would be kicked or prodded with a bayonet: he admitted that after the war, he had hated the Japanese and anything to do with them for half a century.

Then one day he was invited to go on a pilgrimage to Japan. This was organized by a group called Agape, 'Love', founded by a Japanese lady married to an Englishman, who had become a Christian. This lady had discovered in Japan a remarkable memorial, a beautifully maintained garden created by local people in memory of 16 British soldiers who had died as prisoners of war working in a copper mine. This discovery had spurred her to seek to heal the wounds of the past.

Sceptical, the old gentleman went on the pilgrimage. The Japanese family he stayed with sensed his hostility. But then one day he went for a walk down to a river with two of their little girls to feed the fish. Communication was difficult because of the language barrier. But one of the girls, aged seven, knew that the old man looked very unhappy. This is how he described what happened next: 'I felt a little hand slide into mine. I looked down and saw the smiling face of one of the daughters. In that instant, more than 50 years of hatred vanished. I felt great warmth flow through me. I felt so at peace. I thought that I couldn't go on with such bitterness in my heart. These are not the people who tortured us.' He returned to the house recognizably a different person. The terrible nightmares which had dogged him for 50 years ceased.

Five years on, at a celebration he addressed in London, he introduced the girl, now 12, to those gathered, with the words: 'I want you to meet the little girl who saved me. She healed me.'

Jesus said, as he hung pinned to a wooden cross, 'Father, forgive them: for they do not know what they are doing'.

To forgive; to ask God to forgive. It may be one of the hardest things we are ever called on to do. Because it's not just a matter of saying a few words, or trying to block out some bad memories. It's a matter of letting go, deep down. Releasing another person or whole tribe of people from the psychological bind in which we've held them. And in so doing, releasing ourselves. It may take 50 years, sometimes. *But it is possible.*

The opening of the sermon paints a picture of the difficulty of forgiveness, but also seeks to evoke the wonder of it. This is a good-news story – forgiveness happens: and the release is on both sides – for the one forgiving as well as the one(s) being forgiven. (Hence there is no need to find a way of explaining the petition in Lk. 11.4, 'Forgive us our sins, for we also forgive everyone who sins against us' as if we needed to defend Jesus against the charge of making God's grace conditional upon human 'works'. The forgiveness of others is not a mere 'work' such as those contrasted with 'faith' by Paul in Romans 4. It is itself a liberating movement into the sphere of grace.)

In linking the story to the words of Jesus on the cross, there was no suggestion that Jesus himself needed release – as if he had been bearing a grudge – but there is a reminder that these words were not said in a situation of calm reflection, but one of acute agony. To recall Jesus' prayer for forgiveness while forgetting that it was directed towards those crucifying him at that moment would be to trivialize God's atoning work. If forgiveness is costly for us, how much more costly was it for Jesus?

I remember an elderly lady who used to attend regular church gatherings. Her face was lined not only from age but from the bitterness of being unable to forgive the way her late husband had been treated by a colleague in the management of the large firm where he had worked. I moved away. I don't know if she is still alive. I don't know if she ever forgave. But *I know it was possible.*

By naming a situation of non-forgiveness which, as far as I knew, had never been resolved, I further tried to avoid speaking glibly about the subject. The example also brings the subject closer to everyday experience (although as it turned out, there was a member of the congregation who had lost a close relative in the Japanese POW camps: an instance of a sermon turning out to be more pertinent than the preacher imagined beforehand!)

This was the power released by Jesus on the cross. In that scene, it's as if everybody else is blindfolded, apart from Jesus. From his position of bodily and mental torture, he saw what nobody else saw. That the power which the world needs more than any other is the power to forgive. The soldiers, the leaders, the criminal crucified beside him: they all saw Jesus and simply mocked because he had been called Messiah or King. 'He saved others; let him save himself, if he is the Messiah of God, his chosen one!' 'If you are the King of the Jews, save yourself!' 'Are you not the Messiah? Save yourself and us!' For them, the irony of the title above the cross would have been grimly amusing: 'This is the King of the Jews'. Ha!

They took it for granted that the hallmark of being a Messiah or King was a very different sort of power. The sort that talks about stamping out evil by force of arms or bombs in operations with names like 'Phantom Fury'. The sort that's expressed by soldiers rushing into a mosque shouting 'we'll give 'em hell'. The sort that kidnaps and murders innocent women like Margaret Hassan, a woman who loved children and whose knees the children would rush out to hug – yes, that stoops even to that, if it seems to help the cause.

But that was not the hallmark of this Messiah, this King. For him, that was not the way to eradicate evil. For him, kingship meant the giving of royal pardon. And that meant allowing himself to be stripped of all dignity, even his clothes, and being nailed to a cross to suffer a slowly agonizing death. Far from being in a palace with butlers serving fine wine, here was a soldier offering him vinegar.

Faith in the possibility of forgiveness through the power of Christ is greatly strengthened by hearing stories such as the one of the old man returning to Japan. But here I testified that the ultimate source of such faith is the demeanour of the suffering Jesus. I portrayed his words of 'royal pardon' as completely bound up with his own readiness to be on the receiving end of suffering rather than inflicting it. The worldwide implications of this scene of the cross are suggested: Jesus not only makes 'salvation' a reality for individuals, he releases the power of transforming forgiveness into the world.

The allusions to contemporary events in Iraq, in the context of a sermon on forgiveness, were perhaps doubly subversive. On one level, I suggested that some attitudes and behaviour of the Western forces were directly contrary to the way of Jesus (a controversial message in the UK or US context), as were the kidnapping tactics of the terrorists (not at all controversial in this context). But on another level, the implication – as will become clearer as the sermon proceeds – is that all alike both need, and can discover, forgiveness.

It is interesting to reflect here on the political dimensions of preaching. The preacher's prophetic task is not simply to ape journalistic 'opinion' columns. The media readily depict current affairs in black-and-white terms ('pro-war', 'anti-war' etc.) but the preacher is called to go deeper (as do the best journalists). In this case, the question of the rightness or wrongness of going to war was not addressed: the issue was the behaviour of different parties once in a state of war. Further still, the aim was not to pronounce moralistically on that behaviour, but to hold it up beside the figure of Jesus. The Gospels show Jesus presenting examples for his disciples to follow or avoid (e.g. Lk. 10.30–37). The example of Jesus himself is the greatest of all, and here it is contrasted with that of those who mocked him on the cross.[28] But the most significant way in which the sermon seeks to go beyond 'opinion' comment is in the announcement of good news: Jesus not only exemplified forgiveness, he enables it.

And it was as if Jesus could almost see the blindfolds on the eyes of almost everyone around him. Father, forgive them: *for they do not know what they are doing.* This doesn't mean that the soldiers, or the leaders, or anyone else, were innocent: if they were, there would be nothing to forgive. It means that they, like so many today, were caught up in a frightening web of evil so much bigger than themselves, so complex and pervasive, that they can't comprehend their one little part in it: and the only way out is forgiveness, release. Father, *release them.*

And as we hear of bombs and torture directed against, not the obviously evil characters, but the most conspicuously innocent, we look again to Jesus on the cross, the most conspicuously innocent person of all, and we hear his words, pitying those blindfolded tormentors: *Father, forgive them, for they do not know what they are doing.*

And as we hear the fresh-faced young privates from Kansas or Scotland saying, explicitly, I really don't know what we're doing here, do we hear the words from the cross echoing back to them? *Father, forgive them, for they do not know what they are doing.*

The ignorance of those for whom Jesus prays is seen not as an excuse for their sin, but as a fact of their condition which Jesus sees with pity. Scripture presents 'sin' not as simple individual wrongdoing, but a state of being which grips the whole human race. In the Gospels this is seen vividly in terms of the demonic hold of evil forces over people's lives. Similarly, the release that Jesus brings is far more than an assurance that God holds nothing against them. It is an opening of their spiritual eyes to see their situation as it is, and a bestowal of power to live in true humanity under the lordship of Jesus. The refrain 'Father, forgive them' turns the sermon at this point into prayer and aims at an identification of preacher and hearers with the dying Jesus.

And until we have received the royal pardon, until we have felt the influx of *real* Messianic power deep down inside wounded, resentful souls, we all go on in the 'fog of war', not knowing what we are doing. But the release can come.

It can come through looking hard at that scene of the King's death, and asking ourselves which group we would have been found in – which group we *are* found in: and listening again to those words that Jesus spoke.

Are we among those who mock? Those who think all this talk of forgiveness, all this meek submission to cruelty, all this refusal to hit out and hit back, is thoroughly wimpish, not nearly macho enough for our taste?

Are we among the soldiers, caught up in patterns of response to events that seem ultimately beyond our control?

'Father, release them: for they do not know what they are doing'.

Are we among the crowds, looking on, watching, unsure what to make of it all?

Or are we like the one person apart from Jesus without some sort of blindfold on – the criminal who knew that Jesus really was the heir of a kingdom? Let's hear again what Jesus said to him: 'Truly, I tell you, today you will be with me in Paradise'.

The hearers are now invited to see themselves in the scene around the cross: maybe as those who continue 'not knowing what they are doing'; or, like the penitent criminal, already 'released', grasping that the dying Jesus was indeed a powerful King; or, like the crowds, somewhere in between. The listeners are assumed to be for the most part professing Christians, but a return to the cross can be extraordinarily challenging for all believers; we so easily become distant from its reality and its true implications. We may say the Creed, but what we actually think of Jesus will be seen in how we respond to this scene.

The kingdom is real. Forgiveness is possible. Not just for the dying but for the living. So Paul says this is the climax of God's work through the one he has appointed king over all things: to release us from the power of darkness and transfer us into the kingdom of his beloved son, in whom we have the forgiveness of sins. This is the achievement of God through this King: to reconcile to himself all things, whether on earth or in heaven, by making peace through the blood of his cross.

And by a mighty chain reaction, the process continues. Those who are released, release others. A little Japanese girl releases an English pensioner as he feels her hand and looks into her eyes. He releases the figures of his night-mares and is no longer haunted.

And so this morning we will clasp the hands of others in a sign of peace, releasing them, releasing ourselves.

We will pray for a world where the blindfolds are still very evident, and connect with the power of the King to bring release.

We will take bread and wine, and look into the eyes of Jesus who set the process of release in motion.

And we will go *in peace* to love and serve the Lord.

The link from the penitent thief to today's Church is made via the words of Col. 1.13–14, 20, part of the first reading in the service. The dying words of two men utterly shamed in the world's eyes are seen in the light of God's breathtaking, cosmic plan of atonement. And in the indicatives of the sermon's close, the good news that the atonement is still happening is reiterated, first with a reminder of the story with which we began, and then with reference to the liturgy shortly to continue, seeking to show with what pregnant meaning, in the light of the cross, the 'peace', the prayers, the communion and the dismissal are filled.

6

The Word became flesh: John 1.1–14

1. Incarnation and atonement

Talk about the Word becoming flesh evokes memories of candlelit carol services, and of children excitedly waiting for presents. Amidst the crass materialism surrounding Christmas those words serve as powerful reminders of the down-to-earth God who became flesh and dwelt among us. However, while the Prologue to John's Gospel pops up regularly in many Christmas services, it is not the kind of passage which many preachers instinctively turn to when they feel led to preach about atonement.[1] For when it comes to preaching atonement John's Gospel offers so many other attractive possibilities.

For example, preachers may take their cue from John the Baptist who proclaims the atoning significance of Jesus by drawing attention to the 'Lamb of God who takes away the sin of the world' (Jn 1.29). This passage alone could keep the preacher busy for some time, with Don Carson identifying no fewer than nine possible interpretations of the phrase 'the Lamb of God'.[2]

Other homiletical possibilities arise at strategic points in the narrative, where we find the Evangelist foreshadowing the approaching cross with the ominous comments that the 'hour' for Jesus has not yet come (Jn 2.4; 4.21, 23; 7.30; 8.20; see also 13.1; 17.1). It is when some Greeks arrive, seeking Jesus, that the die is cast and Jesus announces that the hour of his glorification, through his lifting up to death on the cross, has dawned (12.20–33). A further invitation to meditate upon the work of Christ comes after the raising of Lazarus, when the High Priest inadvertently highlights the atoning significance of Jesus' death by stating that 'it is better to have one man die for the people, than to have the whole nation destroyed' (11.50). In addition to inviting congregations to look through these windows on the cross,

89

another possibility is to join the long and honourable tradition of those who have focused upon 'the seven words of Jesus' on the cross; because three of them are found in ch. 19 (vv. 26–27, 28, 30).

Faced with such a wealth of material, it is not surprising that preachers tend to overlook the Prologue in their thinking about atonement. However, as George Beasley-Murray reminds us, while the 'death and resurrection of Jesus find no mention in the prologue…that twin event stands as the presupposition of its every line, so surely as the incarnation of the Logos is presupposed through the whole. The Word of whom the prologue speaks is the Christ who revealed the divine glory in his living and dying and rising.'[3]

It is also important to remember the way in which convictions about the person and the work of Christ are so closely bound together. So we find Jürgen Moltmann observing that 'in the history of theology, the doctrine about the person of Christ has always provided the inner premise for the soteriology which is to be substantiated; while soteriology is the outward result of the Christology'.[4] Such an interdependence of the person and work of Christ appears to be at the heart of all doctrines of atonement, because it is the special nature of the person of Christ which makes his sufferings especially effective.[5]

If christology and soteriology are so interdependent, this not only suggests that reflection upon incarnation cannot escape thinking about atonement, but also implies that atonement can be understood as the natural development of the incarnation. This linkage is expressed very powerfully by Hans Urs von Balthasar, who asserts that:

> he who says Incarnation, also says Cross. And this is so for two reasons. The Son of God took human nature in its fallen condition, and with it, therefore, the worm in its entrails – mortality, fallenness, self-estrangement, death – which sin introduced into the world… The second reason…has to do not with the man assumed but with the Logos assuming: to become man is for him, in a most hidden yet very real sense, already humiliation – yes, indeed, as many would say, a deeper humiliation than the going to the Cross itself.[6]

One classic treatment of these overlapping themes of incarnation and atonement is found in Athanasius' famous treatise, *The Incarnation of the Word of God*.[7] Alasdair Heron argues that 'there is material in abundance for preaching in Athanasius'; because 'a theology which is concerned to explore and proclaim the mystery of the movement of God towards man in Christ will always have something to preach'.[8] This chapter picks up that idea by reading Athanasius' reflections on the incarnation alongside John's Prologue, to see what light such a reading may shed upon that profound summary of the gospel contained in Jn 1.14.

2. Creation and fall

The opening words of the Prologue deliberately echo Gen. 1.1. For those with ears to hear, the Evangelist alerts us to the fact that the Word becoming flesh signals the dawn of a new creation. In a fallen world where the darkness constantly seeks to extinguish the light, such a re-creation is only possible because the one through whom all things 'came into being' has now come into the world to begin the work of healing and restoration.

The Prologue signals the divine nature of the Son by talking about the Logos who was with God, and who was God. At the Council of Nicaea in 325 AD, with Athanasius in attendance, the Church defined the nature of the God-Man by saying that the Son was *homoousios*, 'of one substance', with the Father. Heron argues that the phrase '"*homoousios* with the Father" should be seen as the epitome of the Gospel, and the criterion of an authentic evangelical theology'.[9] The rationale for such a claim is that it is only a Christ who is fully divine who is able to reveal God fully, rescue fallen humanity and restore a damaged creation. As Thomas Torrance explains, 'If Jesus Christ the incarnate Son is not true God from true God, then we are not saved, for it is only God who can save; but if Jesus Christ is not truly man then salvation does not touch our human existence and condition'.[10]

Writing at a time of doctrinal controversy in the early decades of the fourth century, Athanasius begins *De Incarnatione* by affirming the divine nature of the Word. Although the technical term *homoousios* is not prominent in *De Incarnatione*, the message is unambiguous. For 'the Word of the Father is Himself divine, that all things that are owe their being to His will and power, and that it is through Him that the good Father gives order to creation, by Him that all things are moved, and through Him that they receive their being'.[11]

Fundamental to his argument is the conviction that the Word through whom 'all things came into being' is the only one who is competent to rescue and restore the originally good creation, which is now on the road to ruin. This means that 'the first fact that you must grasp is this: *the renewal of creation has been wrought by the Self-same Word Who made it in the beginning.* There is thus no inconsistency between creation and salvation.'[12]

Within creation human beings are the special beneficiaries of divine grace and mercy because upon them 'He bestowed a grace which other creatures lacked - namely the impress of His own Image, a share in the reasonable being of the very Word Himself, so that, reflecting Him and themselves becoming reasonable and expressing the Mind of God even as He does, though in limited degree they might continue for ever in the blessed and only true life of the saints in paradise'.[13]

Although human beings are by nature subject to mortality, God has provided a way to keep mortality at bay, through 'constant contemplation' of the one in whose image human beings have been created. For if mortal man 'preserves that Likeness through constant contemplation, then his nature is deprived of its power and he remains incorrupt'.[14]

Sadly, however, paradise has been lost, because human beings have turned away from eternal things and a process of corruption and decay has been set in motion. For 'when this happened, men began to die, and corruption ran riot among them and held sway over them to an even more than natural degree, because it was the penalty of which God had forewarned them for transgressing the commandment'.[15] Now that the prospect of paradise has been lost, the sad fact is that the human race is speeding along the path of self-destruction. This presents a problem not only to fallen humanity, but also to the loving God who created human beings in his own image.

3. The divine dilemma and its solution

The sorry predicament which human beings have brought upon themselves presents God with a dilemma. It is clear that He cannot 'go back upon His word, such that 'man, having transgressed, should not die'. However, 'it was equally monstrous that beings which once had shared the nature of the Word should perish and turn back again into non-existence through corruption'. So with human beings 'on the road to ruin, what then was God, being Good to do?... It was impossible, therefore, that God should leave man to be carried off by corruption, because it would be unfitting and unworthy of Himself.'[16]

It would clearly be unthinkable for such a faithful God suddenly to go back on his word and pretend that nothing serious had happened. However, it is significant to notice that God's involvement in the drama of redemption does not arise from a divine need to satisfy some external law or principle. God is inherently loving and good and the need to initiate redemption arises from his own loving character. ✗

love trumps

At this point Athanasius makes a highly significant observation about what was needed to remedy this sorry situation. For 'had it been a case of trespass only, and not of a subsequent corruption, repentance would have been well enough; but when once transgression had begun men came under the power of the corruption proper to their nature and were bereft of the grace which belonged to them as creatures in the Image of God'.[17] In other words, if salvation had merely been a matter of forgiving sin, then repentance would have been sufficient and God would have been willing to forgive. There is no implication here that Christ had to be punished in order to make God willing to forgive human sin. Athanasius seems to imply that God would have been willing to forgive repentant sinners, but that on its own this would not have been sufficient to deal with the process of decay and corruption which human sin had set in motion. What was needed was the intervention of the only one who was competent to stop the rot and re-create fallen humanity. The only possible candidate for the role of Saviour is the Living Word through whom 'all things came into being'.

So the creative Word of God 'entered the world in a new way, stooping to our level in His love and Self-revealing to us... Thus taking a body like our own, because all our bodies were liable to the corruption of death, He surrendered His body to death instead of all, and offered it to the Father. This he did out of sheer love for us, so that in His death all might die.'[18] Once again it is worth underlining the fact that the motivation for this divine intervention in human affairs was 'sheer love'. The triune God of grace and love is not subject to some external law of justice which he must observe or satisfy. Moved by 'sheer love' the drama of redemption involves the living Word stooping to conquer sin and death; restoring a creation which has been scarred and disfigured by sin and the corruption sin lets loose.

The key characteristic of the body assumed by the Word of the Father was its inherent mortality. The divine Word assumed such a body which was 'capable of death, in order that it, through belonging to the Word Who is above all, might become in dying a sufficient exchange for all'. Such an event has saving consequences for all people because 'the solidarity of mankind is such that, by virtue of the Word's indwelling in a single human body the corruption which goes with death has lost its power over all'.[19] In keeping with all models of atonement, Athanasius assumes that Christ functions as a representative, so that his actions have saving implications for sinful humanity. The defeat of the death which was the consequence of human sinfulness was not the end of the process, because the Word assumed a human body both 'in order that in it death might once for all be destroyed, and that men might be renewed according to the Image'[20] of their Creator. George Bebawi explains that in this saving work, 'Athanasius does not separate the death of Jesus from his resurrection. Salvation is not two steps, death and resurrection; rather, accepting death abolishes its power and re-creates a new life, so the cross and the resurrection go hand in hand.'[21]

What begins to emerge here is a distinctive approach to atonement which stresses the re-creation of fallen humanity by Christ. Athanasius' doctrine of *theosis* or *theopoiesis* ('deification') is summed up in the famous phrase, 'He, indeed, assumed humanity that we might become god' or 'he became man that we might become divine'.[22] Athanasius explores this idea in other writings; but it is important to note that he does distinguish between the way in which the divine Word is God, and the way in which believers share in the divine life. The Word of the Father is the divine Son by nature and in truth, whereas believers become sons and daughters of God by adoption and grace. Hence he asserts that 'we are made sons through Him by adoption and grace, as partaking of His Spirit'.[23]

Athanasius links this claim directly to John's affirmation that 'He came to what was his own, and his own people did not accept him. But to all who received him, who believed in his name, he gave power to become children of God, who were born, not of blood or of the will of the flesh or of the will of man, but of God' (Jn 1.11–13). Reflecting on these verses Beasley-Murray states that 'the positive aspect of the ministry of the Logos is here described: there were those who "received" the Logos, i.e., welcomed the Word in faith. To them he gave authority to become God's children; they were not so by nature (contrary to the Gnostics!), but became such by authorization of the Logos.'[24] It is also worth noticing the way in which such language resonates with 2 Pet. 1.4, which talks about believers becoming 'participants in the divine nature'.[25]

Torrance observes that the approach adopted by Athanasius has sometimes been misinterpreted in ways which create the impression that the incarnation automatically brings about salvation. However, it is important to make clear that the union of the divine Logos with dying humanity does not automatically reverse humanity's sorry state. Having entered into the depths of our human existence, the key thing is to notice how the incarnate Logos acts 'personally on our behalf'... For

through his incarnation the Son of God has made himself one with us as we are, and indeed made himself what we are, thereby not only making our nature his own but taking on himself our lost condition subject to condemnation and death, all in order that he might substitute himself in our place, discharge our debt, and offer himself in atoning sacrifice to God on our behalf. Since sin and its judgement have affected the actual nature of death as we experience it, Christ has made our death and fate his own, thereby taking on himself the penalty due to all in death, destroying the power of sin and its stronghold in death and thus redeeming and rescuing us from its dominion.[26]

Although Christ has taken upon himself the penalty which all deserve, this does not lead Athanasius in the direction of universalism. His purpose in writing is to refute the objections raised by both Jews and Gentiles in his own day, and to deepen believers' faith and trust in Christ. It is clear that he expects people to respond to the sheer love of the divine Word with a faith that leads to a godly life. For the day is coming when Christ will return as Judge, and 'then for the good is laid up the heavenly kingdom, but for those who practise evil outer darkness and the eternal fire'.[27]

4. Death and resurrection

The Word, who became flesh, 'pitched his tabernacle among us' (Jn 1.14); and so shared in the precarious existence of all human flesh. Vinoth Ramachandra draws out the implications of this divine vulnerability by saying that 'the incarnation speaks of a God who *is* entangled with our world, who immerses himself in our tragic history, who embraces our humanity with all its vulnerability, pain and confusion, including our evil and our death'.[28] At this point John is not portraying the divine Son simply as a sympathetic fellow-sufferer. For the one who became flesh, not only endured death, but also overcame death through his resurrection. As the rest of John's Gospel unfolds, it becomes apparent that the incarnate Son has both taken away the sin of the world (1.29), and decisively broken the power of death.

Stephen Sykes argues that:

in the history of Christian thought the balancing of the twin negativities of mortality and sin has been a recurrent problem, over which indeed Greek and Latin Christianity have diverged in emphasis. In the writings of the Greek fathers, up to and including the fourth century, the fundamental problem of man was his corruptibility, his transient hastening to death. In Latin theology, the situation is different. In the highly influential form given to the soteriological structure of theology by Augustine, who combined elements derived from Ambrose and Cyprian, the emphasis is placed rather upon the inevitability and culpability of sin as the prime determinant of the human situation.[29]

In terms of this analysis, Athanasius can be seen as one of those who portrays Christ as the one who has conquered death, for he states that the divine Word 'endured shame from men that we might inherit immortality'.[30] Such a perspective upon why the Word became flesh offers resources for preaching atonement at a time when many people are alleged to be more conscious of their mortality than their sinfulness.

Indeed Athanasius has sometimes been accused of being so concerned with the way in which Christ has conquered death, that he neglects the seriousness of sin, and the need for men and women to be saved from guilt. The evidence, however, suggests that he had a more rounded approach. While it is true that he places great emphasis upon the overcoming of death, he never lets his readers forget that death is the direct outcome of human disobedience to God's clear commands. Human sinfulness means that:

> there was a debt owing which must needs be paid; for...all men were due to die... Thus it happened that two opposite marvels took place at once: the death of all was consummated in the Lord's body; yet, because the Word was in it, death and corruption were in the same act utterly abolished. Death there had to be, and death for all, so that the due of all might be paid.[31]

As his argument moves to a triumphant conclusion, Athanasius playfully says that 'such and so many are the Saviour's achievements that follow from His Incarnation, that to try to number them is like gazing at the open sea and trying to count the waves. One cannot see all the waves with one's eyes, for when one tries to do so those that are following on baffle one's senses.'[32] While a brief commentary cannot do full justice to Athanasius' thinking about the Word who became flesh, the evidence examined here is more than enough to confirm Heron's claim that 'there is material in abundance for preaching in Athanasius'.[33] Likening the Saviour's multiple achievements to the waves of the sea, suggests that the preacher's calling is not to squeeze every aspect of atonement into a neat and tidy system, but rather to encourage people to explore the unfathomable depths of the atoning work of Christ.

Sermon[34]

Early last year the journalist Polly Toynbee received a letter which issued a challenge. And the challenge was this; was she willing to give up her home comforts and live on the national minimum wage of £4.10 per hour for the season of Lent? But to begin with it didn't seem a very good idea and so she put the letter back in the tray.

> It would be impossible. How could I possibly live on £4.10 an hour? That's £164 a week, twice what two of us paid the other night for one local restaurant meal in Clapham, nothing exceptional. Every time I thought about my gold-plated life as a journalist – the taxis, the *Guardian's* car, my mobile phone, eating out, or the gifts for my family and what's called "discretionary spending" on pleasing non-necessities – it seemed undoable. I had to carry out my ordinary working life. How would I get from place to place in a hurry, to press conferences, seminars or interviews, with just a bus pass? What was it Mrs Thatcher said about only failures using buses?

> I thought about my Victorian house bought decades ago and, like most in London, now worth a fortune. I thought about how much comes in each month, never needing to count the cost. It couldn't be done. Or at least, nothing remotely resembling my life could be lived on that sum.[35]

> The more I thought about this project, the closer the time came, the more I was struck by the absurdity of it, too. Several times I almost abandoned the whole idea. It was play-acting, Marie Antoinette as a milk maid in the Petit Trianon. In all my life I have never experienced one moment's financial insecurity, nor even the remotest fear of it. I was born into rock-solid middle-class security reaching back as many generations as I know about on both sides of my family. Like most people who have had well-paid careers for many years, I find it hard to imagine falling far. To make the imaginative leap I have to devise some elaborate scenario that would deprive me of my ability to earn, losing my home, my pension, my savings, my family and friends.[36]

However, despite her misgivings the idea began to grow on her. She'd got some leave from the *Guardian* newspaper and she decided she'd go ahead with this challenge.

Well, one thing led to another and soon she'd got the keys to a Lambeth Council flat on the Clapham Park Estate – a flat which no one else was willing to rent – and so she started her experiment of living on the national minimum wage for the season of Lent in 2002. And over the next few weeks, as she lived in the flat, she went out hunting for jobs at the local Job Centre.

She worked at a telephone call centre.
She worked as a hospital porter; as a school dinner lady; as a cleaner.

She worked in a cake factory and as a care assistant in a nursing home. And she tells her story in the book, *Hard Work: Life in Low-Pay Britain.*

Now, maybe it's because we live in the London Borough of Lambeth – maybe it's because the Clapham Park Estate is just a mile or two up the road – that I think it's an interesting story.

It's an interesting story and alongside that story I want to remind you of another story about a person who sacrificed comfort, and position, and power in a much more dramatic way. For I want to remind you of the story of self-sacrifice that's summed up in those verses which were read to us a few minutes ago. I want to remind you of the story which can be summed up in just ten words – in the ten words which say that '*The Word became flesh and made his dwelling among us*'.

The Word

Tomorrow the Hutton Enquiry[37] resumes, and as various people have given evidence to the Enquiry every word is under scrutiny. Every word is analysed by the judge, by the journalists and by the politicians.

Every word matters because words reveal things. The words I speak reveal the sort of person I am; they reveal where I've come from.

Here in John's Gospel *the Word* is a title describing the Son of God. *The Word* is God's one and only Son; the Son who is the image of the Father. *The Word* was there at the beginning of time. *The Word* was with God and *the Word* was God; and through *this Word* all things were made. *The Word* – who is *the Son of God* – is and was fully divine. And because *the Word* is the eternal Son of God, He is the one who reveals the truth about God.

'*The Word became flesh and made his dwelling among us*'. Now, often we hear those words being read out during our Christmas carol services; and we marvel at the mind-boggling miracle that the eternal Son of God has come to earth in person – in the person of a tiny vulnerable little baby.

But there's more…
As we zoom in on these words about *the Word becoming flesh* we find more and more layers of meaning and miracle.

Polly Toynbee spent just 40 days trying to live on the minimum wage. Her few weeks in that Lambeth Council flat represented a very limited sharing in the life of people on the Clapham Park Estate; and she admits the limitations of what she did. But, when *the Word became flesh*; when the eternal Son of God left the comfort of heaven to come to earth; he didn't come for a few weeks or months; he came for life. He came to share in our life to the full.

You see when it says that '*The Word became flesh and made his dwelling among us*', it doesn't mean that he assumed a cleaned-up version of our human nature. It means that Jesus came in '*the likeness of human flesh*'. This was a complete identification with our fallen human nature, because 'the Son of God took human form in its fallen condition'.[38]

And by taking upon himself our fallen human nature, the Son of God established a link between God and us. One writer puts it like this: 'God did not stay distant from (humanity) remote and isolated; rather in Jesus, God chose to live with humanity in the midst of human weakness, confusion and pain... The incarnation binds Jesus to the "everydayness" of human experience.'[39]

As we zoom in on this summary of the Christian story (Jn 1.14), we see that 'out of sheer love' the Son of God came to share in our fallen human existence.

But there's more...
At the end of her time on the Clapham Park Estate, Polly Toynbee says:

I took the keys back to the housing office, signed away my lease and then set off on the ten-minute walk back to my own home. Traversing the streets between, I looked back on what it had been like to try (unsuccessfully) to live on a little above the minimum wage. I had cheated by clocking up big debts, cheated by eating some meals with family and friends, cheated by going home some weekend nights. None the less, during that time the shape of my life and the shape of the city where I have always lived altered beyond recognition.[40]

Maybe she's a bit harsh on herself to say that she's cheated – but she's honestly explaining that she's avoided some of the most painful bits of being poorly paid.

But when *the Word became flesh*...

he didn't avoid the painful bits of life;
he didn't avoid the painful consequences of his total identification with fallen humanity; and,

he didn't avoid the painful reality of the death which awaits our sinful humanity; the death which is the wages of sin.

Part of what it means, when we read that 'The Word became flesh and made his dwelling among us', is that the Son of God came to die for our sins; he came to deal with our fallenness.

But there's more...

Polly Toynbee's book *Hard Work* provides a glimpse, a snapshot of one part of our society. It pleads for a change in government policy. But probably it won't change very much.

But when 'The Word became flesh and made his dwelling among us', it represented a dramatic change in the relationship between God and the world. For the incarnation, the Word becoming flesh is the first stage in God's rescue plan. By his incarnation, his life, his death, his resurrection and his ascension into heaven, the Son of God was repairing the damage created by sin. He was destroying – putting to death – our sinful human nature, in order to re-create human beings; in order to restore the image of God in us that was damaged by our sin.

As we zoom in on these words about *the Word becoming flesh*, we discover that they signal a new creation, as God's Son comes to create a new humanity – a new race of people reconciled with God and alive with his love.

That's why one writer claims that 'The Word becoming flesh is the decisive event in human history...because the incarnation changes God's relationship to humanity and humanity's relationship to God. The incarnation means that human beings can see, hear and know God in ways never before possible.'[41]

Now I don't imagine that many people on the Clapham Park Estate noticed when the journalist Polly Toynbee was living on their estate for a few weeks. It would've been surprising if they'd noticed. But what is surprising is that when the Son of God came to earth to transform the relationship between God and humanity, most people didn't notice.

He was in the world, and though the world was made through him, the world did not recognise him. He came to that which was his own, but his own did not receive him. Yet to all who received him, to those who believed in his name, he gave the right to become children of God. (Jn 1.10–12)

The great North African Christian leader Athanasius summed this up by saying that 'The Word was made man in order that we might be made divine'. In other words, the Word became flesh in order that we might become God's children.

> Yet to all who received him, to those who believed in his name, he gave the right to become children of God – children born not of natural descent, nor of human decision or a husband's will, but born of God. (Jn 1.12–13)

The Word became flesh
The Eternal Son of God became flesh:

Shared our fallen humanity
Shared our life to the full
Shared in our death
He came to repair the damage caused by sin
He came to transform our relationship with God
He came so that you could become a child of God.

Hard Work: Life in Low-Pay Britain. An interesting story that will provoke all sorts of reactions. It would be interesting to hear your reactions to it.

Much more important, however, is how you respond to the life-changing story that's summed up in these ten words: '*The Word became flesh and made his dwelling among us*'.

Commentary

This sermon is structured simply as an interweaving of two stories. Through the story of Polly Toynbee's adventure of living on the minimum wage for six weeks, the congregation are invited to reflect on the wonder of the Word becoming flesh.

As we stress elsewhere in this book, preachers of the ultimate divine rescue plan are faced with the ultimate challenge: how to speak of a mystery that is unspeakable, yet must be communicated to the very depth of human consciousness and receptivity? The fact that, again and again, the mystery *is* communicated and received is a miracle of God's grace. But, like the incarnation itself, that miraculous grace works through ordinary human means. Our life experiences can become pictures, inadequate of course, of divine truth, sacramental windows through which the glory of God can be glimpsed. Thus the story of a rich journalist's experiment with poverty helps to open up the marvel of the grace of the Lord Jesus Christ who 'though he was rich, became poor, that you through his poverty might become rich' (2 Cor. 8.9).

Of course, as with all our human pictures of supra-human reality, there is a sense that the parallel is illuminating by contrast, as much as by comparison. So the preacher underlines that whereas Toynbee's experience of the housing estate was temporary and comparatively superficial, Jesus' sharing in human nature was complete. She was able to avoid some of the uncomfortable aspects of poverty, whereas Jesus entered the whole human condition, even to the point of 'the death which is the wages of sin'. She hoped to make some political difference, but it is doubtful how far she succeeded; Jesus achieved lasting reconciliation between God and humanity. She probably wasn't noticed; but – and here is a twist at the climax of the sermon – *most people didn't notice Jesus either.* At the very point where one might have expected the contrast to be greatest (surely Jesus' heroic act would have been *recognized*!), the similarity is closest. That is the measure of the self-humbling of God.

The use of Toynbee's experience helps to enforce the sense of an indissoluble link between Christ's coming to earth as a man and his death on the cross, between incarnation and atonement. The idea of one of our wealthy contemporaries taking on, even in a small way, the limitations, inconvenience and messiness of a life of poverty brings home to us the fact that the road to Calvary started right back in Bethlehem. Thus 'Trace we the babe who hath retrieved our loss / From his poor manger to his bitter cross.'[42]

An important image in the sermon is that of 'dwelling' (Jn 1.14). It is perhaps this idea more than any other which enables the hearer first to identify with Toynbee's initial scepticism as to the possibility of taking up the challenge, then feel with her the shock of embarking on a totally different lifestyle, and through that to sense the awesome possibility of what came true in God's taking human flesh. Our dwelling-places are so important to us that the thought of exchanging them for anything less secure is deeply unsettling. Yet in Christ God came to 'dwell' amongst us. He left his safe home to share our vulnerable one.

The sermon gently leads us through the story of John's Prologue to its heart, keeping the momentum through the catchphrase 'but there's more' and the repetition of the key phrase 'The Word became flesh'. The hearers are left to ponder the story, but are surely also invited, implicitly, to place themselves afresh within it. What would it mean to accept among us this God who humbled himself to share our home and die our death?

The unspoken implication – for this recipient – of the movement of the sermon is that it might mean more than gladness and rejoicing. It might mean returning from Bethlehem and Calvary to 'Clapham' – wherever that might be for us – and following the example of a secular journalist, entering the depths of the human condition in a fuller way than was possible for her: extending the reconciling journey of the Word made flesh.

reread "Black like me"

7

The achievement of God's justice: Romans 3.21–26

1. The genre of Romans

Paul's statements about the atonement are made not as part of a handbook of Christian doctrine,[1] neatly arranged, but as part of the rich and complex discourse of letters. These letters vary in tone and content according to the occasion. 2 Corinthians (considered in Chapter 8) is a deeply vulnerable self-defence in the face of powerful threats to the apostle's ministry. Romans is a more irenic but nevertheless passionate account of the gospel, delivered to a church where the issue of the relationship between Jewish and Gentile Christians was clearly a burning one.

The fact that teaching about the significance of Jesus Christ emerges in the context of pastoral letters concerned about particular needs of churches does not in any way diminish its value as 'truth'. It does, however, highlight the nature of such 'truth'. It comes to expression not out of abstract reflection but out of the fires of experience and in the midst of dense argumentation. We therefore fail to do it justice if we abstract it either from that experience, or from the argument in which its expression originally had force. So it is that we must consider Rom. 3.25, which states that God 'put forward' Christ 'as a sacrifice of atonement by his blood, effective through faith' against the backcloth of the entire sequence of Paul's thought, from the beginning of the letter.[2]

2. Paul's argument concerning God's justice

After a salutation heavy with theological freight (1.1–7) Paul offers thanks to God for the Roman Christians and a prayer that he will

105

be able to visit them (1.8–10). He says that he longs for a mutually encouraging encounter with them, during which he would 'preach the gospel' to them, as he has been doing already to many further east in the Roman world (1.11–15).

Already a very significant thing is emerging. Paul is writing to Christians, but he wants to 'preach the gospel' to them (v. 15). Contemporary church parlance sometimes encourages us to believe that the gospel, the *euaggelion*, is what the 'outsiders' or 'unbelievers' need to hear, while the 'insiders' or 'believers' need something else, like 'Christian teaching'.[3] Paul undoubtedly preached the gospel to many an unbeliever and believed fervently in the need to do so. But it seems that he did not draw the neat distinction which we are inclined to do. The *church* needs to hear the gospel – even a church whose 'faith is proclaimed throughout the world' (v. 8).

The corollary of this is that instruction for Christians emerges directly from the gospel itself and is not a detached, add-on 'extra'. This is exactly what we find in this letter. Chapters 12–15 go into detail describing the kind of life God calls his people to lead, not least in respect of the way in which Jew and Gentile are to relate to one another in the church. But it is a mistake to see this as a separate 'ethics' section of the letter, tagged on to the 'doctrinal' section in chapters 1–11.[4] Rather, Paul's pastoral concerns are in view throughout his expositions of 'doctrine', and conversely, his 'ethics' are suffused with the story of Christ. From first to last, Romans is 'gospel' – a majestic overture, as it were, to what Paul wants to say when eventually he meets the letter's recipients.

What, though, is the situation in the Roman church which particularly arouses Paul's pastoral concern? As we only have Paul's side of the correspondence, we cannot be sure. But we can start to imagine intelligently a number of its features as we reflect on the curious statement which is the curtain-raiser for the main argument of the letter, as well as the explanation for Paul's eagerness to visit Rome: 'For I am not ashamed of the gospel' (1.16).

Why on earth, we might wonder, would anyone have thought that Paul was, or could be, ashamed of the gospel? Among the variety of answers which have been given, the following one seems most persuasive. It might well have appeared that the gospel was the last resort of a God whose plan thus far had failed. The calling of Israel as a covenant people, intended to embody his ways in the world, seemed to have foundered. Even exile and return had not taught her faithfulness in a profound and effective way. All the outward signs pointed to the continued absence of God's blessing: a sacred land occupied, rulership in the hands of the pagans. Gentiles, now, were responding in numbers to God's call, to the good news of hope which had come through Jesus Christ. The Jewish people, however, though some believed, as a whole still seemed to be languishing in a state of estrangement. Did this mean that God had given up on his ancient covenant? Did it mean that he had changed his mind about Israel, and decided to try again with a new grouping of people?

One can easily imagine how this kind of question could be aired in a lively and potentially divisive way in a church made up of believers in Jesus from both Jewish and Gentile backgrounds. Were either group 'second-class' beside the other? What about the relations, near or distant, Christian or not, of Roman Jewish Christians in their ancient homeland and elsewhere? What was their status? To what could they look forward? But most pressing of all, what about God? If he really had given up on his covenant with Israel, then not only the Jewish believers, but also the Gentile ones, would have but a flimsy basis for confidence. What if God decided to do the same, if his patience eventually wore out with the waywardness of his *new* family? If that were a possibility, the little churches springing up around the empire would have no stronger foundation or identity than if they had been just another new cult or interest-group, destined to fizzle into nothingness when it failed to deliver to the deity the goods he required.

So Paul states at the outset of his argument that he is *not* ashamed of the gospel. In his very opening verse he has called it the 'gospel of God', and here he asserts that it is 'the power of God for salvation to everyone who has faith, to the Jew first and also to the Greek' (v. 16). He will go on to show how God has not rejected his ancient people: he is indeed a faithful God whose word and work can be trusted by both his old family and his new family. Indeed, the gospel is itself the greatest revelation of God's 'justice' or 'righteousness' (v. 17), his upright character which issues, always, in just acts. Such acts, for the people to whom he has bound himself in love, are *saving* acts, for if he is to be just, he must be faithful to the promises of rescue he has made. Paul will later go on to probe the mystery of God's dealings with Israel (chapters 9–11) and deal sensitively with Jew-Gentile relationships in the church (chapters 14–15). But for now, the main point is made, against the main problem and objection to which the situation in the Roman church in the 50s CE could give rise. Contrary to appearances, *God is just, and the gospel itself is the guarantee of it.*[5]

The gospel is not, however, the first intimation we have of God's justice. By way of introduction to his exposition of the heart of the gospel in 3.21-26, Paul addresses (by implication) one of the main questions a Jewish Christian in Rome might have asked about God's justice: why has not God judged the pagans who have been oppressing God's people all these years – the Jewish people and now the Christians as well? Why has he not done anything about the godless lives which blight the face of the earth, and cause such misery and difficulty to those who seek to live according to the ways of the creator God? Paul's answer is that God *has* in fact shown his justice in this respect and continues to do so. His anger against the sinful ways of the pagan world is shown precisely in his 'giving them up', allowing them to get more and more depraved (1.18–32).

The Jewish person, however (whether Christian or not), should not be lulled into complacency by seeing the anger of God at work in the pagan world. For the reality is that evil pervades the lives of both Jew and Gentile (2.1–29). It may be (Paul seems to say) that *outwardly* Jewish people are upright: but God's judgement is not confined to the present: there will come a decisive time when the *secrets* of all will be judged (2.16). At that time, Jewish people should not think that mere possession of the law, or the covenant badge, circumcision, will be of any avail if they have not been obedient. Conversely, it is entirely possible that Gentiles – yes, even Gentiles from the midst of that world of pagan immorality which Paul has so luridly described in 1.18–32 – will be found to have been truly obedient, even though they have not had the law to guide them (2.14,15). The Jews have been tremendously privileged, but privilege is no guarantee of ultimate acceptability to God: indeed their greatest privilege, the law which God gave, itself served to highlight the all-pervasiveness of sin, which holds Gentile and Jewish worlds alike under its power (3.1–20).

3. The crowning revelation of God's justice

'But now...', says Paul, in one of his great turning points (3.21). In the midst of the continuing revelation of God's wrath in the world, and the continuing revelation of sin to Israel through the law, *now*, at this decisive moment in world history, 'a justice of God has been made public knowledge'. God's upright character, which involves his saving, active faithfulness to his covenant promises to his people, has been made public in a fresh way. How? In this central affirmation of 3.21, 22a, Paul makes three points about how God's justice has been made public.

First, this justice has been made public knowledge apart from the law, but the law and the prophets testify to its reality. We note Paul's balance here. One does not need to know the Jewish law to see that God is faithful and just, because Jesus Christ himself reveals this fact. Yet he reveals it in a way that is completely consistent with all that was said in the Scriptures about God. This was the God whose 'justice', his active loyalty to his covenant pledges, was the ground of hope for his people crying for help (Ps. 143.1). This was the God whose 'justice' had been declared in terms of judgement on his enemies and salvation for his people (Isa. 63.1–6). So what has been made 'public knowledge' in the gospel is not 'new' truth, but something known from ages past, and now seen in decisive action: declared, moreover, in an act of fresh revelation, apart from Torah.

Second, this justice is expressed through the faithfulness of Jesus Christ.[6] In Jesus we see the justice of God embodied, in action. We look at him and we find what being truthful, obedient to God, in right relationship with others looks like. We look at him and we find God actively putting the world to rights. No doubt Paul thought of the *death* of Jesus as the amazing culmination of this process, but thought also of all that he achieved in life, notably in those signs of physical, mental, spiritual, social and cosmic restoration we usually call the 'miracles'.[7]

Third, this justice has been exercised 'towards', i.e. in favour of, all who believe. This is not to be thought of as a limiting statement, as we shall see presently; the emphasis is, rather, on the 'all'. The beneficiaries of God's justice, that is, are not limited to members of historic Israel, but *all* believers. Paul's emphasis is not that of a Calvinist 'limited atonement' theory, that God only had in his sights those he knew would be believers when he enacted his justice through Jesus. Nevertheless, belief (i.e. in Jesus) is clearly the prerequisite for tasting and enjoying this saving power, this just promise-keeping of God; and, importantly for Paul's overall argument, it is in and through those who do believe in Jesus that the justice of God, made known decisively in Christ, continues to be made 'public'.

There then follows a short explanatory clause ('for there is no distinction', v. 22b), which is itself backed up by four whole verses of explanatory material (vv. 23–26), completing the long sentence that began in v. 21. Paul's introduction of the fact that 'there is no distinction' (i.e. between Jews and Gentiles) betrays the ongoing, immediate pastoral concern in his argument. This is precisely what he wants to stress: neither Jew nor Gentile has a claim to superiority – both are the beneficiaries of God's justice.

Verses 23–26, in which Paul's statement about the atoning death of Christ is embedded, unpack this crucial fact that 'there is no distinction'. They begin with a terse recapitulation of the entire argument of 1.18–3.20: 'all have sinned'. This is expanded by an allusion to the belief that humanity was made in God's image, to reflect his glory (Gen. 1.27) – an image which has become tarnished, so that as a race we now 'lack' or 'fall short of' his glory, whether we are Jews or Gentiles. This being the case, though, says Paul, a wonderful reversal also applies. All have sinned, but all are now *justified*. What is the meaning of this remarkable assertion?

To 'justify' is a term drawn from the lawcourt, and is of course related to the 'justice' which is the dominant theme of Paul's argument. It means to declare someone acquitted, in the right. It refers to the *pronouncement* of the judge – a pronouncement which is effective. It does not refer to a judge's or jury's assessment of whether the person in the dock in actual fact committed the crime. It is the pronouncement which enables an accused person to walk free and begin a new life in the community – whatever they may or may not have done. It reflects precisely the nature of justice in Scripture as an *active* concept: God's being just does not mean merely that God gives a 'correct' verdict; it means that God is actively putting the world to rights. To declare someone 'in the right', to 'justify' them, is to allow them to put their past behind them and begin again. That, says Paul, is what God has done for us in Christ.

All, then, being sinners, are also justified: but on what basis? What is the origin and wellspring of this marvellous fact? Paul makes clear that this is no automatic 'right'. It comes freely. God is not coerced into it. It comes from his grace. He could have finished the world off, as he nearly did in the days of Noah. Instead he chooses to start setting it to rights, by pronouncing his human creatures, the pinnacle of creation, acquitted, free. And he does it 'through the redemption that is in Christ Jesus'. Jesus Christ is the new Moses, the Messiah who has come to lead his people out from their slavery to sin, the 'Egypt' of their past, into the promised land of a new creation. But how does this redemption happen? Here indeed we come to the heart of the matter.

God presented Jesus Christ, the Redeemer, as a *sacrifice of atonement* (v. 25). This translates the word ἱλαστήριον (*hilasterion*), which can mean 'a means of expiation' or 'a place of propitiation'. In either case it alludes to the Jewish sacrificial system; and the word probably carries echoes of both meanings. As a *means of expiation* Christ dealt with sin itself, blotting out its stain. As a *place of propi-*

tiation (the word is used for the 'mercy seat' in the LXX of Exod. 25.17–22) he took on himself, and averted from humanity, the wrath of God against sin.[8] The fact that Paul starts his defence of God's justice by pointing to the operation of his wrath (1.18–32) strongly suggests that we are right to hear the overtones of 'propitiation' in this verse as well as those of 'expiation'. Paul's assertion of the universality of human sin in the preceding chapters has implied that there is divine wrath to be poured out over and above that which is already manifest in the excesses of pagan culture. This verse shows where that wrath was born.

We shall return to this central phrase in a moment, but first let us note how Paul expands it: God presented Christ as a sacrifice of atonement *through faith, by his blood. Through faith* should perhaps be translated *through his* (i.e. Christ's) *faithfulness* (cf. v. 22). Christ's own covenant loyalty and obedience to the Father are seen thus as the appropriate condition and means of his executing the Father's justice. And it happened by his *death*. 'Blood' here is a metonymy, an aspect of death standing for the thing itself, alluding to the central importance of the shedding of blood in the old sacrificial system. Paul was not here encouraging a blood-fixation in Christian piety, but rather using a reticent circumlocution for a gruesome fact.

It is the shared awareness of the story of Jesus' death on the part of Paul and his readers which makes his interpretation of Jesus' death here so striking, and helps to set it apart from both Jewish and pagan notions of sacrifice. In the Jewish system, the animals offered in sacrifice had to be of the highest quality, spotless. But here Paul was alluding to a *human* death in circumstances of the utmost shame. *This* event served to expiate sin; *this* event was the mercy-seat, the place of propitiation of the wrath of God.[9] Moreover, this was no merely human attempt to get on the right side of God, whether on one's own behalf or that of others. Contrary to standard pagan notions of expiation and propitiation, it was God himself who initiated this momentous act: he is the subject of the clause.[10] The notion of *hilasterion* thus undergoes a radical redefinition in Paul's hands: rather than merely adopting Jewish and pagan concepts to 'explain' Jesus' death, he transforms them.

Thus a careful reading of Paul's language safeguards against two common misapprehensions about what he is saying, which drive a wedge between God and Christ: that a wrathful God was arbitrarily punishing an innocent Jesus, and conversely that an innocent Jesus was seeking to appease a wrathful God. Although the whole section of the letter, as we have seen, concerns God's *justice*, Paul is very circumspect in what he suggests about Christ's death as a *punishment*. He seems to have been anxious to avoid reducing the death of Jesus to the kind of pagan transaction that this language could have suggested. At the same time, though writing before the age of detailed trinitarian formulations, he appears very careful to avoid driving a wedge between God and Christ. God did not 'punish' Christ, as it were subject-to-object: he 'set him forth' as expiation and propitiation, offered him to us as the acceptable means of dealing with sin and wrath.[11] Christ, on his side, did not set out to appease an alien and angry God. His death was, rather, simply the inevitable outworking of his *faithfulness*. He led an obedient life, in the most intimate fellowship with God, and this was where it led him: a shameful death on behalf of humanity, as the LORD's servant (cf. Isa. 53). The passage suggests one of the profound paradoxes of the atonement, that it was the Messiah's complete identification with the will of God which led to the utter desolation of the cross, in which he was equally identified with the plight of humanity. In short, Calvary was the result of the unity of Father and incarnate Son, not of their somehow being pitted against each other, and its achievement was the unity of God with his human creatures.

Paul now returns to the overall theme of his argument, to stress the purpose of the Messiah's faithful death and complete the picture opened up in v. 21 concerning the revelation of God's righteousness. Twice he says it: this happened *to demonstrate his justice* (vv. 25, 26). He expands this in three ways.

First, God's justice is demonstrated in the death of Jesus because it showed him dealing with sins which previously he had 'passed over'. As a patient merciful God, he had not exercised the wrath which he could have done on sinful humanity, whether Gentile or Jewish. The death of Jesus shows him closing this account, making an end of that chapter in the life of the world, so that humanity and the world might begin afresh.

Second, God's justice is demonstrated 'at the present time' in the death of Jesus. It is vital to Paul's whole notion of justification that it happens *now*: it is an *anticipation* of the verdict of the last judgement. God has brought the time of the verdict forward.

Third, God's justice is demonstrated in the death of Jesus *in order that he might be both 'just' himself, and justify the one who has faith in Jesus*. Although, inexplicably, the RSV and NRSV do not translate the words 'that he might himself be just' in v. 26a, they are surely crucial to Paul's thinking. God wishes not only to demonstrate that he is just; he wants, further, to *be* just. And he could not *be* just while at the same time declaring sinful people justified, without some appropriate dealing with sin and aversion of wrath.

4. Preaching the justice of God

As we have seen, Paul's great statement of the atonement here is embedded in the detailed argument of a pastoral letter. This fact gives us the first clue about preaching on the atonement from this passage. The good news of God's action to set the world to rights is something of which *Christians* need constantly to be reminded, for its consequences for the life of the Church are direct and immediate.

It is interesting to observe, indeed, that the language of 'sacrifice', 'expiation' or 'propitiation' with reference to Christ's death emerges precisely in such pastoral letters (cf. 1 Jn 4.10; Hebrews *passim*). The sermons in Acts, addressed to unbelievers, suggest that early evangelistic preaching focused simply on the story of Jesus, linked in to that of Israel. Perhaps today we need to re-learn this emphasis. Those who know little or nothing of the gospel may best be introduced to it in narrative form, with the invitation to become a part of the narrative. As they find themselves caught up into God's great plan, deeper reflections on the meaning of it all become possible and desirable.

What is it, especially, which we should stress concerning the atonement if we are to be faithful to Paul's thinking here?[12]

First, we should point to the divine reality to which Paul bears witness. The good news – of which Paul is not ashamed – is good news *of God* (1.1). It is 'a righteousness *of God*' which has now been made public knowledge (3.21). It is God who has set forth Jesus the faithful Messiah as a sacrifice of atonement (3.25), and whose grace has prompted him to justify those who believe. Any preaching on the atonement which places the main emphasis on humanity and its strivings simply misses the heart of the good news. *God* has been faithful to his covenant, and has acted with saving justice to restore both Jew and Gentile to their true human dignity – and through them, as he will show, the world itself (8.18–25).

Second, however, we should stress the immediate consequences for us of this stupendous divine event. Not to do so would be to abstract Paul's witness to it quite arbitrarily – and dangerously – out of its context. Clearly, for those who do not yet believe, the immediate consequence must be that having heard it announced, they should put their trust in Jesus the Messiah (cf. 10.8–15). But as we have seen, this letter is addressed to believers. For them, the immediate consequence must be the realization that Jew and Gentile are now in the same position before God: having both been liable to his judgement, both are now the beneficiaries of his act of justification (3.23, 24). There is therefore no room for boasting by one group over against the other (3.27–31).

The truth of God's justification of believers cannot therefore be grasped without a constant impact on our perception of ourselves and of those around us. The stress by the advocates of the so-called 'New Perspective on Paul'[13] on the social dimension of the doctrine of justification by faith, both in its origins and in its implications, should not be misheard as denying what the doctrine has traditionally affirmed about the new standing of individuals before God which he has given. It is rather that the individual and social dimensions are inseparable and go hand in glove. We cannot see ourselves as justified, given a fresh start by God's grace, without seeing that others are in the same position – and that this has radical implications for how we relate to them, and they to us. At least, if we do, we have not heard what Paul says in this passage; we have completely missed the word 'all' (3.23): all have sinned, all are justified.

Divine action and human response therefore form a seamless, logical whole in Paul's thinking, which it is quite artificial to separate. Preachers should present the atonement neither as if our own initiative, desires or efforts were primary – which would not be good news! – nor as if the consequences of God's act in our perceptions of and behaviour towards others were a matter in principle separable from it – which would be a truncated and perverted good news. Christian history offers examples of both these errors.

We should further note that the passage also raises in acute form the issue of the metaphors in which the truth of the atonement is expressed. Biblical images such as 'expiation' or 'propitiation' are, indeed, foreign to many people today. It is therefore a challenge for the preacher to proclaim the gospel of God's act in Christ in a way that is simultaneously faithful to the original proclamation and accessible to contemporary hearers. Gunton[14] has very helpfully shown how even the more alien or 'primitive' sounding biblical atonement-words, when probed, in fact open up profound and near-universal perceptions concerning the nature of the human predicament and the need for cosmic resolution. This is certainly not – either for Gunton or the present authors – a sign that Christian atonement teaching is merely one religious 'solution' to be set alongside others; but it is a telling exposure of the renewable life of the ancient metaphors. The sermon which follows is based upon the three central pictures of atonement to appear in our passage, and demonstrates how one may on a single preaching occasion *both* 'teach' the force of the metaphors in their original context, *and* 'proclaim' them effectively for today.

Sermon[15] and commentary

'Thanks be to God', says Paul, 'for his inexpressible gift!' Indeed, how could anyone express the unfathomably deep gift of the atonement, the impenetrable mystery of God's merciful righteousness towards his sinful creatures? Writing to the Roman Christians, Paul has surely not forgotten his own earlier words to the Corinthians about the difficulty of expressing the inexpressible gift of God (2 Cor. 9.15). Yet, he is determined to keep trying to describe God's saving work in Christ as well as he can. Paul will not rest until he has communicated the gospel (good news) of God's love.

An opening such as this clearly assumes a group of hearers broadly familiar with Christian teaching and language: and that, of course, is the kind of audience most preachers nowadays have – though the degree of familiarity will vary widely. This is broadly parallel to the composition of Paul's own readership. But rather than plunging straight into the passage, the preacher sets it within the wider, and fundamental, perspective of Paul's being grasped by the gospel of God's grace. Importantly, the point is made that all Paul's attempts (and by implication, ours) to express the grace of God in words will be inadequate – but that that is no reason not to go on trying. This sets the sermon's subsequent focus on Paul's metaphors of atonement in its proper context.

A word about the context. Few scholars today would agree with the older view that Romans is 'a compendium of Christian doctrine', an elaborate treatise where one can look up the answers to theological questions about nature and grace, faith and works, predestination and free will, or other such matters. Instead, Romans is best read as a real letter, written to real Christians living in real house churches, engaged in real controversies about practical matters of real importance to them and to Paul. The Romans Christians haven't met Paul yet, but they've heard a great deal about him – not all of it good – so before his planned visit, he writes them a very long rather formal letter introducing himself and, much more importantly to Paul, introducing his gospel.

He calls it 'the gospel of God, which he promised beforehand through his prophets in the holy scriptures concerning his Son' (1.1–2). It is the story of God's love for his lost and endangered creatures, a story that Paul summarizes elsewhere in Romans in one sentence: 'God shows his love for us in that while we were yet sinners Christ died for us' (5.8). But how will Paul tell that story in the context of his long and complex letter to the Roman Christians? How can he possibly express to them God's inexpressible gift?

Here the preacher distils crucial elements of scholarship, but with pastoral, not just scholarly intent. For many Christians, the danger with the Bible as a whole (not only Romans!) is precisely that it be treated as a 'compendium of Christian doctrine'. Its vibrant dynamics, the real-life setting behind its individual books, the rich narrative shape of the whole and many of the parts can all get lost in the process. One of the preacher's challenges is to open up these aspects of Scripture for those who have lost sight of them or may never have seen them.

If 'a picture is worth a thousand words', Paul's rhetorical strategy is a wise one indeed. He uses three powerful word pictures or metaphorical images to describe God's saving work in Christ in Rom. 3.21–26. Although those few verses admittedly comprise one of the densest and most difficult sections of his argument, they point with unerring directness to the mysterious atonement accomplished in the death and resurrection of Jesus Christ. Each of these word pictures represents a different way of telling the same wonderful story of God's love for sinful humanity. Paul piles them on top of one another in rapid succession, perhaps to suggest the way God dazzles and overwhelms us with grace. All three of Paul's atonement metaphors are found together in two verses (3.24–25) and together they attempt the impossible: to express God's inexpressible gift.

The simple structure of what follows is introduced: we are going to contemplate three of the key word pictures Paul uses to tell the story of atonement. A picture, if painted in fresh colours by the preacher, can become as arresting as when it was first used.

The first word picture Paul uses is 'justification' or 'rectification' since by it God rectifies (puts right) the relationships between himself and humanity that have gone wrong because of our wrongdoing since the time of Adam and Eve. Here the metaphorical image is the condemned prisoner in the dock, already declared guilty and sentenced to death. God loves us so much, says Paul, that he was willing to pay all our fines, to serve all our time in prison, and even to die on our behalf, in order to restore us to himself in love. Now Paul knows as well as we do that no analogy is perfect, no metaphor captures everything there is to say. Telling the story of God's love this way stresses the danger we were in and the wrongdoing and guilt that properly belonged to us. But it doesn't say much about how we were set free or cleansed from our sin. For those ideas, Paul will need to use other metaphorical images.

Paul's second word picture is 'redemption' or 'liberation from slavery'. Here the metaphorical image is the group of Hebrew slaves in bondage to cruel Pharaoh in Egypt until God leads them out with a strong arm and with signs and wonders. 'Redemption' means buying back lost family members who have been kidnapped, or retrieving lost property that has been wrongfully impounded. Israel understood God to be her redeemer at the Exodus, when, against all odds, a tiny group of slaves defeated a great tyrant and escaped into the wilderness across the Red Sea. God loves us so much, says Paul, that he was willing to venture far away into Egypt to find his lost people, to fight on their behalf for their freedom from slavery, and to bring them out to a place where they could worship him without fear. The 'redemption' metaphor underlines the helplessness of those enslaved to sin and the distortion of perspective that results from sinning. Like addicts in detoxification, at first the Israelites actually longed for the pleasures of Egypt, conveniently forgetting their slavery unto death. It has been well remarked that it was easy for God to get Israel out of Egypt; but it took 40 years to get Egypt out of Israel! Paul's redemption metaphor also stresses the high price God paid for our liberty when we had managed to enslave ourselves to the forces of sin and death as a result of our complicity with Adam and Eve.[16]

Finally, Paul uses a third word picture: God put Jesus Christ forward as 'hilasterion', that is, as an atoning sacrifice for sin. This is the boldest and most shocking metaphor of all, not only because it makes it clear that the saving death of Jesus Christ on the cross is God's work, but also because the death of an executed criminal on a Roman (pagan) cross is so far away conceptually from the sacred liturgical duties of Israel's high priest in the Holy of Holies on the Day of Atonement, Yom Kippur. The blood poured out there on the mercy seat, the golden cover of the ark of the covenant, is the means by which God 'covers' the sins of the people and cleanses them from every iniquity. God loves us so much, says Paul, that he poured out himself, his very own Son, as a sacrifice for sin, as the blood by which the new covenant was cut and sealed. The metaphor of the priestly work of sacrifice is further developed, of course, in the letter to the Hebrews, written by one of Paul's contemporaries. And in Romans as well it reminds us that through the power of God, as shown in the resurrection of Jesus Christ from the dead, we are made clean again and purified from every stain or defilement that we imagine could separate us from the love of God. Paul's word picture stresses that God's holiness and righteousness is not compromised by his merciful forgiveness of sins. It is God's own atoning sacrifice that makes us whole.

Note how for each of the pictures, the preacher both stays faithful to their background in Paul's thought world, and relates them to today's. The notions of a criminal in the dock, the liberation of a nation, an addict in detoxification, even of the stain that we imagine separates us from God's love, are all ones which in different ways we can relate to. Through a new word – 'rectification' – and taking a congregation back to an original Greek word – 'hilasterion' – she has helped to give fresh life to the concepts of 'justification' and 'propitiation' or 'expiation'.

So in three different ways, Paul has described the atonement. With three quite remarkable word pictures, he has attempted to paint the story of God's love for Israel and for us, as those grafted into Israel through baptism into Christ's death on the cross. In three striking metaphorical images, Paul has expressed, as well as he could, God's inexpressible gift. In these word pictures – rectification, redemption, hilasterion – Paul has hinted at the power of God's unfathomable aweful love. Mindful that the actions of the Father, the Son, and the Spirit are the actions of the One God of Israel, it may be helpful for us to associate Paul's threefold account – not explanation! – of God's love with one great story told three ways or in three voices or from three perspectives. Or it may help us to think about the ways we 'sign' atonement liturgically: rectification in confession and absolution; redemption and release through the waters of baptism; the broken body and poured-out blood of the eucharistic sacrifice of praise and thanksgiving. No one metaphor can tell the whole story; no one 'sacramentum' or mystery can fathom the depths of God's love.

I like to think of Paul as a poet here, and I turn for help to the poet Robinson Jeffers who managed to capture the frustration of trying to express the inexpressible. This poem is entitled, 'Love the Wild Swan'.[17]

> I hate my verses, every line, every word.
> Oh pale and brittle pencils ever to try
> One grass-blade's curve, or the throat of one bird
> That clings to twig, ruffled against white sky.
> Oh cracked and twilight mirrors ever to catch
> One color, one glinting flash, of the splendor of things.
> Unlucky hunter, Oh bullets of wax,
> The lion beauty, the wild-swan wings, the storm of the wings.
> – This wild swan of a world is no hunter's game.
> Better bullets than yours would miss the white breast.
> Better mirrors than yours would crack in the flame.
> Does it matter whether you hate your ... self? At least
> Love your eyes that can see, your mind that can
> Hear the music, the thunder of the wings. Love the wild swan.

No theologian, no poet, not even the apostle himself can begin to capture the beauty, the power, or the profundity of what God has done for us in Christ Jesus. Finally, in attempting to speak of the atonement, we must end where Paul himself ended: in doxological wonder at what cannot be spoken. 'O the depth of the riches and wisdom and knowledge of God! How unsearchable are his judgements and how inscrutable his ways!' (11.33). 'Thanks be to God for his inexpressible gift!'

The sermon ends as it began with a reflection on the inadequacy of all of our language to express the wonder of God and his grace, not least as we seek to speak of his atoning work: a reflection which of course applies not only to Paul and the other biblical writers, but also to every preacher. Having looked at the pictures of rectification, redemption and hilasterion, we are reminded that even they are but 'cracked and twilight mirrors' to catch the splendour of what God has done.

8

The reconciliation of the world: 2 Corinthians 5.11–6.2

1. The defence of a ministry

In contrast to Romans, an expansive, rather formal letter to a church Paul had not yet visited, 2 Corinthians is a very personal missive to a church he had founded and knew well. Here he is concerned with defending his apostleship, and through that the very foundation of the church's life. He darts from one topic to another with a sense of pained urgency, not to mention distaste that he has to be dealing with such matters at all. Although it lacks the majestic sweep of Romans' treatment of God's great purposes, 2 Corinthians has a profound consistency arising, ultimately, from Paul's deep sense of identification with Christ.[1]

The note of defence first becomes explicit in 1.12–14; in chapters 10–12 it becomes most intense, but is in fact present throughout the argument from 1.3 onwards. There are passages of heavy irony; Paul wants to put 'clear blue water' between himself and those who employ the tactics of the orator to 'defend' themselves with elaborate rhetoric, as in a court of law. He will boast, certainly, but he will do so as a 'fool' – of his weaknesses and sufferings (11.1–12.10). He stresses that he is arguing not for his own sake, but for his readers' (12.19). Why did Paul find it necessary to defend his ministry like this?

Apparently there were some travelling people who called themselves 'apostles' and who sought influence (and money) by getting one church to 'recommend' them to another. Paul sees these people as a threat to his own apostolic ministry. The first allusions to such rival leaders are in 2.17 and 3.1. Paul pulls no punches in identifying the basic problem with these rivals: they proclaimed a different Jesus (11.4). Paul's fear that there may be continuing immorality in the church (12.19; cf. 6.14–7.1) is surely not coincidental to his fear that

121

the Corinthians are being lured away by other 'apostles'. The 'gospel' of these travelling 'peddlers of the word' (2.17) was not one which could effect a radical change in people's lives.

These rivals, it seems, have poisoned at least some of the Corinthians against Paul; they have sown doubt about his apostolic credentials. What was it about Paul's own testimony to Christ which the Corinthians had been led to see as suspect, and which he has to defend and explain? The answer to this question leads us to the heart of this letter's distinctive presentation of the atonement.

It appears that Paul's rivals belittled or ridiculed him because of the weakness and suffering that continually and obviously attended him in his ministry. Paul's answer is that the weakness and suffering of God's servants is perfectly consistent with the saving work of God, which was itself accomplished through the weakness and suffering of the Messiah. Indeed, such weakness and suffering is the *mark* of authentic ministry, rather than a negation of it. A gospel which stressed the triumph of Christ without his suffering was a dangerous half-truth. This message is the dominant thread which can be traced through the letter, from Paul's opening praise to the God who strengthens him in his troubles that he might strengthen others (1.3–17) right through to the statement near the end that he is glad when he is weak but they are strong (13.9).

Thus, as in Romans, we shall see that Paul's explicit teaching on the atonement in 2 Cor. 5.11–21 is embedded in an entire argument rooted in particular pastoral need. It is because he needs to defend his own weakness that he stresses the weakness of Christ. Again, this does not mean that the truth which thus emerges is merely local or temporary. On the contrary, it is precisely as we see the immediate relevance and consequences of the truth of the atonement for Paul and his readers that we shall grasp the fact that this is no merely abstract doctrine, nor one that can be grasped by detached mental assent, but a truth which embraces all of life and issues in a radically new vision of what in Christ we are meant to be.

2. Appearance and reality

The climax of Paul's account of God's atoning work in this letter comes in the famous verse 5.21, expressing what Luther called 'the great exchange': 'God made him to be sin who knew no sin, so that we might become the righteousness of God in him.' Familiarity with Christian doctrine may lead us to miss the full force of this startling paradox. Paul says that one who had died the most shameful of deaths was yet one who 'knew no sin'. And he says that an event which by all human standards was incomparably ignominious was God's chosen means of making people 'righteous'.[2]

The crucifixion turns human expectations on their heads. What appears to signal utter defeat, in fact signals ultimate achievement. What appears to epitomize human sin and shame, in fact epitomizes innocence and brings about righteousness. If we are to begin to appreciate what Paul is saying here, we need to see that this statement in 5.21 comes as the culmination of a sustained argument, pointing out that with God, things are *very often* not what they seem. The shocking, amazing truth of Calvary, uniquely significant though it is, is replicated in all sorts of ways in the life of God's servants.

The truth that God works through weakness and through the ordinary vicissitudes of human life was something which, it seems, the Corinthian Christians found strange and hard to grasp: they were still accustomed to a 'surface' vision which did not discern the mysterious reality beneath. Paul therefore had to draw special attention to this truth, as the central plank of his defence against his detractors.

The theme is first seen in 1.3–11. Here Paul points to the fact that his own sufferings (surprisingly, no doubt, for many) have a good purpose. As God strengthens him in them, so he is enabled to strengthen others. In 1.15–22; 2.12–16 Paul writes of his changes of plan. The Corinthians, apparently, had been made suspicious that these were the result of inconsistency or impulsiveness. Paul assures them, again, that things are not what they seem on the surface. The mundane matter of his movements, his decisions when to travel where, remain within the plan of God and serve Paul's testimony to God's faithfulness (1.15–22). It also reflects Paul's love for the Corinthians (1.23). Believe it or not, this bruised and buffeted apostle, far from shifting helplessly to and fro, is in a triumphal procession (2.14)![3]

In 1.23–2.11 Paul tries to get his readers to see that the discipline which is rightly exercised in the Christian community must be carried out in the spirit of love. Here too he seems to be resisting a crude fixation on appearances. On the one hand, his own recent absence (when they were expecting him to visit) is not a sign that he does not care: on the contrary, it is a sign that he did not want to cause them further pain (1.23) – the discipline already exercised was, he thought, sufficient. On the other hand, he wants *them* to recognize when 'enough is enough' (2.5–11). They must learn not only to see through to the motivating heart of *his* actions, but also reflect that motivation in their own dealings with others in their community. It is as if they have 'seen' only their temporary, external task of punishing the 'sinner', not the constant underlying call to love him.

Paul goes on to speak of the 'ministry of justification' with which he had been entrusted by God (2.17–4.15). He strongly asserts the 'glory' of this ministry 'that brings righteousness' (3.9). Equally, however, he points out that the 'treasure' is appropriately carried in homely 'clay jars' (4.7), so that it may be God's power which is on display. The Corinthians should surely not expect God's messengers to display a glory of their own which would distract people from God's! They must look beneath the unpromising surface to the treasure within.

An obvious aspect of Paul's weakness was his nearness, in fact and in feeling on a number of occasions, to death (1.8, 9). Death seems to have been a Corinthian taboo, something they preferred to avoid facing (see 1 Cor. 15). Paul, by contrast, characteristically asserts a paradox: that even the prospect of death does not diminish his confidence (4.16–5.10). As one who can discern the working of the unseen God, and has grasped in the present God's future purpose, which includes a new 'heavenly dwelling' for his people (5.2), he can face death head-on without shame or terror. Indeed, for Paul, facing up to death is not only a possibility; it is a requirement, and his brushes with it are therefore salutary. Otherwise there is a danger of forgetting the reality of future judgement (5.9, 10). Living under the illusion of the permanence of our present existence, our whole outlook will be skewed and we will forget our ultimate accountability to God.

So, Paul is saying through these early chapters of the letter, God's glory has been 'revealed' in strange ways, the perception of which calls for the penetrating eyes of faith. God's true servants are suffering,[4] but he is using them for good purposes now, and is preparing them for ultimate glory beyond imagining. If there are 'alternative' apostles who claim superiority on the grounds that they embody God's glory more manifestly now, the church should look beneath the gloss, discover the reality, and unmask the deception.

3. The heart of Paul's motivation

Thus we reach 5.11–21. Within this passage it is vv. 14–21 which focus on God's reconciling work in Christ, but these verses follow seamlessly from vv. 11–13, in which Paul continues to defend not only his ministry, but even the self-defence in which he is engaged as he writes. Verses 14–21 appear, in fact, not as an isolated statement of belief, but as a central plank in Paul's argument for the authenticity of his ministry.

Verse 14 is the crucial hinge verse, in which Paul is led into his affirmations about Christ by his assertion of what motivates him: 'The love of Christ impels us, because we are convinced that one has died for all...' From v. 11 the focus of the argument has been on himself; from now until the end of the chapter his focus will be on Christ.

In verses 11–14 Paul lays bare what drives him, the motor which propels his life and mission. This is a twofold disposition: the fear of the Lord (v. 11), who knows his heart and who, Paul has just reminded his readers, will be our judge;[5] and Christ's love for all people (v. 14a: this seems to be the logical meaning of 'the love of Christ' here – Christ's own love, which led him to 'die for all', indwelling Paul). Paul is at pains to point out that his activity as a 'persuader' (including the writing of this very letter) is *not* to be construed as mere self-promotion (v. 12) – in contrast to his rivals who liked to be 'commended' (cf. 3.1). On the contrary, he is wanting to give his *readers* a defence against those who would lead them astray, who would entice them to concentrate on outward appearance rather than the heart reality which God is interested in (cf. 1 Sam. 16.7). That is, Paul's ministry among them arises out of these twin foci of his life: he does it for God's sake, and out of love for them.

Paul goes on to assert that these twin foci explain an apparent contradiction in his behaviour: 'If we are out of our mind, it is for God; if we are in our right mind, it is for you' (v. 13). It seems as if Paul was sometimes accused of being crazy for his willingness to endure such hardship, yet his churches and his opponents also well knew the clarity and force of his words, which were far from being those of a madman. Thus Paul once more points beyond appearance to reality; the apparent inconsistency in behaviour stems simply from his fear of the Lord and Christ's love working through him.

Now in vv. 14–21 Paul opens up the full grandeur of what lies beyond, beneath and above his unimpressive, sometimes puzzling, face as an apostle. He is in fact caught up in nothing less than the mighty movement of God's atoning work, his reconciliation of the world to himself.

As noted above, v. 14a seems to refer not to Paul's love for Christ, but to the love which Christ has for people. And Paul, surely, is not saying merely that the loving disposition seen in Jesus is a mighty example and inspiration, though it is certainly not less than that. He is saying that as a man who is 'in Christ', Christ's love actually catches him up into its great outward-moving flow. But this is more than some mystical, inarticulate experience or emotion. It entails a clear-eyed intellectual conviction about the significance of the historical event of Jesus' death: 'we have concluded that one has died on behalf of all, so all have died' (v. 14). What does Paul mean?

Clearly, Paul is interpreting the death of Jesus as the supreme expression of his love as the Messiah who came to save his people. Jesus' death as an expression of love implies that it was a gift: Jesus *went ahead* of us, doing *for* us, *instead* of us, something which we need never do for ourselves.[6] In this sense it is natural to speak of Jesus' death as *substitutionary*. It is hard to see how the Messiah's death could be an expression of true love without this dimension. Yet at the same time Paul says that the Messiah took us *with him*: the consequence of his death was 'all have died'. A *substitutionary* death alone, if that were all it was, would leave humanity unchanged. Thus it is necessary to speak of Jesus' death also as *inclusive*.[7] Not only did he die *for us*; *we* died *with him*.

This is the language of paradox: in v. 15 Paul makes it clear that he knows very well that plenty of human beings are still alive! But this is the very paradox of death-in-life to which he keeps returning throughout the letter (cf. 1.8, 9; 4:10, 11). We should not soften this paradox by saying that Paul is just using colourful language meaning no more than 'turned over a new leaf'. 'Died' here is the only word which will do for what Paul means, which is that in the death of Jesus, the old order of humanity has come to an end. Moreover, a new order has begun. The resurrection of the Messiah signals the rebirth of the race, totally reoriented, with a new goal. He died for us, we died with him, we live for him (v. 15).

Paul's use of the word *all* (three times in vv. 14, 15) is noteworthy. It foreshadows the unmistakeably cosmic terms in which Paul will shortly speak of God's reconciling work. We ought not to allow our understanding of a verse like this to be overly dictated by post-Reformation debates about the extent of the atonement; rather, we should let the verse critique the terms of those debates. It is clear both that Paul sees the scope of Christ's loving death as gloriously, breath-takingly universal, and that he is making no predictions concerning the number of those who will or will not let themselves be a part of God's project in Christ. To Paul, it would have been an alien idea that it might be a slur on God's omnipotence to suggest that some of those 'for whom' Christ died might not avail themselves of what he has done, as in the theory of 'limited atonement'.[8] The very picture Paul draws throughout this letter of himself as a vulnerable apostle, suffering, pleading, is defended against misconstrual precisely by his assertion that in this process he is caught up with Christ, identified with him. In Christ, God appears not as a tyrant coming to suppress all opposition, but as a human risking rejection. This is not to deny his power to carry out his purpose of reconciling the cosmos to himself – a purpose which, with wonderful faith, Paul will shortly declare to have been achieved in Christ – but simply to assert that he continues to face rejection from human beings, rejection which he cannot and will not summarily reverse. It is a rejection now directed immediately against his servants.[9]

We ought also to note here Paul's continuing self-defence against his rivals. In contrast to the factionalism promoted by alternative apostles, Paul stakes out his ground as an apostle of the one Messiah, who shares in that one Messiah's love for all people. That is the love which leads him into precisely the situations of suffering and shame which some in the church found so hard to understand, but which, for those with eyes to see, were the clearest signs of his identification with Christ. Rather than preying, parasitically, on believers, like his rivals – flattering them and seeking their approval – Paul is engaged in the serious business of preaching to an unbelieving world the news of its reconciliation. No wonder he suffers. His doctrine of 'unlimited atonement', and the hardship which went along with declaring it, may have much to say to those who today prefer the safety of rival cliques within the murky world of ecclesiastical politics to the bracing business of proclaiming to the world Christ's love for it.

As he continues to unpack the 'love of Christ' for all people, which is his own galvanizing force, in v. 16 Paul returns explicitly to the theme which he has never really left behind, that of appearance and reality. In v. 11 he has spoken about how God sees into his heart – and he hopes the Corinthians, by and large, do too, even if his opponents do not. Now he speaks about how he, Paul, regards other people. This is a consequence of the truth of Christ's death 'for all' which he has declared in v. 15. He does not look at them 'according to the flesh', weighing them up by the standards of a sinful world. He is not impressed by an outward appearance of intense piety, or dynamic leadership, or striking giftedness. Nor, conversely, does he dismiss those who seem weak and insignificant. He looks at anyone and everyone and sees a person who is dead because Christ has brought the old order of humanity to an end. That is the all-controlling reality, whatever the outward appearance may be.

This new perspective on other people derives directly from the new perspective on the Messiah himself which Paul gained on the Damascus road (v. 16b). Previously, it seems, he had regarded Jesus as a blasphemer, a dangerous subversive, who had got his just deserts in the shame of the crucifixion. Now he knows that he had then been judging Jesus by appearances; that it was precisely in his death that his Messiahship was most clearly revealed.

But Paul sees not only a lot of dead people as he looks around. He sees some risen ones, too: those who, like him, are 'in Christ'. Here is the next great consequence of Christ's death for all (note the repeated conjunction ὥστε, 'so that', at the start of both vv. 16 and 17): 'if anyone is in Christ, there is a new creation' (v. 17).[10] The form of words here (literally 'if anyone in Christ, new creation') suggests not only that the person concerned has been made new, but also that they are the signs of a vastly greater 'new creation' coming into being. This emphasis is borne out by the second half of the verse: 'the old things have passed away, new things have come into being'.

It is vital to Paul's whole strategy of defence of his apostleship – on which depends the Corinthians' very adherence to the gospel – that he can show that God himself is at work in him, just as God was at work through Christ. This stress on the sovereignty of God has been present from the start of the letter, where Paul praises God for the strength he gives him in his troubles, and the purpose he discerns in them. Now in a bold conjunction of clauses Paul asserts that the 'ministry of reconciliation' which he – and his colleagues – exercise, comes from God himself, the same God who 'reconciled us to himself through Christ' (v. 18). '*All* this is from God' – not only the Messiah's love for all people, taking him to his death, but also the Messiah's indwelling of Paul and others which impel them to continue what he decisively began. Thus Paul stresses that what *he* stands for, proclaims and lives out is the work of God – and, by implication, that those who oppose him are standing in the way of God himself.

The point is underlined in v. 19, where for the first time in the passage the full majesty of the extent of God's reconciling work comes into view: 'since it was God who in Christ was reconciling the world to himself, not reckoning their transgressions against them and placing in us the word of reconciliation'. The continued use of 'us' suggests that Paul is not thinking of his self-defence in narrow terms: what he says about the ministry entrusted to him applies to his fellow-workers and, in principle, to all Christians. In this great summary statement, note the two movements of God's activity: reconciling us to himself through Christ, and giving us the ministry or 'word' of reconciliation. The two go together: Paul could not think of what Christ had done for him without in the same moment thinking of what Christ had called him to be. This is entirely consistent with the picture of the disciples in the gospels. They are called not just to receive the benefits of the kingdom, but to be instruments in its advancement: 'follow me, and I will make you fishers of human beings' (Mk 1.17).

What is this 'reconciliation' of which Paul speaks in vv. 18, 19? 'To reconcile is to end a relation of enmity, and substitute for it one of peace and goodwill'.[11] On whose side, then, was the estrangement? The answer, it is natural to assume, is on *both* sides, as indeed Paul elsewhere states (Rom. 1.18–32): humanity as a whole was hostile to God; God therefore was angered and aggrieved with humanity. 'Reconciliation' is here like a summary of the whole process of 'justification' and its consequences. Since God has declared us acquitted and free, and shown in Christ that he does not hold our transgressions against us, the relationship is re-established, and can now flourish afresh on a new footing. Those who are reconciled to God become the agents of bringing others too into that new relationship. And of course, those who are reconciled to God are logically, inexorably, reconciled also to each other. Here still Paul may be casting a sidelong glance at his rivals. In contrast to their legacy of division, Paul burns with the vision of unity flowing from the action of the one God in the one Christ.[12]

We shall only feel the force of Paul's argument here when we think of the story of Jesus' suffering and death, familiar to the Corinthians and no doubt to the rival apostles, but, it seems, too frequently forgotten by them. Paul is appealing from the greater to the lesser: if we accept that God was at work in *that death*, the death of the Messiah himself, can we not accept that he is at work in his servants who suffer similar degradation and pain? *This* Christ, to whom the Corinthians (and the rival apostles) owed allegiance, and paid at least lip service: *this* Christ, who suffered a death that made him accursed in Jewish eyes and the most degraded criminal in Gentile ones: *God* was at work in him, reconciling the world to himself, declaring to the world that he was not going to hold its rebellion against it. And it was God who, in those same hours of Christ's desolation, was entrusting to 'us' – the apostles, the church – the 'word' of reconciliation. So, implies Paul: is it not natural that we, like Christ, should suffer pain and weakness, and appear the objects of shame and scorn? Is it not inevitable? That was God's chosen way of reconciling the world to himself – through Christ, and now through us.

Paul now in vv. 20, 21 sums up the argument of this section of his defence. Just as Christ died 'on behalf of' all, so Paul sees himself as an 'ambassador' on *Christ's* behalf.[13] Once again Paul is pointing to the reality beneath the appearance: he may not look like the trusted ambassador of God's anointed King; but then you remember what the King himself looked like, and it all falls into place. And as *God* was in Christ, so God also makes *his* appeal through Paul, as Paul uses all the diplomacy at his command to seek to 'persuade' people. His mission is to beseech people to be reconciled to God; to avail themselves of the amnesty he has offered. Although this may be a general statement (i.e. 'this is our business – to implore you [or anyone] to be reconciled to God'), its stark application to the Corinthians is clear, and underlined in 6.1–2. They themselves, professing Christians though they were, needed to be reconciled to God. All the way through, that is Paul's implication: that the effect of following the rival apostles was, and would be, estrangement from God. And all the way through, this is Paul's ultimate goal: not restoration of his own good name, but the reconciliation of people to God, *via reconciliation to him and the gospel he embodied.*

Finally, in as paradoxical terms as he can muster, Paul returns to the heart of the matter: the work of God in Christ. Verse 21 contains two examples of *catachresis*, that category of metaphor which is used because no other expression will do. Paul does not here speak of Christ as a *sacrifice* for sin: he goes still further and says God *made* him sin, on our behalf (ὑπὲρ ἡμῶν). All the opprobrium, all the shame, all the estrangement of humanity through the centuries, was heaped on his head: God said, as it were, *there* is sin – and there's an end of it. Equally startling is the second metaphor: 'that we might *become* the justice of God in him'. Again, Paul goes further than saying that in Christ we are forgiven, and can be obedient, wonderfully true though those things are. *We become what Christ was*: the embodiment of God's justice, his faithful upright character, in the world. The glorious 'great exchange' is there, but the gift we have received because of Christ's becoming 'sin' is not just a status passively enjoyed, but a calling actively to pursue. God's 'justice' is always an active justice, putting the world to rights, and that is exactly what Paul – and all who share and imitate his faith – are caught up in.[14] This part of Paul's defence is clinched: all his suffering, all his labours, all the twists and turns of his travels, all his earnest arguing and pleading, all his words of persuasion – *this* is what they are: the carrying-out of God's justice in the world, leading to reconciliation: achieved in Christ, but worked out through his servants.

4. Preaching God's reconciling work

This passages exemplifies, like Rom. 3.21–26, the need for *Christians* to hear the message of the atonement. But here there is a different twist, for what Paul is stressing as a consequence of God's act in Christ is not the equal standing of Jew and Gentile in God's economy, but the need to recognize that suffering and shame are still the paradoxical marks of authenticity in God's servants. *when does white patready give it ones*

Preaching which gets to the heart of this passage is almost bound to contain an element of self-reflection, as the preacher is engaged in the very activity of which Paul writes in vv. 18–20: being an ambassador for Christ, holding out the 'word of reconciliation'. Preachers often prefer not to speak of themselves, and for good reason; but the awesome truth told by Paul here is that we cannot drive a wedge between the work of God in Christ and the work of God in the Church. Of course the crucifixion indicates the extraordinary *uniqueness* of God's work in Christ. What he did and what we do are of a different order. But for Paul, being reconciled and being a reconciler went inseparably together. The logic of this is that as we continue to preach Christ today, we proclaim not only the unfathomable paradox of what happened on Calvary, but also the mystery of God's continuing appeal through us, his unlikely ambassadors. Conversely, in the words of P. T. Forsyth, God's work and words continue in ours:

> No true preaching of the cross can be other than part of the action of the Cross... The preacher, in reproducing this Gospel word of God, prolongs Christ's sacramental work. The real presence of Christ crucified is what makes preaching... This is the work of God, this continues His work in Christ... We do not repeat or imitate that Cross, on the one hand; and we do not merely state it, on the other. It re-enacts itself in us.[15]

We therefore see atonement here as a narrative decisively begun in Christ, but continuing according to the same pattern in and through his followers. It is not a matter of a select and fixed number being 'saved' through Christ's death. It is a matter of an old order of humanity dying with Christ who 'became sin', and a new order coming to birth with him in his resurrection. It is a matter of an estranged world being reconciled to its creator, and therefore of its creatures, above all the human ones, being reconciled to one another. And since the news of this does not travel automatically, or easily, it is a matter, finally, of those who have availed themselves of the amnesty and entered into the reconciliation revealing in their words and their

own pattern of suffering service the nature of the God who has reconciled us to himself, and appealing to others – to all – with the humility,
earnestness and love of Christ.[16]

Sermon[17] and commentary

'From now on, we regard no one from a human point of view', Paul declares.
Easier said than done! What could such a claim conceivably mean? Having
discovered the principle of the fulcrum, Archimedes supposedly exulted, 'Give
me a place to stand on, and I can move the world.' Indeed!

In Paul's case, the oddity involved in his assertion is more than the
practical impossibility of climbing outside one's own skin. Something has
clearly gotten *under* his skin. If anything is evident in this prickly apologia
to the congregation at Corinth, it is that Paul's perspective is 'human, all
too human'. Defensive at best, egoistic at worst – Paul seems to embody
the antithesis of what he asserts. (Not the only preacher to suffer from a
problem with consistency!)

Paul is anything but reconciled to the situation he finds in Corinth. He
excoriates the 'apostles' who proclaim what he regards as 'another gospel'.
In doing so, he is surely further exacerbating the fissure between himself and
his intended audience. This poor congregation seems caught in a withering
crossfire between duelling preachers! 'From now on, we regard no one from
a human point of view'? Indeed!

*The preacher begins by highlighting the obvious humanness of Paul in his pained
communication to the Corinthians. This is an honest move, which may well name a
problem which congregations who read Paul have with this letter. In Eugene Lowry's
terms, Schlafer has identified 'trouble in the text'[18] as his starting-point. Is Paul's claim
to regard no one 'from a human point of view' really credible? The sermon's opening
ensures that the 'message of reconciliation' on which it, like Paul, will focus remains
earthed in the dynamics of Paul's own relationships and ministry, and emerges from
them, rather than being abstracted as a 'purple passage'.*

Reconciliation – the ways we commonly use the word all but mock its meaning,
do they not?

'I've reconciled myself to the inevitable', he says, throwing up his hands,
bitterly lamenting a broken marriage. Reconciled – Resigned.
'We've reconciled the books at last', she says, wiping her face in relief.
Reconciled – Balanced, accounts equal on both sides of the ledger – penny
for penny.

'After months of discussion, we've reconciled our differences for the good of the country', the legislative negotiators say (issuing a joint statement to the press). Reconciled – Compromised; cut the best deal we could with opponents bent on doing the same.

Reconciliations – all of these – from a human, very human point of view.

Do you sense the underlying energy in all of these? If you missed it, it doesn't mean you weren't paying attention – for that 'energy' is all but flat line, barely pulsing. The lowest common denominator in 'resigned', 'balanced', 'compromised'? It's a feeling of relief.

'No need to struggle any more (at least no point in trying). We've found a way to stand down, to cease and desist from all the hassle. Lower the volume, will you? Let's have some peace and quiet. Things will even out; let's get on with business as usual.'

As Rodney King put it (the black man whose battering by police sparked the Los Angeles riots), 'Can't we all just get along?'

Here the focus shifts from the apparent problem of Paul's own inconsistency (ironically, of course, one of the very charges levelled against him by some at Corinth) to the tired uses of the word 'reconciliation' in contemporary language. This names another obstacle, a straightforward linguistic one, which many readers or hearers of the text will encounter. Note the echoes of some kinds of traditional atonement language in the contemporary usages enumerated: balancing the books, accounts equal. This section acts as a dark foil for the bright jewel of the gospel which is now to be announced.

Is that the message of reconciliation Paul, the ambassador, is charged to bring? If so, it isn't good news, it isn't even news. Maybe this contrary preacher, with feisty language, and 'in your face' demeanour, is not as contradictory as he sounds. Maybe reconciliation – real reconciliation – requires a way of seeing, speaking, acting that is, in fact, radically different from 'a human point of view'.

At this point the preacher both introduces 'real' Pauline reconciliation, and suggests that the first impressions of Paul described at the start of the sermon may not give the whole story. Like the Corinthians themselves, we are being called to look beyond appearance to reality.

Many of you may remember, among all the other incendiary tragedies attending the war in Iraq, the bombing of the United Nations headquarters, and the resulting death of Sergio de Mello, the UN representative in charge. As de Mello lay dying, pinned amid the rubble of collapsed walls and ceilings, he was heard to say by an associate who was also trapped but later rescued, 'Whatever you do, don't let the UN pull out of Iraq! What we are doing here may well be the only hope for peace.'

Sergio de Mello is seen not only as illustrating Christ's peace-bringing death, but as also in some sense a contemporary embodiment of the 'ministry of reconciliation' with which Paul believed he had been entrusted. A wide, cosmic view of atonement is here hinted at: not only did Christ die 'for all'; all may potentially be the bearers of his pacific life, and death.

That is the kind of 'reconciliation' Paul has in mind. The death of Jesus balanced no moral books – negotiated no moral deals. Jesus, as Paul understands it, did not, for all practical purposes, commit suicide – political and physical – standing up to the powers that be, dying the death of an idealistic martyr for a noble, hopeless cause. Nor was the death of Jesus simply some combination of inspiration and injunction – 'if *he* can do it, by God, you and I can do the same!'

But if not that, then what?

Forgiveness – feisty forgiveness. Not 'It's all right; it didn't really hurt.' Not 'Shame on you for all you've done to make me suffer so!' Not 'I won't hold it against you this time; but don't let it happen again!'

But 'Your hate is hereby countered with my love! Your fear is, at this moment, taken up into my trust. The devastation of war, wrought by generation upon generation, until no one knows any other mode of being than self-destruction – that devastation is not magically deleted from the screen of history. But it *is* engaged and responded to with a different language, a different imagination, a different mode of being. That which is no longer from a human point of view – but which humanity was made for, and can be recreated into.'

The preacher strongly asserts the personal character of what Christ has done, which lifts 'atonement' far above any merely mechanical act, and his genuine historical achievement, which makes 'atonement' far more than merely symbolic or exemplary.

Paul is convinced that he has been somehow empowered by such forgiveness to set such forgiveness loose upon the world. That forgiveness is totally compatible with savvy political strategies ('Wise as serpents, innocent as doves' is a line that comes to mind.) The forgiveness that Paul has experienced, and aches, in longing frustration, for the Corinthians to experience as well, is fully capable of raising its voice, and calling easy answers and cheap grace exactly what they are – damned nonsense.

In a world still scarred by warfare, this is an important paragraph, for the preacher does not want to be heard announcing a 'soft option' that ignores harsh realities. There is an echo here of Paul's own bluntness which at first sight we can find so problematic. Somehow, in the very midst of this rough world, not merely on some Utopian planet, the forgiveness announced by the gospel is possible.

Paul is under no illusion that his participation in such salvation strategies will usher in a Disneyland of Happily Ever After. He knows that it will get him seriously killed. And yet, what can he do, whatever it costs, but bear witness with his body to what the body of Jesus has somehow done for him? For Jesus, as Paul sees it and says it, has taken his angle of vision, a very human point of view, and turned it 180 degrees. So now Paul sees everything the same, and from an utterly opposite angle.

Distorted as my perspective is, I long to see life, speak of life, and live a life like that, don't you? Even as I draw back instinctively from what such a celebration of feisty forgiveness costs. And when the absolutely necessary seems utterly impossible, Paul offers me a single, simple suggestion: look at the cross.

The difference between Paul's gospel and a mere 'Disneyworld' of escapist bliss is starkly stated. This is indeed a gospel which catches up its heralds into the very movement of the story it tells, a story of suffering and death as the means to life and hope. In the final paragraph the preacher is at his most personal. Like Paul, the preacher cannot speak of Christ without also speaking of Christ's investment in him, and his in Christ, and makes his appeal on that basis. Acknowledging the inevitable distortion of all our perspectives, he yet recognizes the truth of what Paul was striving to say when he announced that he regarded no one 'from a human point of view', and ends by summoning us to look again at the place where all our perspectives are transformed.

9

The decisive victory: Colossians 2.8–15

1. Good news for a postmodern world?

In his search for a fresh vision for the Church's mission in a postmodern world, Robert E. Webber looks for connections with classical Christianity. He reflects upon the three main ways in which the work of Christ has been interpreted through the centuries. While many Christians since Anselm and Calvin have placed the emphasis upon a sacrificial understanding of the cross, others, inspired by Abelard, have viewed it as an example which has power to transform lives. The third, often neglected, approach is the proclamation that Christ's 'death and resurrection constitute *a victory over the powers of evil*'.[1]

At this point his analysis repeats the point made famously in the 1930s by Gustaf Aulén in his advocacy of the *Christus Victor* motif as the 'classic' way of interpreting atonement.[2] However, Webber moves on to make what, for some, may be the surprising claim that 'the classical view that God in Christ is the cosmic redeemer is the message that will be most readily heard in the postmodern world'.[3] This tantalizing suggestion leads us back to Col. 2.8-15, verses which are central to any exposition of the *Christus Victor* theme.

2. Issues in the text

Before focusing directly upon this theme it is worth noting, briefly, that preachers turning to this passage have no shortage of material to wrestle with. Some of the issues which the commentaries examine in depth are as follows.

a. The nature of the problems in Colossae

James Dunn suggests that 'what was being confronted was not a sustained attempt to undermine or further convert the Colossians, but a synagogue apologetic promoting itself as a credible philosophy more than capable of dealing with whatever heavenly powers might be thought to control or threaten human existence'.[4]

b. Who or what are 'the elemental spirits of the universe'?

In a society where astrology continues to fascinate many, it is interesting to note how many writers highlight the astrological dimension of these elemental spirits which exert such an oppressive force upon people. Hence, Dunn suggests that the reference here 'is to the belief that was no doubt then common (as still among not a few today) that human beings had to live their lives under the influence or sway of primal and cosmic forces, however precisely conceptualized'.[5]

c. The uniqueness of Christ

The inextricable interdependence of the person and work of Christ is evident in v. 9, which focuses upon the one in whom 'the whole fullness of deity dwells bodily'. In a religiously pluralist world, how can the uniqueness and particularity of Christ be proclaimed in appropriate ways?

d. What is the nature of the written record which has been nailed to the cross?

Peter O'Brien's preference is to understand this document

> as the signed acknowledgment of our indebtedness before God. Like an IOU it contained penalty clauses (see Job 5:3; Phlm. 19). The Jews had contracted to obey the law, and in their case the penalty for breach of this contract meant death (Deut. 27.14-26; 30.15-20). Paul assumes that the Gentiles were committed, through their consciences, to a similar obligation, to the moral law in as much as they understood it (cf. Rom. 2.14, 15). Since the obligation had not been discharged by either group the "bond" remained against us.[6]

Even if some of the details are open for debate, the overall impact of the imagery is clear. 'God has canceled the bond by nailing it to the cross – this is a vivid way of saying that because Christ was nailed to the cross our debt has been completely forgiven.'[7]

e. Victory over the powers

In vv. 11–15 a range of metaphors is employed to express the significance of Christ's death. Circumcision (v. 11), burial and resurrection (v. 12), death and new life (v. 13), erasing the incriminating record (v. 14), and disarming the powers and public victory (v. 15) are all pressed into service to explain the saving power of the cross. At the climax of this complicated list comes the proclamation of Christ's victory over the powers.

Dunn sums up the shocking and surprising nature of this claim in a memorable way. He says that

> to treat the cross as a moment of triumph was about as huge a reversal of normal values as could be imagined, since crucifixion was itself regarded as the most shameful of deaths... But in this letter it is simply of a piece with the theological audacity of seeing in a man, Jesus the Christ, the sum and embodiment of the divine wisdom by which the world was created and is sustained (1.15–20). The key can only be to recognize that for Paul, as for the first Christians generally, the cross and resurrection of Christ itself constituted such a turning upside down of all that had previously determined or been thought to determine life that only such imagery could suffice to express its significance. The unseen powers and invisible forces that dominated and determined so much of life need no longer be feared. A greater power and force was at work, which could rule and determine their lives more effectively – in a word 'Christ.' Triumph indeed.[8]

3. The wondrous duel

If there is a possibility that the *Christus Victor* message is 'the good news for a postmodern society',[9] then it is worth taking some time to get better acquainted with this way of understanding atonement. One example which classical Christianity offers is Martin Luther, whose *theology of the cross* contains this *Christus Victor* motif.

At a number of points Luther portrays Christ's death as a 'wondrous duel', with Christ battling against the law, sin, death and the curse which is divine wrath against the whole world. While these cruel tyrants appear to be victorious, they all end up serving God's purpose. So, for example, the law gleefully attacks and kills the Son, who has taken the sins of all upon himself, with the result that 'by this deed the whole world is purged and expiated from all sins and thus is set free from death and from every evil'.[10]

In similar ways sin, death and the curse seek to annihilate the blessing, but are instead annihilated by it. Christ is victorious in this wondrous duel by virtue of the invincible righteousness and immortality inherent in his divine nature. As he was a divine and eternal person it was therefore impossible for death to hold him, and he rose again freed from the constraints of law, sin and death. Luther makes it clear that only a divine person could possibly achieve such a victory and so his comprehensive understanding of the work of Christ requires a high view of the person of Christ. 'Therefore it was necessary that He who was to conquer these in Himself should be true God by nature.'[11]

At times Luther describes the law as one of the cruel tyrants which oppresses men and women. There is, however, a divine purpose hidden behind this law which humiliates sinners and confronts them with the thunder of hell and the lightning of divine wrath. The law serves God's purpose by thus reducing people to hopelessness and despair in the hope, and with the intention, that they will turn in faith to God as Saviour.[12] At times he writes about the devil using these instruments to reduce sinners to despair; but even if the devil is the immediate cause of the despair, it is the love of God which is ultimately responsible for it.

Thus the law is part of God's 'strange work' (*opus alienum Dei*), which serves the purpose of preparing the way for God's 'proper work' (*opus proprium Dei*) which is the work of love, forgiveness and justification.[13] In addition to the law, Luther also includes sin, death, the curse and the wrath of God within the scope of God's 'strange work'. Hidden within them all, discernible only to the eye of faith, is the 'proper work' of God and so it becomes clear that, for Luther, 'God's wrath is his penultimate and not his final word'.[14]

A further dimension of God's 'strange work' is described by Luther as '*Anfechtung*'. Death, the devil, the world and Hell launch such an 'assault' on men and women that it reduces them to despair. Once again it is God who is ultimately behind this assault or temptation, because his intention is that such attacks will lead people to a state where they will turn to him for the mercy he is longing to give them. On the cross Christ endured the most severe form of *Anfechtung* on our behalf, thereby effecting the marvellous exchange that opens the way to salvation.[15]

Yet another aspect of God's 'strange work' is seen in the stratagem whereby God used the devil's weapon of death in order to defeat death and produce life. 'God promotes and perfects his proper work by means of his alien work, and by a marvellous wisdom compels the devil to work through death nothing else than life itself, with the consequence that as the devil is working his damnedest against the work of God, he is by dint of his own work but working against himself and forwarding God's work.'[16] In this way the devil was deceived and defeated by the Son of God whose divine nature could not die eternally. In this context it is again clear that Luther's convictions about the divinity and the humanity of Jesus Christ provide the essential foundations for his soteriology.

Luther's 'theology of the cross' clearly contained this dramatic emphasis on Christ's battle with evil forces. It spoke powerfully to an age which was conscious of the malign influences of evil powers. Without necessarily adopting all of Luther's analysis of evil there may be insights here which continue to have relevance to an age which is also, for different reasons, painfully aware of the destructive power of evil and the demonic.

4. Victory – human and divine

The strangeness of Luther's language may distance us from this classic understanding of atonement. The impression we get is that Christ succeeded in this wondrous duel, by virtue of the powers inherent in his divine nature. Such a divine victory may be something to celebrate, but it may also create the feeling that this battle takes place far away from everyday human experience.

In his evaluation of Aulén's use of the *Christus Victor* model, Colin Gunton asserts that it is important to stress that, in the New Testament, the victory is as much human as divine; and his comments apply equally well to Luther's approach. Within the Gospels, Jesus achieves victory over the powers of evil by obeying the will of his Father. 'It is the refusal to succumb to temptation that is Jesus' victory... The victory is at once human and divine – a divine victory only because it is a human one – and although the Synoptic Gospels do not explicitly describe the ministry of Jesus as a victory, they clearly see it as in part a conflict between the authority of God represented by Jesus and that which would deny it.'[17]

Gunton moves on to consider the cash value of the language of the demonic, arguing that 'in the beginning, nothing is demonic in itself, not even Satan (see, again, Job 1). The demonic is what happens when what is in itself good is corrupted into its opposite... If the created order, or a part of it, is treated as god, then it behaves like god for those who so treat it, but for destructive rather than creative ends.'[18] So, if sex, money or other things become idols, they become demonic powers which end up exerting a destructive influence over people.

William Placher argues that the imagery of this battle against evil forces us to face the reality that

> evil has its own kind of power. Whether it's the logic of warfare that seems to require murdering innocent people, or the sexual affair that gathers its own momentum, or the economic situation that forces a factory closure, or the history of abuse that goes down the generations in a family, there are countless situations in which the evil that surrounds us seems greater than the sum of the bad deeds of the human agents involved.[19]

In the face of such overwhelming powers and forces, it is easy to end up feeling powerless; and on the first Good Friday it appeared as if Jesus Christ himself was powerless in the face of them. But the resurrection reveals that the power of God's love will ultimately be victorious.

So as we await God's final victory over evil, what weapons are available to help us in this battle between good and evil that continues to rage within our lives, and within the world? The cross reveals that it is inappropriate to fight evil using its own weapons, because that simply perpetuates the powers of evil and violence. At the cross we see how 'Christ confronts evil with no weapons but sinlessness and love, and triumphs not through violence but through willingness to suffer'.[20] Christ's prayer from the cross, that his enemies might be forgiven, is but one example of the victory of his love and obedience over hatred and evil.

Such considerations point to the conclusion that the cross is not only an event in history where God defeated evil, but that it is also the event which manifests God's way of overcoming evil *now*, through obedient, suffering love. Such love triumphs over evil, not by exercising superior force, but by absorbing evil at great personal cost. 'And this is the victory that conquers the world, our faith' (1 Jn 5.4).

5. Christ's royal office

Robert Sherman has recently argued that a helpful account of atonement can be developed by expounding the person and work of Christ in terms of his threefold office as Prophet, Priest and King.[21] Reflection on the decisive victory which Christ accomplished on the cross contributes to thinking about Christ as king, because the victory of Christ over evil is essential to any consideration of the kingly office of Christ.

For John Calvin, the kingly office of Christ makes a difference to the life of the baptized because 'God surely promises here that through the hand of his Son he will be the eternal protector and defender of his church'.[22] Calvin notes how 'Paul with good reason, therefore, magnificently proclaims the triumph that Christ obtained for himself on the cross, as if the cross, which was full of shame, had been changed into a triumphal chariot! For he says that "Christ nailed to the cross the written bond which stood against us...and disarmed the principalities...and made a public example of them" [Col. 2:14-15].'[23] As the risen, victorious king, Christ is armed with such eternal power 'that the perpetuity of the church is secure in his protection'.[24] This protection is guaranteed because God has appointed his Son eternal King by immutable decree.[25]

The royal office of Christ has direct bearing on matters of salvation because 'Christ enriches his people with all things necessary for the eternal salvation of souls and fortifies them with courage to stand unconquerable against all the assaults of spiritual enemies'.[26] God has entrusted all power to the Son, so that through the Son he can 'nourish, and sustain us, keep us in his care, and help us'. As their king and pastor the Son rules over his people but another vital dimension of his royal power is that he will bring about judgement upon the ungodly. This means that the Last Judgement 'may also be properly considered the last act of his reign'.[27]

In his teaching, and in his death upon the cross, Christ the King calls into question traditional assumptions about power and authority, and sets the agenda for different forms of leadership and service (Mk 10.45).

6. Good news for a postmodern world!

The *Christus Victor* model faces the reality of evil in this turbulent world, with a hope based on the resurrection. The good news for a despairing world is that 'no matter how effectively the powers of evil now rage, they are doomed. Evil is not ultimate. Evil is not the final word in human existence. The final word is Jesus Christ. The vision of new heavens and a new earth is not fantasy. It is the reality, the truth. Therefore, it is the hope that lies behind everything we do as Christians.'[28] As we await the new heavens and the new earth, the preacher's calling is to proclaim the good news of the one who broke the power of evil at the cross. Confident in Christ's ultimate victory over evil and death, we are called to use the loving weapons of the crucified in the ongoing battle against principalities and powers.

Sermon[29]

Through the letterbox the other day popped a rather sombre letter.

> *Dear Mr Stevenson*
> *It's not a pleasant thought we know.*
> *But if you died would you family face financial difficulties?*
> *Would your partner be able to pay all the family bills and expenses your income takes care of now? Could they earn enough?*
> *And take care of the home and children at the same time?*
> *Would your savings be enough to fall back on?*
> *It could be difficult...*

So, here's a cheerful way to start the day.

Life is fragile
We live in an unpredictable world
We're all going to die...

But before you choke on your morning corn flakes – don't worry.
Never fear, says the bank, because as their letter puts it

> *We have the answer!...*
> *...and the answer is... Life Insurance.*

> *And if you sign up before your next birthday it's even cheaper.*
> *Isn't your family's future worth from 47p a day?*

Now, if life insurance isn't what you have in mind – don't worry.

Yes life is fragile
We do live in an unpredictable world,

But never fear because the astrologers also say: *We have the answer.*

According to the astrologers all you have to do to find out what life has in store for you is to phone the tarot line.

> All you have to do is concentrate hard on the question on your mind, then call the phone number above. You'll be asked to punch a number between one and 78 into your keypad – this guides the computer to select three cards, which will then be read to you. Listen to the interpretation of the cards and see how it may affect your life.
> *(Calls cost 75p per minute and last 4½ minutes)*

A few weeks ago Channel 4 ran a series of programmes which they called Psychic Night. And during Psychic Night they had a series of programmes exploring various aspects of spiritualism, with people trying to contact the dead. And the climax of this Psychic Night on Channel 4 was a programme at 10.30 p.m. which claimed to tell us about the top ten ways to contact the dead.

Yes life is fragile
We do live in an unpredictable world,
We're not certain what the future may bring
And people are unsure about what happens when we die.

And that uncertainty breeds uncomfortable feelings of fear.
And in that uncomfortable situation there are plenty of
Psychics,
   Astrologers
      Life-guides and other gurus
Who say in effect:
Never fear –
We have the answer.

Now our Bible reading from Colossians chapter 2 reveals that this is not a new phenomenon. For our Bible reading takes us back to the city of Colossae in the first century, to that part of the world we now call Turkey.

And as we read through the apostle Paul's letter to the Christians in Colossae
we get the impression that:
many people in first century Colossae felt helpless
they believed that their lives were not entirely under their own control
that they were subject to the iron grip of fate: *Que será será…*

They believed, as the astrologers still do,
that their lives were dictated and determined by the movements of the stars
and the planets.
that their lives were dominated by the elemental, basic principles of this world.
that they were the victims of invisible principalities and powers.
that their lives were at the mercy of unseen evil forces.

And people who felt so vulnerable were longing to find some answers to the
mysteries of life. They were on the look-out for anything that would help them
discover freedom and life in all its fullness.

And back there in first-century Colossae there were various people who said
in effect:
Never fear –
We have the answer.

We know the sacred mysteries.
We have the special knowledge you need if you're going to succeed in this
world and the next.
So, believe what we teach
Do as we say
Perform the rituals and ceremonies we command
Observe the holy days we will tell you about
Worship the heavenly beings we identify
And then you'll find the path to freedom and fullness of life.

So when the apostle Paul writes his letter to the Christians in the city of
Colossae he says very bluntly

Beware
Look out
Be on your guard.

'See to it that no one takes you captive through hollow and deceptive
philosophy, which depends on human tradition and the basic principles of this
world rather than on Christ'.

Be on your guard for people who're peddling:
man-made ideas
home-brewed philosophies which claim to make sense of life.

Watch out! Because far from finding freedom,
you'll end up becoming enslaved to false ideas.

Watch out! Avoid these dead-end teachings.

Watch out! for those who say *We have the answer* –
because the truth is that *Christ is the answer.*

Some time ago I was delivering leaflets, inviting people to special services at church. And at one door a gentleman invited me in for a chat, because his son and my son were in the same class at school.

It turned out that this man was a practising Muslim and he asked:
'Why do Christians believe that Jesus was more than just a prophet?'

It's the sort of question many people ask in our tolerant, pluralist society.

Yes, Jesus was…
A prophet
A great religious teacher
One amongst several great religious teachers.

But surely it's inappropriate and insensitive nowadays to claim anything more than that?

Now when we turn back to first-century Colossae, we find the apostle Paul living and working in a religiously pluralist society where people worshipped many gods.

And yet he still makes a staggering claim about Jesus, for he says…

'In Christ all the fullness of the Deity lives in bodily form, and you have been given fullness in Christ, who is the head over every power and authority.'

Now the apostle Paul's not claiming that Jesus is one of the world's great religious teachers – he's claiming something much, much more than that,

Because he's stating clearly that the Eternal Son of God through whom all things in heaven and earth were created has come to earth.

God has come to earth in person – in the person of his Son, Jesus Christ.

And in Christ, all the fullness of the Deity lives in bodily form.

The full content of the divine nature lives in Christ, in his humanity (Good News Bible).

So if you want the full truth about God – look no further.

The full truth, and nothing but the truth, is there in Christ staring you in the face.

So if you want to experience the full life and power of God – look no further.

Because all the fullness of God is in Christ, and in union with Christ that power flows into our lives and begins to change us and transform us.

During August there was a programme called 'Restoration' which ran on BBC 2 for several weeks. Twice a week, on Tuesdays and Fridays, the programme visited different parts of the country and each programme featured three more buildings
which were run down;
which had fallen into disrepair;
which were on their way to wrack and ruin;
buildings which desperately needed to be rescued and restored.

Eventually, after lots of votes came in by phone, the Victoria Baths in Manchester was chosen as the building to be restored; and using the miracle of computer graphics the viewers were given a glimpse of what the buildings would look like after they'd been restored and rebuilt.

As we look at our world, and as we look at ourselves;
we can see how human sin and rebellion against God has caused death and decay.
Our human nature is riddled, not with dry rot, but with sin and self-centredness.

But in Christ we see the full truth about God
And in Christ the full power of God is released
The power of God which can repair the damage caused by sin
The full power of God which can restore and re-create human beings in the image of Christ (see Col. 3.10).

So, there's no need to add
circumcision
or special diets
or special prayers
or special ceremonies
or special experiences.

Our salvation is complete in Christ in every respect because
'In Christ all the fullness of the Deity lives in bodily form.'
And so we need look no further – we need look nowhere else.

Many today make the claim *We have the answer!*
But today it remains the case that *Christ is the answer*, because

'In Christ all the fullness of the Deity lives in bodily form.'

Now, it's not just letters inviting me to take out life insurance that pop through our letterbox. There are other letters, other bits of paper, invoices and bills which come to tell me how much I owe.

But what if we were to receive through the letter box a statement about how much we owe God? What state would the account be in?

The apostle Paul uses that sort of language as he goes on to talk about the atoning death of Christ because he talks about *a written code, or a certificate of our indebtedness* which Christ has dealt with.

Many Jews believed that when Israel entered into a covenant with God they were accepting an obligation to obey God's law – and that they'd be liable to death (Deut. 27.14–26; 30.15–20) if they failed to obey the law.

And maybe what Paul has in mind is a document which clearly shows how Jews and Gentiles alike have clearly failed to obey God.
Or maybe it's a document listing all their evil deeds?

What is clear is that 'all have sinned and fall short of the glory of God' (Rom. 3.23).

If we're honest, God has more than enough evidence on the charge sheet to prove that all we like sheep have gone astray, each of us going our own way.

But the good news which Paul announces is that when Christ died for our sins, he nailed humanity's criminal record to the cross.

'God made you alive with Christ. He forgave us all our sins, having cancelled the written code, with its regulations, that was against us and that stood opposed to us; he took it away, nailing it to the cross.'

The debt of sin which we could never pay has been paid in full by Christ.

One preacher puts it like this:

'If it was a bill of indictment, it was revoked.
If it was a bill of obligation it was paid by another.
If it was a document of (our) evil deeds kept in heaven, it was rendered void.

All record of our debt was removed.
The wonderful news of the cross is that the IOU of sin has been cancelled.
The debt we owe to God has been eradicated once and for all by being nailed to the cross.'[30]

Many still claim – *We have the answer!*

Many still claim that
Our plan
Our diet
Our scheme
    Will make you happier.

But today the good news is still that *Christ is the answer,*

Because Christ alone can wipe the slate clean
Because Christ alone can give us a new start, a new beginning
Because through his death he has dealt with our sins, nailing them to the cross.

Last autumn my wife Susan and I spent a few days in Belgium visiting the historic city of Bruges. And in one of the museums there they have on display a guillotine. Not one of those little guillotines that you see in the office which chops up bits of paper. But a large-scale guillotine modelled on the ones used during the French revolution to chop people's heads off.

The guillotine is just one of the many brutal ways that people have invented over the years to execute people. And at the heart of the Christian faith stands the cross which represents another bloody and brutal form of execution. Crucifixion was such a barbaric form of execution that it was reserved as a way of punishing rebels against the state and runaway slaves.

And when Jesus died a criminal's death upon the cross it must have seemed to friend and foe alike that he had been defeated – that the powers of evil had succeeded in frustrating God's work through Jesus.

But once again we find the apostle Paul saying something quite amazing here, because he explains that the cross was not the place where Jesus was defeated; but rather the cross was the place where Jesus accomplished an amazing victory over the powers of evil.

'He forgave us all our sins, having cancelled the written code, with its regulations, that was against us and that stood opposed to us; he took it away, nailing it to the cross. And having disarmed the powers and authorities, he made a public spectacle of them, triumphing over them by the cross.'

Over the last few weeks there have been many sad reports from the Middle East. First we hear of a suicide bomber causing an explosion in Jerusalem killing many people. Then we hear of Israeli troops moving into Palestinian areas and attacking and killing suspected terrorists.

It's tit for tat
It's an eye for an eye
And the spiral of hatred and violence just goes on and on.

But with the death of Jesus we see something very different at work.

For at the cross when Jesus is on the receiving end of
evil
hatred
injustice

violence
death
he doesn't retaliate.

He doesn't allow himself to become possessed by bitterness, anger or hatred.

But he prays 'Father forgive them…'

He absorbs all that hatred, sin and violence;
at great personal cost he absorbs the violence and breaks the spiral of revenge and violence.

For you see his prayer from the cross that his enemies might be forgiven, represents the victory of love and forgiveness over hatred and evil.
And the love that is victorious at the cross proves to be more potent and more powerful than all the combined forces of sin, and evil and death.

At the beginning of his ministry, Jesus was tempted by the devil (see Luke 4.1–12), and that battle between Jesus and the devil continued throughout his ministry.

And in that battle between good and evil
Jesus won the victory
He resisted temptation
He overcame the devil
by obeying God
by being obedient to God
by being obedient unto death, even death upon the cross.

The key to Christ's victory over evil was his obedience.

As we look at our troubled world we can see that the battle between good and evil is still raging.

That battle is still there inside each one of us too.

But we celebrate that the decisive battle has been won.
We need not fear any evil power because 'He that is in us is greater than he that is in the world'.

Christ has triumphed decisively over evil powers through his death upon the cross,

And he calls us to take up the cross and to follow him, relying upon the weapons he used,
the weapons of faith and obedience,

the weapons of love and forgiveness.

He calls us in the power of the Spirit not to be overcome by evil, but to overcome evil with good (Rom. 12.21).

Thinking about Christ's victory over evil reminds me of some prayers from a Ghanaian Christian lady called Afua Kuma. These prayers clearly convey the sense that believers are involved in a spiritual battle. And they express a strong confidence that Christ has been victorious in the battle with evil forces.

Jesus! You are the one
who has gone out to save the nations.
You wear a chief's crown
The flag of a conqueror leads you in battle.

Strong-armed One!
You are the one who has tied death to a tree
So that we may be happy.

...the strong-hearted One,
whose works are indeed stout-hearted:
you stand at the mouth of the big gun
while your body absorbs the bullets
aimed at your followers.

If you go with Jesus to war,
No need for a sword or gun.
The word of his mouth is the weapon
Which makes enemies turn and run.

If we walk with him and we meet with trouble
We are not afraid.[31]

A Christian magazine recently recruited two advertising agencies to devise an advertising campaign to attract people back to church. And the advertising experts came up with a campaign featuring images of lonely goldfish and giraffes which they believed would provoke a response from non-Christians about church.

Advertising gurus have claimed that the Church needs to tone down the cross and promote friendship in order to attract new members...

The agencies said that people outside the Church would not connect with typical images of Church and religion, for example, Jesus on the cross.

'We don't think people like to be preached at. The key is to get people through the door of the church and let them make up their own minds,' said Guy Lipton, Managing Director of Link ICA.[32]

Now I'm all for promoting friendship...but tone down the cross?

We need to proclaim the cross because
The one who died upon the cross is the one in whom the fullness of deity lives in bodily form.

We need to proclaim the cross because
The cross of Christ is the place where God deals with humanity's criminal record and wipes the slate clean.

We need to proclaim the cross because
It gives us hope by pointing us to the Christ who has broken the power of the evil that destroys our world.

In Christ crucified and risen *we have the answer* that meets the deepest needs and longings of human beings.

Tone down the cross? No!
Celebrate it.
Proclaim it.
Live it. YES!

Commentary

This sermon sets Paul's proclamation of the victory of Christ on the cross within the context of his pastoral concern for the Christians at Colossae. Paul wants to warn them against being taken captive 'through hollow and deceptive philosophy', and forcefully remind them that 'Christ is the answer'. Therefore, just as in the case of his letters to the Romans and Corinthians, his exposition of God's atoning work in Christ is directed to believers, and with a very practical purpose.

The preacher follows Paul, earthing his message in the reality of the seductive appeals from various quarters today, purporting to offer security in a fragile world. The structure of the sermon reflects this concern to let Paul's message about the uniqueness and achievement of Christ have its impact in contemporary life, and especially in the priorities of the Church. Built around the linking phrase 'we have the answer', it moves from the deceitful answers, in contemporary Britain and Colossae, to Paul's declaration that 'Christ is the answer'. The story about the advertising agency at the end is a reminder that the pressures *on Christians* to shrink from proclaiming the cross, where the achievement of Christ is focused, are as alive now as they were in the first century, and to be resisted.

The sermon begins by describing the kind of alluring junk-mail offer likely to be familiar to all the hearers, moving on to the more sinister appeals of astrology and spiritualism. This enables the preacher then to move into the biblical world and show the connection between the atmosphere in which we live and that in which Paul wrote. When the opening of the text, Paul's warning in v. 8, is first spoken, we are thus well prepared to hear it with its full force. The foundation is also now laid for the assertion that 'Christ is the answer', but before the reading of vv. 9, 10 in which Paul starts to expound this, the preacher tells a story reminding us that the claim is controversial in a pluralist society. This in turn prepares the way for us to hear vv. 9, 10 more clearly, for we are reminded that Paul's society too was pluralist. The claim of Christ's uniqueness is made with courtesy but clarity.

The rest of the sermon, similarly, allows us to hear Paul's words with fresh understanding, through carefully relating his words to concepts familiar today. As the preacher unpacks the various images Paul uses to expound Christ's achievement, he helps us to grasp them through vivid contemporary pictures. Our human nature, so in need of the 'fullness of life' which only Christ can bring (v. 10), is likened to a building desperately needing restoration. The 'written code' or 'certificate of indebtedness' (v. 14) is compared to the constant reminders we receive of money owed for one reason or another. Crucifixion itself, as a barbaric form of execution in the ancient world, is compared to the guillotine: now also a thing of the past, but much nearer in time to us, and still visible in museums.

The paradox at the heart of the cross, victory through shame and apparent defeat, is explored in terms of Christ absorbing the violence of humanity and breaking the spiral of revenge (vv. 13c–15). The very concrete 'answer' this offers to the world today is suggested by the reference to continuing retaliatory attacks in the Middle East.

Thus through an interweaving of the biblical and contemporary worlds (note especially the links between one section and another), the preacher proclaims Paul's message of the cross, bringing Paul's own words to life. Note that he sees no need to deal with every verse (vv. 11, 12 are omitted): every sermon must be clearly focused, and this one focuses on the contrasting 'answers' available, the false and the true. We see too how not only the meaning, but also the triumphant mood of Paul's words has been caught.[33] The prayers of Afua Kuma bring a spirit of praise to the final section of the sermon. It then concludes with the reminder, much in keeping with Paul's whole thrust, that the victory of Christ on the cross is to be not only enjoyed, but also celebrated, proclaimed and lived.

10

The final sacrifice:
Hebrews 9.11–14

1. The trouble with sin

Eugene Lowry advises preachers to go looking for '*trouble*, in, around, with and about the text'[1] because he believes that this can help the preacher to hear the text in a fresh way. Anyone foolhardy enough to wrestle with Heb. 9.11–14 has plenty of trouble to contend with. It is not that there is great trouble in understanding what the passage is saying; for there are plenty of commentaries which helpfully fill in the background to the text. The trouble lies in making connections between the passage's concerns about the blood of bulls and goats, and twenty-first century hearers who are more concerned about mobile phones, pension plans and interest rates. In a sin-denying culture where problems are usually someone else's fault, bloody sacrifices for sin are not high on most people's agendas.

Thomas Long suggests that Hebrews is addressed to exhausted believers who are keen to give up. 'Tired of walking the walk, many of them are considering taking a walk, leaving the community and falling away from faith.' Faced with such a contemporary sounding problem, Long argues that 'what is most striking about Hebrews is that the Preacher, faced with the pastoral problem of spiritual weariness, is bold enough, maybe even brash enough, to think that christology and preaching are the answers'.[2] All of which raises questions about the nature of the christology which is being advanced in this epistle as the antidote to spiritual drift.

2. The high priest

At first glance the christology in question does not appear to be one
that is likely to resonate with our contemporaries, because it presents
Christ coming on the scene 'as a high priest of the good things that
have come' (9.11). Such language conjures up a long-lost world of
temples and animal sacrifices which may be of historic interest to
some, but feels remote to many more. However, before rejecting it out
of hand it is worth taking time to put this priestly picture in context.

Throughout this letter, the author has argued that although Christ
does not qualify as a priest on the basis of his human ancestry, he
nevertheless deserves to be seen as a priest for ever according to the
order of Melchizedek. He is qualified to mediate between God and
humanity because, as ch. 1 announces, the Son is fully divine and able
to speak God's word decisively and authoritatively. At the same time
he is also able to sympathize with fallible human beings because, as
ch. 2 declares, he has 'become like his brothers and sisters in every
respect' (2.17). Having endured temptations, and having learned
obedience in the garden of Gethsemane, and on the cross (5.7–10),
he has become perfectly qualified to represent human beings before
God.

Human mortality means that other priests can only fulfil their
representative functions for a limited period. However, 'through the
power of an indestructible life' (7.16), the risen and ascended Christ
'holds his priesthood permanently because he continues for ever'
(7.23–25). Step by step the author constructs his argument to prove
that Christ can be seen as the great high priest, according to the order
of Melchizedek, who ever lives to make intercession for his people
(7.20–25).

At various points along the way there are hints that this priestly
work will involve offering sacrifice to make atonement for human sins
(2.18; 5.1; 7.27; 8.3). Here in 9.11–14, the author boldly affirms that
this high priest has once and for all presented a sacrifice which deals
with the problem of sin finally and effectively.

For many today this stress upon the atoning action of the high
priest is not only old-fashioned and strange, but also contains some
offensive elements. Talk about sacrifices for sin implies that sin is still
a problem which needs to be dealt with. That sits uneasily with an
age of do-it-yourself morality, where people claim the freedom to do
whatever they want to do.

The idea that Christ the high priest has acted on my behalf may
also offend deeply held convictions about the sacred autonomy of the

individual, which is one of the legacies of Enlightenment thinking. In a world where one of the watchwords is 'be who *you* want to be', the idea of someone acting on my behalf, without even asking my permission, rubs somewhat against the grain.

However, even in an individualistic age, it is clear that the actions of some representative figures have massive implications for others. When the President of the United States and the Prime Minister of the United Kingdom decided to wage war against Iraq, their representative actions affected millions of people, irrespective of whether or not people agreed with them.

Moving back to Old Testament times it is evident that both kings and high priests were recognized as representative figures. Once a year, on the Day of the Atonement (Leviticus 16), the high priest entered the Holy of Holies to represent the people before God. John Calvin saw a clear parallel between the representative actions of Israel's high priest, and the atoning work of Christ. In his *Commentary on Hebrews* Calvin explained that

> the high priest used to enter the holy of holies not only in his own name, but in that of the people, as one who in a way carried all the twelve tribes on his breast and on his shoulders, because twelve stones were woven into his breastplate and their names were engraved on the two onyx stones on his shoulders to be a reminder of them, so that they all went into the sanctuary together in the person of the one man.

For Calvin this clearly prefigures the priestly ministry of Christ, and implies 'that our High Priest has entered heaven, because He has done so not only for Himself, but also for us'.[3]

Having reflected upon the way in which the representative actions of the high priest had implications for others, it is necessary now to move on to consider the sacrifice which the High Priest offered.

3. The final sacrifice

The Old Testament describes many sacrifices which were God-given ways of dealing with the problem of sin. It also pointed forward to a new covenant which would provide a permanent solution to the problem of human sinfulness (Jer. 31.31–34). Hebrews confidently announces that the sacrificial death of Jesus Christ has sealed this new covenant, and dealt with the problem of sin once and for all (7.27; 9.12, 26–29). But what is it that makes the sacrifice of Christ so special?

One answer is along the lines advocated centuries ago by Anselm who saw the divinity of Christ adding infinite value to the sacrifice being offered. At one point in *Cur Deus Homo*,[4] Anselm argues that the greatest evil imaginable would be to kill the one who is perfect God and perfect man. The converse of this is that the life and death of the God-man must therefore be of 'infinite value'. 'If then to lay down life is the same as to suffer death, as the gift of his life surpasses all the sins of men, so also will the suffering of death'.[5] The God-man freely gave his life for the honour of God and this priceless offering makes 'ample satisfaction' for the sins of the whole world, and infinitely more'.[6] The consequent remission of debt clears the way for women and men to inherit the eternal life God created them to enjoy.

However, the author of Hebrews does not try to calculate the mathematical value of the divine Son's offering, but he draws our attention instead to the obedience of Christ (10.3–10). Although the divine Son shared in our fallen humanity, and was thus exposed to the full force of temptation, yet by the power of the Holy Spirit he was enabled to resist temptation and to offer to God a life of perfect and complete obedience.

Centuries later, the Puritan theologian, John Owen, focused on Christ's '*unspeakable zeal* for, and *ardency of affection unto, the glory of God*' and concluded that 'these were the coals which with a vehement flame, as it were, consumed the sacrifice'.[7] The inherent connection between godly zeal and obedience means that obedience is a major atoning element within Owen's understanding of Christ's final sacrifice.

> It was not, then, [by] the outward suffering of a violent and bloody death, which was inflicted on him by the most horrible wickedness that ever human nature brake forth into, that God was atoned, Acts ii. 23; nor yet was it merely his enduring the penalty of the law that was the means of our deliverance; but the voluntary giving up of himself to be a sacrifice in these holy acts of obedience was that upon which, in an especial manner, God was reconciled unto us.[8]

The atoning significance of Christ's obedience was similarly evident to Calvin who said: 'Now someone asks, How has Christ abolished sin, banished the separation between us and God, and acquired righteousness to render God favourable and kindly toward us? To this we can in general reply that he has achieved this for us by the whole course of his obedience.'[9]

William Lane helpfully explains that

Christ's sacrifice was qualitatively superior to the blood of goats and calves because it consisted in the offering of his life to God (9.14, 25, 26). The antithetic formulation of v. 12a suggests a stark contrast between the involuntary, passive sacrifice of animals and the active obedience of Christ who willingly made himself the sacrifice for sins (9.26; 10.5–10).[10]

Hebrews adds to our thinking about atonement by proclaiming that it is the sacrifice of a life of perfect obedience, perfected in death, which atones for sin and establishes the new covenant whereby God promises to remember his people's sins no more. By entering into God's presence this great high priest achieves salvation for us, by bringing us with him into the Holiest Place. The separation between sinful people and God has been removed, because Christ our representative has taken us with him into the very presence of the living God.

Another way in which Hebrews describes the atoning work of Christ on the cross is to talk about 'the blood of Christ', which Lane describes as 'a graphic synonym for the death of Christ in its sacrificial significance'. He notes how

the writer rhetorically contrasts the limited efficacy of 'the blood of goats and bulls' with the surpassing efficacy of 'the blood of Christ.' The effectiveness of the blood of Christ derives from the qualitatively superior character of his sacrifice. His sacrifice achieved what the old cultus could not accomplish, namely, the decisive purgation of conscience and the effective removal of every impediment to the worship of God.[11]

Although many assume that sacrificial language about the 'blood of Christ' has lost its power to communicate with people today, Robert Sherman argues that the reality is rather different. Noting the widespread use of phrases such as 'blood is thicker than water', 'blood money' and 'cold-blooded murder', he suggests that 'metaphorical uses of the word "blood" are far from meaningless and obsolete. On the contrary, they may well reflect something utterly primal and perduring in human experience...When "blood" is invoked the matter is not trivial, it is serious, indeed, often a matter of life and death.'[12] The preacher's task is to communicate the death, resurrection and ascension of Jesus Christ in ways which show that they continue to be life and death issues for people today.

Another perspective on the topic is opened up as the author explains that by entering into the Holy Place by means of his own blood, Christ has obtained 'eternal redemption'. Paul Ellingworth

says that 'it is difficult to be sure whether the idea of liberation (as
in Exodus from Egypt) or of payment (as in the ransoming of the
firstborn; e.g. Lev. 15.29) predominates' in this passage. 'Since neither
aspect is directly related to the Day of Atonement liturgy' which exerts
such an influence upon Hebrews he suggests that other aspects of
liberation should also be taken into account.[13] Fred Craddock takes
this a step further by noting how the idea of 'redemption' sometimes
refers 'to freedom from slavery, sometimes from prison, sometimes
from death, sometimes from sin'. As the author of Hebrews does not
make one particular view explicit, Craddock suggests that 'it seems
best to leave it as open as it is in the text'.[14]

As Hebrews stresses the final sacrifice which deals with sin and
cleanses our consciences, it seems reasonable to conclude that freedom
from the slavery of sin and guilt is integral to the eternal redemption
accomplished by Christ. If the purpose of Christ's coming was also to
'free those who all their lives were held in slavery by the fear of death'
(Heb. 2.14–15), then freedom from the slavery of death must similarly
form part of this eternal redemption.

4. Through the eternal spirit

The redemption accomplished by Christ can be described as eternal
because it is permanent, final, once and for all. It will never cease to
be effective because there is something eternal about its origin, for it
was 'through the eternal Spirit' that Christ 'offered himself without
blemish to God' (Heb. 9.14).

Although Hugh Montefiore denies any reference to the Holy Spirit
at this point, preferring to interpret Heb. 9.14 in terms of Christ
offering himself to God 'in his eternal nature',[15] it seems much more
likely that the reference here does point to the Holy Spirit. Hence
Ellingworth states that 'it was the power of the eternal Spirit which
enabled Christ to be at the same time both high priest and offering.
Other priests depended on animal sacrifices to cover their own sins;
Christ was supernaturally empowered to be himself an unblemished
offering; or conversely it was the power of the eternal Spirit which
made Christ's unique sacrifice eternal in its effect.'[16]

John Owen rejected the idea that the 'eternal Spirit' being referred
to in verse 14 was the divine nature of the Son, and insisted instead
that the person of the Holy Spirit was in view, so that 'the Lord
Christ offered up himself unto God as a sacrifice by the eternal Spirit'.
Amongst the graces imparted to the incarnate Son by the Spirit, his

'*unspeakable zeal*' and his '*ardency of affection unto the glory of God*' were the things which helped to make his sacrifice effective.[17]

More recently Jürgen Moltmann has drawn upon Heb. 9.14, in his reflections upon a trinitarian theology of the cross. He asserts that 'the surrender through the Father and the offering of the Son take place "through the Spirit". The Holy Spirit is therefore the link in the separation. He is the link joining the bond between the Father and the Son, with their separation.' Although the language at this point might be criticized as being somewhat impersonal, the trinitarian pattern of his thinking is evident. Building on these ideas Moltmann moves on to claim that the 'form of the Trinity which is revealed in the giving up of the Son appears as follows:

- The Father gives up his own Son to death in its most absolute sense, for us.
- The Son gives himself up, for us.
- The common sacrifice of the Father and the Son comes about through the Holy Spirit, who joins and unites the Son in his forsakenness with the Father.'[18]

It would be unwise to dismiss such trinitarian reflections as matters of abstract, academic interest. Some preachers of the cross are criticized for creating models of atonement which give the impression that a loving Son needed to placate an angry Father. To avoid such distortions it is worth pausing to reflect on Heb. 9.11–14, which offers useful resources for a trinitarian understanding of atonement. For at this point we see the divine Son, obeying the will of the Father (10.3–10), in the power of the Spirit. This alone should be sufficient to demonstrate that there is no conflict within God over matters of atonement, because these verses point to the way in which the Father, Son and Spirit are mutually involved and implicated in this one divine work of salvation.

5. Past event and present salvation

One evening early in my ministry a young Christian couple brought a Muslim colleague round to our home. An interesting discussion evolved and at one point our Muslim guest asked a question which provoked some serious thought. The gist of his question was about how the death of Jesus Christ nearly 2000 years ago could possibly make any difference to people today. I have thought about that question many times over the years and I am grateful for an encounter which forced me to think deeply about how the past events of crucifixion and resurrection connect with our present experience of salvation. The longer I reflect upon that question the more convinced I become that the work of the Holy Spirit is a vital dimension of any model of atonement seeking to explain how the story of Jesus can also be the story of my redemption today.

This passage's reference to Christ offering himself 'through the eternal Spirit' invites reflection upon the work of the Spirit in the life and death of Jesus Christ, and upon the Spirit's work within the believer today. For the same Spirit who empowered the suffering servant to resist temptation, and to be obedient unto death on a cross, is now available to all who believe. As Sherman puts it, 'Christ's atoning work as priest is not a matter restricted simply to the past. Rather, it is ongoing and ever present, as his benefits are made effective each moment in the power of the Holy Spirit.'[19] Through the secret working of the Spirit the believer is united to the one who is seated at the right hand of the Father.

6. The desire of divine love

Some models of atonement concentrate on the past event of the cross to such an extent that it is sometimes difficult to see how the Christ event in the distant past has any real connection with Christian living today. In sharp contrast to that, the priestly understanding of atonement developed by John McLeod Campbell in *The Nature of the Atonement* sought to explore not only what human beings have been saved from, but also what they have been saved for. He argued that 'the atonement is regarded as that by which God has bridged over the gulf which separated between what sin had made us, and what it was the desire of the divine love that we should become.'[20]

Tom Wright notes how a

generation ago, liberal thought managed to get rid of sin; and, with sin, most theories of atonement were dismissed as odd and unnecessary. But in our own generation we have rediscovered guilt; we have shame and violence in plenty; we have alienation at all levels. And we don't know what to do with it, either at a personal or at a corporate level. Cleansing of the conscience is what is required, and the only way to do that is by the total offering of the human life to God.[21]

Hebrews announces that the sacrificial death of Christ provides that long-awaited total offering of life to God. Now, the once-and-for-all sacrifice of Christ penetrates to the depths of our humanity, and succeeds in purifying 'our consciences from dead works to worship the living God' (9.14). This sacrifice is more effective than the sacrificial rituals performed by other high priests, year after year, which could only deal with external matters of ritual defilement.

In this way Heb. 9.11–14 not only makes clear what Christ has saved us *from*, but also highlights what Christ has saved people *for*. For the purpose of this deep-seated cleansing of the human conscience is not simply to supply a superior form of spiritual and emotional therapy. The desire of the divine love is to free people from sin and guilt, in order that they might serve and worship the living God. Hence Craddock observes that 'the end and purpose of Christ's sacrifice for us is in order that we may worship ("serve," NIV) the living God. The verb "to serve" (λατρεύω, *latreuo*) comes from the cultus and has the immediate sense of worship, but throughout the NT it includes service to God much more broadly (12.28; Lk. 1.74; Acts 27.23; Rom. 1.9; Phil. 3.3).'[22]

7. An antidote to spiritual drift?

The inclusion of Hebrews in the New Testament canon suggests that the diet of christology and preaching proved effective responses to the spiritual crisis facing its first readers. That still leaves open our earlier questions about the relevance of such answers for a culture which is less familiar with religious language and imagery.

Derek Tidball observes that our contemporary 'world is full of secular priests who, having renounced the significance of God, still seek to relieve people of guilty consciences and offer wisdom for living... The secular priest acts as a mediator who puts clients in touch with themselves, their feelings, their true identity or the forgotten past.'[23] A context where so many are searching for meaning and wholeness provides opportunities for preachers to point to the one who can relieve guilty consciences and offer wisdom. The one who has both shared in the painful realities of human existence, and also made the lonely journey through the death we fear, is uniquely qualified to act as a reliable life coach in this world and the next.

James B. Torrance suggested that 'the epistle to the Hebrews contrasts two forms of worship: true worship, which means reposing on and participating in the self-offering of Christ who alone can lead us into the "Holy of Holies" – the holy presence of the Father – and false worship, with its false reliance on what we do by following our

own devices or traditions'. In the light of this it becomes clear that fevered pleas for people to try harder, which place the emphasis upon what we have to *do*, will inevitably lead to spiritual exhaustion. The antidote to spiritual tiredness lies in a trinitarian understanding of atonement which enables the worship which is 'the gift of grace to participate through the Spirit in the incarnate Son's communion with the Father – the way of joy and peace and confidence'. [24]

Sermon[25]

In the church I attended as a teenager, the Pastor ran a series of Bible studies looking at Old Testament themes. One year he got someone to build a large model of the Tabernacle used by the people of Israel in the wilderness. Another year he had a life-sized model dressed in the garments of the high priest; and week by week he drew out spiritual lessons about the symbolism of the tabernacle or the garments worn by the high priest.

Now I have to confess that in over 25 years of preaching and teaching I've never felt tempted to run a series examining the garments of the high priest; because talk of priests and sacrifices, and the blood of goats and calves all seems so remote and old-fashioned.

In the 21st century who needs a High Priest?

Last Saturday evening you may've seen a programme on Channel 4 about *The New Ten Commandments*. And in preparation for the programme, Channel 4 had polled 65,000 people across the UK to discover which of the original Ten Commandments they felt were still relevant to living a moral life in the modern world.

Only two of the original Top Ten Commandments survived:

Do not kill
Do not steal

And some of the original Ten Commandments like:
Don't commit adultery, and
Respect your mother and father,
failed to make it into the Top Ten, but were still in the Top Twenty Commandments.

The New Ten Commandments, in reverse order were:

10. Protect your family
9. Never be violent
8. Look after the vulnerable
7. Protect the environment
6. Protect and nurture children
5. Do not steal
4. Be honest
3. Do not kill
2. Take responsibility for your actions
1. Treat others as you would have them treat you

Now, I don't know if you noticed, but looking at this list it's significant that the commandment which says '*You shall have no other god before me*' has disappeared entirely; to be replaced by a commandment in the Top Twenty Commandments which says '*Be true to your own god*'.

In a world where we:

create our own commandments
make our own rules, and
choose our own gods

Who needs a high priest?

And yet, strange as it may sound, it appears to be the case that lots of people are looking for someone who sounds very much like a high priest. For at a time, in the UK, where fewer and fewer people are going to church, more and more people are turning to psychiatrists, psychologists, psychotherapists, counsellors and life coaches. And in Britain the number of qualified counsellors has tripled over the last ten years to keep up with rising demand.

And why is there a rising demand for the help of someone who sounds very much like a high priest?

Might it be that it's easy enough to create Ten New Commandments; but it's not so easy to find the power to put them into practice?

Might it be that it's not too difficult to make up our own rules for living; but it's much more difficult to handle the pain and disappointment which comes when you fail to live up to your own rules, and others fail to observe them too?

Might it be that it sounds a good idea to *be true to your own god*; but what if deep down inside your heart is still restless and dissatisfied?

In spite of all our desires to

> create our own commandments
> make our own rules, and
> choose our own gods;

there's still a niggling sense for many people that life's not as it should be, and many people are looking for someone who'll help them deal with painful matters of conscience and who'll offer them wisdom for living.

And into a world where people are longing for healing and wholeness, the book of Hebrews announces that Jesus Christ is the one who fits the bill. He's the one people are looking for, whether they realize it or not; because he is the high priest who has offered once and for all the final sacrifice which deals with sin and its painful consequences.

> For if the blood of goats and bulls, with the sprinkling of the ashes of a heifer, sanctifies those who have been defiled so that their flesh is purified, how much more will the blood of Christ, who through the eternal Spirit offered himself without blemish to God, purify our conscience from dead works to worship the living God! (Hebrews 9.13–14 NRSV)

It was meant to be just a simple blood test – and as the nurse got ready to put the needle in my arm, she said, 'you're not going to faint on me, are you?' Well, I had no intention of fainting, but the next thing I knew I'd collapsed, and not only the nurse but one of the doctors was looking over me as I came around. They were rather anxious because my heart rate stayed low and before I knew it, I was in the back of an ambulance on the way to King's College Hospital. And when the doctor in casualty came to see me, the first thing he said was, 'We'll need to do a blood test...'

When we start talking about 'blood', it touches a raw nerve; and yet our language is saturated with references to blood. We talk about 'cold-blooded murder'. We talk about people who are 'blood-brothers'. We talk about paying 'blood money'. We talk about things which make your blood boil, and we talk about people who're 'hot-blooded'.

And when we use the word 'blood' in those ways, it's a way of saying that:

this thing is serious,
this thing is important, and
this thing is a matter of life and death.

And when the Book of Hebrews talks about 'the blood of Christ' it's pointing to something serious, something that's of life and death importance.

I don't know what style of church music you're into; but in our congregation we don't tend to sing many hymns about being 'washed in the blood of the Lamb'. But before we reject language about 'the blood of Christ' as being out of date or irrelevant, we do well to remember that the phrase 'the blood of Christ' is a vivid and dramatic way of describing the sacrificial death of Christ.

And in these verses Jesus is portrayed as the one:
who has shared in our human existence,
who has faced the full force of temptation,
who, in the power of the Spirit, has resisted temptation and remained obedient to God,
who has offered himself to God in death through the power of the Holy Spirit,
who is the perfect sacrifice which repairs the damage caused by sin,
who removes the sin which separates us from God,
who reunites fallible, flawed, sinful people like us to the living God.

In the past God has provided a system of sacrifices to keep sin under control; but now in Christ the final, costly sacrifice has been offered through the eternal Spirit. And by the power of the Spirit the benefits of Christ's death are applied to our lives today.

but this does keep sin under control

A few days ago a brochure came through the letterbox announcing:
At last. Something new is coming that will change your perspective forever.

And what is it that will transform your perspective forever? Well, it turns out to be a very expensive retirement home for elderly people a few miles down the road in Purley.

Now with much greater justification, the author of the book of Hebrews announces that something new has come that will change your perspective forever, because Christ has come as the 'high priest of the good things that have come'. Jesus the great high priest has acted as our representative. And by his life, death, resurrection and ascension into heaven he has acted decisively:

[handwritten marginal note, partly illegible: "Ok but now I cho but Paul says … subject … but I do"]

to set us free from the burden of failure,
to cleanse and heal our troubled consciences, and
to set us free from sin's power so that we can be free to serve the living God.
For 'how much more will the blood of Christ, who through the eternal Spirit offered himself without blemish to God, purify our conscience from dead works to worship the living God!' (Hebrews 9.14)

At a time when so many people are looking for someone who will bring them healing, wholeness and hope, the Church is called to point people to the one who is uniquely qualified to act as a reliable life coach in this world and the next.

But as we seek to proclaim this Jesus it's also important to remember that Jesus Christ is not just a superior life coach, who offers better therapy which can make us feel better. Jesus Christ is the high priest, who has come to deal with the mess and muddle in our lives, so that he can set us free to worship and serve the God whose service is perfect freedom.

For 'how much more will the blood of Christ, who through the eternal Spirit offered himself without blemish to God, purify our conscience from dead works to worship the living God!' (Hebrews 9.14)

Commentary

The preacher turning to Hebrews will probably find it comparatively easy to preach from texts such as 11.8, where the reference to Abraham's faith calls to mind the twists and turns of the Old Testament narratives. Chapter 12 invites sermons about running the race of faith with our eyes fixed on Jesus; and 13.8 focuses attention on the one who is the same yesterday, today and forever.

Preaching from Hebrews 9 presents a different set of issues. The brief reference here to the 'high priest of the good things that have come' calls to mind the lengthy discussions of the high priest that run throughout the letter. All of that may have been very familiar to first-century hearers and readers of this letter, but it is not so familiar to many western Christians today.

This particular sermon was preached during a service which formed part of a residential training weekend for a group of people preparing for lay leadership within the Anglican Church. It seeks to build, therefore, upon the biblical and theological background which the hearers brought to the occasion.

David Schlafer suggests that 'throughout all the varieties of Scripture forms three basic related, but distinctive motifs can be consistently found. Whether a text is a hymn of praise, a terse teaching, a historical account, a parable, or a theological essay, it communicates by using *images, narratives* and *arguments*'.[26] This leads him to suggest that when it comes to constructing the sermon one of these three – image, story, or argument – can be used as the integrating principle to give shape to the whole sermon. In his opinion, effective sermons normally employ only one central strategy, so that 'one of the three is chosen as the means best suited for *this* preacher at *this* time with *this* text for *these* people. Images, stories and arguments serve as sermon-shaping strategies, as vehicles for an experience of the Word that is genuinely sacramental.'[27]

In preparing this sermon it was necessary to wrestle with questions about which of these three motifs might help to hold the sermon together. One option was to consider making *story* the sermon shaping strategy. For it would be possible to design a narrative sermon, drawing upon the story of the first recipients of this letter, who were being tempted to give up on faith for one reason or another. It could also be argued that as the passage is developing a detailed theological argument about the person and work of Christ, a 'form-sensitive' sermon might take the form of a theological *argument*.

In the event the choice was taken to allow the *image* of the high priest offering a sacrifice to function as the integrating principle for the sermon. In a variety of ways the sermon reflects on that central image and seeks to remove some of the layers of misunderstanding which might prevent people from identifying with it. In exploring this image, which is central to Hebrews, it was appropriate to employ aspects of story and argument at various points along the way.

From another perspective this sermon could be viewed as a *problem-resolution* sermon. It identifies the *problem* at the outset, with the refrain *who needs a high priest?*, and then tries to help the hearers feel that, whether people realize it or not, many people are actually looking for someone who will perform those priestly functions of bringing peace and wholeness into troubled lives. Having identified this deep-seated human need, which Christ the high priest is uniquely qualified to meet, the sermon encourages the Church to point people to Christ with renewed confidence.

The language of Hebrews 9.11–14 is rich in theological images and ideas, and decisions had to be made about which of those images could be included on this occasion. The decision was also made not to try to explain everything, but to announce and release some of these powerful words; taking the risk that these words have their own inherent power to communicate to hearers at a variety of levels.

Bibliography

The Alternative Service Book (London: Hodder and Stoughton, 1980).

Anselm, *St Anselm: Basic Writings* (trans. S. N. Deane; La Salle: Open Court, 1962).

Antoine, Gérald, 'The Sacrifice of Isaac: Exposition of Genesis 22:1–19', in Bovon and Rouiller (eds.), *Exegesis*, pp. 177–82.

Athanasius, 'Four Discourses Against the Arians', in Schaff and Wace (eds.), *St. Athanasius*, pp. 303–447.

—— *The Incarnation of the Word of God: De Incarnatione Verbi Dei* (trans. anon; London: Geoffrey Bles, 1944).

—— *Contra Gentes and De Incarnatione* (trans. Robert W. Thomson; Oxford: Clarendon Press, 1971).

Auerbach, Erich, *Mimesis: The Representation of Reality in Western Literature* (trans. Willard R. Trask; Princeton, NJ: Princeton University Press, 1953 [1946]).

Aulén, Gustav, *Christus Victor: An Historical Study of the Three Main Types of the Idea of the Atonement* (trans. A. G. Hebert; London: SPCK, 1961 [1931]).

Balentine, Samuel E., *Leviticus* (Interpretation: A Bible Commentary for Teachers and Preachers; Louisville, KY: John Knox Press, 2002).

Balthasar, Hans Urs von, *Mysterium Paschale: The Theology of the Easter Mystery* (Edinburgh: T&T Clark, 1990).

—— *The Epistle to the Romans* (BNTC; London: A & C Black, 1962).

Barrett, C. K., *A Commentary on the Second Epistle to the Corinthians* (BNTC; London: A & C Black, 1973).

Bartholomew, Craig, Joel B. Green and Anthony C. Thiselton (eds.), *Reading Luke: Interpretation, Reflection, Formation* (Milton Keynes: Paternoster; Grand Rapids, MI: Zondervan, forthcoming, 2005).

Bauckham, Richard J., *2 Peter, Jude* (WBC, 50; Dallas: Word, 1992).

Beasley-Murray, George R., *John* (WBC, 36; Waco: Word, 1987).

Bebawi, George, 'Atonement and Mercy: Islam between Athanasius and Anselm', in Goldingay (ed.), *Atonement*, pp. 185–202.

Black, Kathy, *A Healing Homiletic: Preaching and Disabililty* (Nashville: Abingdon Press, 1996).

Bovon, François, and Grégoire Rouiller (eds.), *Exegesis: Problems of Method and Exercises in Reading (Genesis 22 and Luke 15)* (trans. Donald G. Miller; Pittsburgh Theological Monograph Series, 21; Pittsburgh, PA: Pickwick Press, 1978).

Bruce, F. F., *This is That: The New Testament Development of Some Old Testament Themes* (Exeter: Paternoster Press, 1968).

Brueggemann, Walter, *Genesis* (Interpretation: A Bible Commentary for Teachers and Preachers; Atlanta: John Knox Press, 1982).

—— *Isaiah 40–66* (Westminster Bible Companion; Louisville, KY: Westminster John Knox Press, 1998).

Burridge, Richard A., *Four Gospels, One Jesus* (London: SPCK, 1994).

Calvin, John, *Institutes of the Christian Religion* (LCC, 20; ed. J. T. McNeill; Philadelphia: Westminster Press, 1960).

—— *The Epistle of Paul the Apostle to the Hebrews and the First and Second Epistles of St. Peter* (Grand Rapids, MI: Eerdmans, 1963).

Campbell, Douglas A., 'The Story of Jesus in Romans and Galatians', in Bruce W. Longenecker (ed.), *Narrative Dynamics in Paul*, pp. 97–124.

Campbell, John McLeod, *The Nature of the Atonement* (London: Macmillan, 6th edn, 1906).

Carson, D. A., *The Gospel According to John* (Leicester: InterVarsity Press, 1991).

Chamberlain, Jane, and Jonathan Rée (eds.), *The Kierkegaard Reader* (Oxford: Blackwell, 2001).

Childers, Jana (ed.), *Birthing the Sermon: Women Preachers on the Creative Process* (St. Louis, MI: Chalice Press, 2001).

—— (ed.), *Purposes of Preaching* (St Louis, MI: Chalice Press, 2004).

Childs, Brevard S., *Isaiah: A Commentary* (The Old Testament Library; Louisville, KY: Westminster John Knox Press, 2001).

Clarke, Anthony, *A Cry in the Darkness: The Forsakenness of Jesus in Scripture, Theology and Experience* (Oxford: Regents/Smith & Helwys, 2002).

—— 'Violence and the Cross: God and the Death of Jesus', in *idem* (ed.), *Expecting Justice*, pp. 24–43.

—— (ed.), *Expecting Justice, but Seeing Bloodshed: Some Baptist*

Contributions to Following Jesus in a Violent World (Oxford: Whitley Publications, 2004).

Clemens, Deborah R., 'Dialogue between the Testaments', in Lazareth (ed.), *Reading the Bible in Faith*, pp. 71–77.

Craddock, Fred B., 'The Letter to the Hebrews', in Keck (ed.), *The New Interpreter's Bible*, XII, pp. 1–173.

Dodd, C. H., *The Apostolic Preaching and its Developments* (London: Hodder & Stoughton, 1936).

Dunn, James D. G., *Jesus and the Spirit: A Study of the Religious and Charismatic Experience of the First Christians as Reflected in the New Testament* (London: SCM Press, 1975).

—— *The Epistles to the Colossians and to Philemon: A Commentary on the Greek Text* (Carlisle: Paternoster, 1996).

Edwards, James R., *The Gospel according to Mark* (Grand Rapids, MI: Eerdmans, 2002).

Ellingworth, Paul, *The Epistle to the Hebrews: A Commentary on the Greek Text* (Carlisle: Paternoster, 1993).

Evans, Craig A., *Mark 8:27–16:20* (WBC, 34B; Dallas: Word, 2002).

Fiddes, Paul S., *Past Event and Present Salvation* (London: Darton, Longman & Todd, 1989).

Florence, Anna Carter, 'Put Away Your Sword! Taking the Torture out of the Sermon', in Graves (ed.), *What's the Matter*, pp. 93–108.

Forsyth, P. T., *Positive Preaching and the Modern Mind* (Carlisle: Paternoster, 1998 [1907]).

Girard, René, *Things Hidden since the Foundation of the World* (London: Continuum, 1987).

—— *I See Satan Fall Like Lightning* (Maryknoll: Orbis, 2001).

Goldingay, John (ed.), *Atonement Today* (London: SPCK, 1995).

Gowan, Donald E., *Reclaiming the Old Testament for the Christian Pulpit* (Edinburgh: T&T Clark, 1980).

Graves, Mike, *The Sermon as Symphony: Preaching the Literary Forms of the New Testament* (Valley Forge: Judson Press, 1997).

—— (ed.), *What's the Matter with Preaching Today?* (Louisville, KY: Westminster John Knox Press, 2004).

Green, Joel B., 'Jesus on the Mount of Olives (Lk. 22.30–46): Tradition and Theology', *JSNT* 26 (1986), pp. 29–48.

—— *The Theology of the Gospel of Luke* (New Testament Theology; Cambridge: Cambridge University Press, 1995).

—— *The Gospel of Luke* (NICNT; Grand Rapids, MI: Eerdmans, 1997).

Green, Joel B., and Michael Pasquarello III (eds.), *Narrative Reading, Narrative Preaching: Reuniting New Testament Interpretation and Proclamation* (Grand Rapids, MI: Baker Academic, 2003).

Greidanus, Sidney, *Preaching Christ from the Old Testament: A Contemporary Hermeneutical Method* (Grand Rapids, MI: Eerdmans, 1999).

Grieb, A. Katherine, *The Story of Romans: A Narrative Defense of God's Righteousness* (Louisville, KY: Westminster John Knox Press, 2002).

Gunton, Colin E., *The Actuality of Atonement: A Study of Metaphor, Rationality and the Christian Tradition* (Edinburgh: T&T Clark, 1988).

—— *Yesterday and Today: A Study of Continuities in Christology* (London: SPCK, 2nd edn, 1997).

Hahn, Scott W., 'Kingdom and Church in Luke–Acts: From Davidic Christology to Kingdom Ecclesiology', in Bartholomew *et al.* (eds.), *Reading Luke*.

Hartley, John E., *Leviticus* (WBC, 4; Dallas: Word, 1992).

Hays, Richard B., *Echoes of Scripture in the Letters of Paul* (New Haven and London: Yale University Press, 1989).

—— *The Faith of Jesus Christ: The Narrative Substructure of Galatians 3:1–4:11* (Grand Rapids, MI: Eerdmans, 2nd edn, 2002).

Heron, Alasdair I. C., 'Homoousios with the Father', in Torrance (ed.), *Incarnation*, pp. 58–87.

Hill, Charles E., and Frank A. James III (eds.), *The Glory of the Atonement* (Downers Grove: InterVarsity Press, 2004).

Hooker, Morna D., *The Gospel according to Saint Mark* (BNTC; London: A & C Black, 1991).

Hurtado, Larry W., *Mark* (NIBC, 2; Peabody: Hendrickson, 1989).

Jeffers, Robinson, *Selected Poems* (New York: Random House, 1965).

Jones, L. Gregory, 'Crafting Communities of Forgiveness', *Int* 54.2 (2000), pp. 121–34.

Josipovici, Gabriel, *The Book of God: A Response to the Bible* (New Haven and London: Yale University Press, 1988).

Kaiser, Walter C., Jr, 'The Book of Leviticus', in Keck (ed.), *The New Interpreter's Bible*, I, pp. 983–1191.

Keck, Leander E., *The New Interpreter's Bible*, I (Nashville: Abingdon Press, 1994).

—— *The New Interpreter's Bible*, IX (Nashville: Abingdon Press, 1995).

Keck, Leander E., *The New Interpreter's Bible*, XII (Nashville: Abingdon Press, 1998).

—— *The New Interpreter's Bible*, X (Nashville: Abingdon Press, 2002).

Kierkegaard, Søren, 'Fear and Trembling', in Chamberlain and Rée (eds.), *Kierkegaard Reader*, pp. 72–107.

Kok, Joel E., 'The Test', in Lazareth (ed.), *Reading the Bible in Faith*, pp. 83–88.

Kuma, Afua, *Jesus of the Deep Forest: Prayers and Praises of Afua Kuma* (Accra: Asempa Press, 1981).

Lane, William, *Hebrews 9–13* (WBC, 47B; Dallas: Word, 1991).

Lazareth, William H. (ed.), *Reading the Bible in Faith: Theological Voices from the Pastorate* (Grand Rapids, MI; Cambridge, UK: Eerdmans, 2001).

Long, Thomas G., *Hebrews* (Louisville, KY: John Knox Press, 1997).

Longenecker, Bruce W. (ed.), *Narrative Dynamics in Paul: A Critical Assessment* (Louisville, KY and London: Westminster John Knox Press, 2002).

Longenecker, Richard N. (ed.), *The Challenge of Jesus' Parables* (McMaster New Testament Studies, 4; Grand Rapids, MI: Eerdmans, 2000).

Lowry, Eugene L., 'Surviving the Sermon Preparation Process', *Journal for Preachers* 24.3 (Easter 2001), pp. 28–32.

—— *The Homiletical Plot: The Sermon as Narrative Art Form* (Louisville, KY: Westminster John Knox Press, 2nd edn, 2001).

Luther, Martin, 'De Servo Arbitrio' (LCC, 17; London: SCM Press, 1969), pp. 99–334.

—— *Lectures on Galatians 1535* (Luther's Works, 26; St. Louis: Concordia, 1963).

—— 'Lectures on the Epistle to the Hebrews 1517–18' (LCC, 16; London: SCM Press, 1962), pp. 19–250.

—— 'The Heidelberg Disputation' (LCC, 16; London: SCM Press, 1962), pp. 274–307.

Mathewson, Steven D., *The Art of Preaching Old Testament Narrative* (Grand Rapids, MI: Baker; Carlisle: Paternoster, 2002).

McGrath, Alister E., *Luther's Theology of the Cross* (Oxford: Blackwell, 1985).

McKinney, Richard W. A. (ed.), *Creation, Christ and Culture: Studies in Honour of T.F. Torrance* (Edinburgh: T&T Clark, 1976).

Michaels, J. Ramsey, 'Atonement in John's Gospel and Epistles', in Hill and James (eds.), *Glory*, pp. 106–18.

Moessner, David P., 'Reading Luke's Gospel as Ancient Hellenistic Narrative: Luke's Narrative Plan of Israel's *Suffering* Messiah as God's Saving "Plan" for the World', in Bartholomew *et al.* (eds.), *Reading Luke.*

Moltmann, Jürgen, *The Crucified God* (London: SCM Press, 1974).

—— *The Trinity and the Kingdom of God* (London: SCM Press, 1981).

—— *The Way of Jesus Christ* (London: SCM Press, 1990).

Montefiore, Hugh, *A Commentary on the Epistle to the Hebrews* (BNTC; London: A & C Black, 1964).

Moule, C. F. D., *Forgiveness and Reconciliation and Other New Testament Themes* (London: SPCK, 1998).

Murphy, Patrick, 'Lessons in Love', *Church Times*, 15 October 2004, p. 18.

O'Brien, Peter T., *Colossians, Philemon* (WBC, 44; Milton Keynes: Word, 1987).

O'Day, Gail, 'The Gospel of John', in Keck (ed.), *The New Interpreter's Bible*, IX, pp. 491–865.

Owen, John, *The Works of John Owen*, III (ed. W. H. Goold; London: Banner of Truth, 1965).

—— *The Death of Death in the Death of Christ* (Edinburgh: Banner of Truth Trust, reprint edn, 1983 [1650]).

Peskett, Howard, and Vinoth Ramachandra, *The Message of Mission* (Leicester: InterVarsity Press, 2003).

Placher, William C., 'Christ Takes Our Place', *Int* 53 (1999), pp. 5–20.

—— *Jesus the Savior: The Meaning of Jesus Christ for Christian Faith* (Louisville, KY: Westminster John Knox Press, 2001).

Renquist, Thomas A., 'The Music of Failure', in Lazareth (ed.), *Reading the Bible in Faith*, pp. 77–83.

Rouiller, Grégoire, 'Augustine of Hippo Reads Genesis 22:1–19', in Bovon and Rouiller (eds.), *Exegesis*, pp. 343–61.

—— 'The Sacrifice of Isaac (Genesis 22:1–19): First Reading', in Bovon and Rouiller (eds.), *Exegesis*, pp. 13–42.

—— 'The Sacrifice of Isaac (Genesis 22:1–19): Second Reading', in Bovon and Rouiller (eds.), *Exegesis*, pp. 413–35.

Sawyer, John F. A., *The Fifth Gospel: Isaiah in the History of Christianity* (Cambridge: Cambridge University Press, 1996).

Schaff, P., and H. Wace (eds.), *St. Athanasius: Select Works and Letters* (Nicene and Post-Nicene Fathers of the Christian Church, 2nd series, vol. 4; Edinburgh: T&T Clark, 1891).

Schlafer, David J., *Surviving the Sermon: A Guide to Preaching for Those who Have to Listen* (Boston: Cowley Publications, 1992).

Sherman, Robert, *King, Priest, and Prophet: A Trinitarian Theology of Atonement* (New York and London: T&T Clark International, 2004).

Southall, David, *The Meaning of δικαιοσύνη Θεοῦ in Paul's Epistle to the Romans* (MTh Dissertation; London: Spurgeon's College, 2002).

Speers, Samuel H., 'The Founding Vision of Covenant Community', in Lazareth (ed.), *Reading the Bible in Faith*, pp. 89–94.

Sykes, Stephen W., 'Life after Death: the Christian Doctrine of Heaven', in McKinney (ed.), *Creation, Christ and Culture*, pp. 250–71.

Taylor, Barbara Brown, 'Bothering God', in Childers (ed.), *Birthing*, pp. 153–68.

Thompson, James W., 'Reading the Letters as Narrative', in Green and Pasquarello (eds.), *Narrative Reading*, pp. 81–105.

Thompson, Michael B., *The New Perspective on Paul* (Grove Biblical Series, 26; Cambridge: Grove Books, 2002).

Tidball, Derek, *The Message of the Cross* (Leicester: InterVarsity Press, 2001).

Torrance, James B., *Worship, Community and the Triune God of Grace* (Downers Grove: InterVarsity Press, 1996).

Torrance, Thomas F., *The Trinitarian Faith: The Evangelical Theology of the Ancient Catholic Church* (Edinburgh: T&T Clark, 1988).

—— (ed.), *The Incarnation: Ecumenical Studies in the Nicene-Constantinopolitan Creed A.D. 381* (Edinburgh: Handsel Press, 1981).

Toynbee, Polly, *Hard Work: Life in Low-Pay Britain* (London: Bloomsbury, 2003).

Tuckett, Christopher M., *Luke* (New Testament Guides; Sheffield: Sheffield Academic Press, 1996).

Turner, Mary Donovan, 'Disrupting a Ruptured World', in Childers (ed.), *Purposes*, pp. 131–40.

Van Dyk, Leanne, *The Desire of Divine Love: John McLeod Campbell's Doctrine of the Atonement* (New York: P. Lang, 1995).

Van Harn, Roger (ed.), *The Lectionary Commentary: Theological Exegesis for Sunday's Texts* (3 vols.; Grand Rapids, MI: Eerdmans; London: Continuum, 2001).

Vanstone, W. H., *The Stature of Waiting* (London: Darton, Longman & Todd, 1982).

Volf, Miroslav, 'The Social Meaning of Reconciliation', *Int* 54. 2 (2000), pp. 158–72.

Wainwright, Geoffrey, *For Our Salvation: Two Approaches to the Work of Christ* (Grand Rapids, MI: Eerdmans, 1997).

Webber, Robert, *Ancient-Future Faith: Rethinking Evangelicalism for a Postmodern World* (Grand Rapids, MI: Baker Books, 1999).

Wenham, Gordon J., *The Book of Leviticus* (London: Hodder & Stoughton, 1979).

Williams, James G. (ed.), *The Girard Reader* (New York: Crossroad, 1996).

Willis, E. David, *Calvin's Catholic Christology: The Function of the So-called Extra Calvinisticum in Calvin's Theology* (Leiden: E. J. Brill, 1966).

Wright, N. T., *Following Jesus: Biblical Reflections on Discipleship* (London: SPCK, 1994).

—— *Jesus and the Victory of God* (London: SPCK, 1996).

—— 'The Letter to the Romans', in Keck (ed.), *The New Interpreter's Bible*, X, pp. 393–770.

Wright, Stephen I., 'Christ the King, Year C', in Van Harn (ed.), *Lectionary Commentary. 3. The Gospels*, pp. 455–58.

—— 'Parables on Poverty and Riches', in Richard N. Longenecker (ed.), *Challenge*, pp. 217–39.

Young, Frances M., *Sacrifice and the Death of Christ* (London: SCM Press, 1975).

Young, Frances M., and David F. Ford, *Meaning and Truth in 2 Corinthians* (London: SPCK, 1987).

Notes

Introduction

1   A famous account of three of the main ones was given by Gustav Aulén in *Christus Victor: An Historical Study of the Three Main Types of the Idea of the Atonement* (trans. A. G. Hebert; London: SPCK, 1961 [1931]).

2   From the service for 'The Ordination or Consecration of a Bishop', in *The Alternative Service Book* (London: Hodder & Stoughton, 1980), p. 388.

Chapter 1: The cost of a father's commitment: Genesis 22.1–19

1   Lit. 'binding', from the root   found in v. 9.

2   See especially the treatment of Augustine, discussed in Grégoire Rouiller, 'Augustine of Hippo reads Genesis 22:1–19', in François Bovon and Grégoire Rouiller (eds.), *Exegesis: Problems of Method and Exercises in Reading (Genesis 22 and Luke 15)* (trans. Donald G. Miller; Pittsburgh Theological Monograph Series, 21; Pittsburgh, PA: Pickwick Press, 1978), pp. 343–61. The passage is one of the traditional readings for the Easter Vigil.

3   The rhythm and restraint of the story was brilliantly described in Erich Auerbach, *Mimesis: The Representation of Reality in Western Literature* (trans. Willard R. Trask; Princeton, NJ: Princeton University Press, 1953 [1946]), pp. 7–12, in the context of a contrast drawn between the biblical and Homeric narrative styles. See also the insightful treatments of Gérald Antoine, 'The Sacrifice of Isaac: Exposition of Genesis 22:1–19', in Bovon and Rouiller (eds.), *Exegesis*, pp. 177–82, and Grégoire Rouiller, 'The Sacrifice of Isaac (Genesis 22:1–19): Second Reading' in Bovon and Rouiller (eds.), *Exegesis*, pp. 413–35.

4   On parallels between this story and that of Job see Walter Brueggemann, *Genesis* (Interpretation: A Bible Commentary for Teachers and Preachers; Atlanta: John Knox Press, 1982), p. 189.

5   This is stated most starkly in Amos 3.6b ('When disaster comes to a city, Has not the LORD caused it?') and Isa. 45.7 ('I form the light and create darkness, I bring prosperity and create disaster'). For a further discussion of this theme as it relates specifically to the atonement see Ch. 3 below.

6   Søren Kierkegaard, 'Fear and Trembling', in Jane Chamberlain and Jonathan Rée

181

(eds.), *The Kierkegaard Reader* (Oxford: Blackwell, 2001), pp. 72–107.

7 Cf. Auerbach, *Mimesis*, pp. 11-12.

8 See Kierkegaard's incisive comments on the irony of this verse in 'Fear and Trembling', p. 103. Brueggemann points to the centrality of this statement in the structure of the story (*Genesis*, p. 186). It is the only time Abraham utters a complete statement beyond the 'here I am' of vv. 1, 7, 11. On the latter expression as evoking 'a sense of reciprocal trust between Abraham and God, Isaac and Abraham', see Gabriel Josipovici, *The Book of God: A Response to the Bible* (New Haven and London: Yale University Press, 1988), p. 174.

9 Cf. this comment of Auerbach: 'But here, in the story of Abraham's sacrifice, the overwhelming suspense is present; what Schiller makes the goal of the tragic poet – to rob us of our emotional freedom, to turn our intellectual and spiritual powers (Schiller says "our activity") in one direction, to concentrate them there – is effected in this Biblical narrative, which certainly deserves the epithet epic' (*Mimesis*, p. 11).

10 For a good summary of modern objections to this story and responses to them, see Samuel H. Speers, 'The Founding Vision of Covenant Community', in William H. Lazareth (ed.), *Reading the Bible in Faith: Theological Voices from the Pastorate* (Grand Rapids, MI; Cambridge, UK: Eerdmans, 2001), pp. 89–94.

11 Deborah R. Clemens stresses that 'Christians cannot speak of Genesis 22 without it being absorbed into the Resurrection': 'Dialogue between the Testaments', in Lazareth (ed.), *Reading the Bible in Faith*, pp. 71–7 (76). Thomas A. Renquist cites Origen, Augustine, Luther and Calvin as interpreting the story as one of faith in the resurrection: 'The Music of Failure', in Lazareth (ed.), *Reading the Bible in Faith*, pp. 77–83 (78f.). Clearly their original cue was Hebrews 11. Certainly the resurrection is our indispensable hermeneutical lens as Christians; and the resurrection sets the seal on God's atoning work. But if we are to do justice to the story before rushing too quickly to a gospel perspective, we have to say that it gives no hint either that Abraham believed that Isaac would be raised, or that the narrator believed that God could/would have done it.

12 Douglas A. Campbell, 'The Story of Jesus in Romans and Galatians', in Bruce W. Longenecker (ed.), *Narrative Dynamics in Paul: A Critical Assessment* (Louisville, KY and London: Westminster John Knox Press, 2002), pp. 97–124 (especially 105, 113–16). I am grateful to David Southall for drawing my attention to this article. On p. 114, n. 24, Campbell notes the (quite sparse) other literature on the connection between the two passages. In his notes 25 and 26 (pp. 114–15) Campbell suggests that Genesis 22 may also lie behind parts of 1 Corinthians and Galatians.

13 ἐφείσατο (Rom. 8.32), ἐφείσω (Gen. 22.12).

14 Cf. Campbell, 'Story of Jesus', p.115, n. 28: 'Notice that this shifts the moral framework of the story, resolving many of the potentially problematic dimensions in the original narrative (that so exercised Kierkegaard).'

15 Anthony Clarke, 'Violence and the Cross: God and the Death of Jesus', in *idem* (ed.), *Expecting Justice, but Seeing Bloodshed: Some Baptist Contributions to Following Jesus in a Violent World* (Oxford: Whitley Publications, 2004), pp. 24–43 (on the Genesis 22 allusion, see p. 33). Clarke also discusses Acts 2.23; 3.17f.; 4.27f.; Rom. 3.25; 2 Cor. 5.21.

16 In this connection, Clarke discusses the accusation of Dorothée Sölle that Jürgen Moltmann had presented a God who on the Cross inflicts as well as endures violence ('Violence and the Cross', pp. 34–5).

17 Clarke, 'Violence and the Cross', pp. 32–4. Clarke refers especially to the treatment of W. H. Vanstone, *The Stature of Waiting* (London: Darton, Longman & Todd,

1982). Vanstone saw the frequent use of παραδίδωμι in the passion narratives as emphasizing the passivity of Jesus, and from this makes an argument for passivity being at the heart of God's own disposition in the atonement: God waits, and lets humanity do its worst.

18 On these see Grégoire Rouiller, 'The Sacrifice of Isaac (Genesis 22:1–19): First Reading', in Bovon and Rouiller (eds.), *Exegesis*, pp. 13–42 (29–30, 38–9). A close association was made between the *Akedah* and Passover.

19 Something similar can be said of Jesus' story of the Prodigal Son (Lk. 15.11–32), which defies attempts to see it as an allegory of atonement or salvation, in which the father plays the role of God, not least because the returning son declares to his father 'I have sinned against heaven [i.e. God!] *and* before you' (v. 21).

20 It is possible, of course, to preach on Genesis 22 without bringing in the atonement: Abraham can be seen simply as an example for us of costly obedience. Such an approach is exemplified in Steven D. Mathewson, *The Art of Preaching Old Testament Narrative* (Grand Rapids, MI: Baker; Carlisle: Paternoster, 2002), pp. 161–75. The danger here is that the appalling nature of what Abraham was asked to do may be trivialized in the interests of making an 'application' to today.

21 For an exploration of the significance of 'echo' in the New Testament see Richard B. Hays, *Echoes of Scripture in the Letters of Paul* (New Haven and London: Yale University Press, 1989).

22 Renquist sets the test, and Abraham's obedience to it, in the context of Abraham's previous failures, notably his initial lack of faith at God's promise of a son (Gen. 17.17): it was because of these failures that such a test was necessary ('The Music of Failure', p. 82). This is an important reminder of the need to look at the wider narrative, but cannot fully address or explain the problematic nature of the story.

23 Brueggemann discusses the parallel tension, evident in the story, between God as tester and God as provider (*Genesis*, pp. 191–3).

24 Each of these six synoptic references has the phrase ὁ υἱός μου ὁ ἀγαπητός (cf. Gen. 22.2 LXX: τὸν υἱόν σου τὸν ἀγαπητὸν ὃν ἠγάπησας, lit. 'your beloved son whom you have loved'), though Lk. 9.35 has ἐκλελεγμένος, 'chosen', as an alternative in some MSS to ἀγαπητός.

25 Colin E. Gunton, *The Actuality of Atonement: A Study of Metaphor, Rationality and the Christian Tradition* (Edinburgh: T&T Clark, 1988), pp. 124–5.

26 Gunton, *Actuality*, p. 125.

27 This further underlines the need to see Paul in Rom. 8.32 as seizing upon a vivid picture, rather than fully expounding *either* Genesis 22 *or* a doctrine of atonement.

28 The ram of Gen. 22.13 is only one among many possible sources for this designation of Jesus. See D. A. Carson, *The Gospel According to John* (Leicester: InterVarsity Press, 1991), p. 149.

29 Cf. Gunton, *Actuality*, p. 120f.

30 On this see further especially Chapters 5, 7, 8 and 9 below.

31 See especially Lk. 24.26, 46–47.

32 In some brief but pregnant remarks on the literary qualities of the story, Antoine points to the symbolic quality of the victim Isaac, whose emotions and reactions are treated sparsely in the extreme, and who indeed eventually drops out of sight altogether (see v. 19): in other words, it is the quality of Abraham's obedience, not the experience of Isaac, which is clearly at stake in the story: 'The Sacrifice of Isaac', pp. 81–2. John Calvin saw a spiritual anguish in Abraham: he proposed that the main cause of Abraham's grief would have been that 'in the person of his son, the

whole salvation of the world seemed to be extinguished and to perish': cited in Joel
E. Kok, 'The Test', in Lazareth (ed.), *Reading the Bible in Faith*, pp. 83–8 (85).

33 By David Southall, Research Fellow of Spurgeon's College, London and Minister of
Brighton Road Baptist Church, South Croydon, UK.

34 The Greek παραβολή means literally 'something laid alongside', and this derivation
illuminates (though of course it does not exclusively define) the function of 'parables'
in Scripture.

35 Professor Frances Young has stressed how 'atonement' in classic Christian theology
concerns not just the relationship of God to human beings, but his relationship to
the cosmos itself (Conference on Atonement, High Leigh, UK, July 2004).

36 *Mimesis*, pp. 11–12.

Chapter 2: Taking away their iniquities: Leviticus 16.15–22

1 Walter C. Kaiser, Jr, 'The Book of Leviticus', in Leander E. Keck (ed.), *The New
Interpreter's Bible* (Nashville: Abingdon Press, 1994), I, pp. 983–1191 (1073).

2 Gordon J. Wenham, *The Book of Leviticus* (London: Hodder & Stoughton, 1979),
p. 231.

3 John E. Hartley, *Leviticus* (WBC, 4; Dallas: Word, 1992), pp. lxix–lxxii (lxix–lxx,
lxx, lxxii).

4 Wenham, *Leviticus*, p. 228.

5 Wenham, *Leviticus*, p. 230.

6 Samuel E. Balentine, *Leviticus* (Interpretation: A Bible Commentary for Teachers
and Preachers; Louisville, KY: John Knox Press, 2002), p. 4.

7 Balentine, *Leviticus*, p. 129, original italics.

8 Balentine, *Leviticus*, p. 130, original italics.

9 Anselm, *Cur Deus Homo*, in *St Anselm: Basic Writings* (trans. S. N. Deane; La Salle:
Open Court, 1962), pp. 191–302.

10 Gunton, *Actuality*, pp. 91–2.

11 Kaiser, 'Leviticus', p. 1111, original italics.

12 Lev. 17.11. See Paul S. Fiddes, *Past Event and Present Salvation* (London: Darton,
Longman & Todd, 1989), pp. 61–82; Frances M. Young, *Sacrifice and the Death
of Christ* (London: SCM Press, 1975).

13 Hartley, *Leviticus*, p. 238.

14 Balentine, *Leviticus*, p. 130.

15 Hartley, *Leviticus*, p. 238.

16 Hartley, *Leviticus*, p. 245.

17 René Girard, *Things Hidden since the Foundation of the World* (London:
Continuum, 1987); *idem, I See Satan Fall Like Lightning* (Maryknoll: Orbis, 2001);
James G. Williams (ed.), *The Girard Reader* (New York: Crossroad, 1996).

18 Girard, *Things Hidden*, p. 27.

19 William C. Placher, 'Christ Takes Our Place', *Int* 53.1 (1999), pp. 5–20 (8).

20 Girard, *I See*, pp. 154–5.

21 Girard, *Things Hidden*, pp. 205–15.

22 Girard, *Things Hidden*, p. 210.

23 Girard, *I See*, p. 2.

24 'Epilogue: The Anthropology of the Cross: A Conversation with René Girard', in
Williams (ed.), *Girard Reader*, pp. 262–88 (280).

25 Girard, *I See*, p. 155.

26 Placher, 'Christ Takes Our Place', pp. 14–15.
27 Preached by Peter Stevenson at Chatsworth Baptist Church, West Norwood, London, on 10 August 2003.
28 'Hospital boss "forced" to leave', *BBC News, http://news.bbc.co.uk/1/hi/england/2537847.stm* (accessed 8 August 2003).
29 '"Scapegoat" claim over abuse case', *BBC News, http://news.bbc.co.uk/1/hi/scotland/2338259.stm* (accessed 8 August 2003).
30 'Blame culture', *Guardian Unlimited, http://society.guardian.co.uk/socialcarestaff/comment/0,1141,959874,00.html* (accessed 8 August 2003).
31 'Don't blame the scapegoat', *BBC News, http://news.bbc.co.uk/1/hi/uk/1170645.stm* (Accessed 8 August 2003).
32 Derek Tidball, *The Message of the Cross* (Leicester: InterVarsity Press, 2001), p. 72.
33 Tidball, *Message*, p. 74.
34 Hartley, *Leviticus*, p. 241.
35 Tidball, *Message*, p. 74.
36 Ps. 103.11–12.
37 Jn 11.49–50.
38 Heb. 13.12–13.
39 2 Cor. 5.21.
40 Ps. 103.11–12.
41 Lev. 16.29–31.
42 Wenham, *Leviticus*, p. 236.
43 Donald E. Gowan, *Reclaiming the Old Testament for the Christian Pulpit* (Edinburgh: T&T Clark, 1980), pp. 95–9.
44 Gowan, *Reclaiming*, p. 95.
45 Barbara Brown Taylor, 'Bothering God', in Jana Childers (ed.), *Birthing the Sermon: Women Preachers on the Creative Process* (St. Louis: Chalice Press, 2001), pp. 153–68 (156).
46 Taylor, 'Bothering God', p. 157.
47 Taylor, 'Bothering God', p. 157.
48 Balentine, *Leviticus*, p. 138.
49 Some of the hermeneutical issues are helpfully explored in Sidney Greidanus, *Preaching Christ from the Old Testament: A Contemporary Hermeneutical Method* (Grand Rapids, MI: Eerdmans, 1999).
50 The high priestly ministry of Christ is explored further in ch. 10, 'The Final Sacrifice'.

Chapter 3: The suffering of a servant: Isaiah 52.13–53.12

1 The designation 'servant song' applied to this and three earlier passages from Isaiah 40–55 goes back a century to Bernhard Duhm: this separation of these passages from their surrounding context is now widely questioned. See John F. A. Sawyer, *The Fifth Gospel: Isaiah in the History of Christianity* (Cambridge: Cambridge University Press, 1996), p. 187.
2 For a treasure-trove of examples of the varied use of Isaiah in Christian history see Sawyer, *Fifth Gospel*.
3 Dr Christina Baxter, for instance, recently cited Isaiah 53 as one of the main 'drivers' for the conservative evangelical emphasis on 'penal substitution' as the heart of the atonement (Conference on Atonement, High Leigh, UK, July 2004). See further section 3b below.

4   Brevard S. Childs, *Isaiah: A Commentary* (The Old Testament Library; Louisville, KY: Westminster John Knox Press, 2001), p. 420. For a recent re-airing of the 'minimalist' position see C. F. D. Moule, *Forgiveness and Reconciliation and Other New Testament Themes* (London: SPCK, 1998), p. 63. For a fuller picture presenting Isaiah 53 as a crucial part of a web of Scriptural influences on Jesus, see N. T. Wright, *Jesus and the Victory of God* (London: SPCK, 1996), pp. 597–605. Wright stresses that this does not mean that Jesus 'regarded himself as "the servant"', 'as though second-Temple Jews had anticipated modern criticism in separating out the "servant songs" from the rest of Isaiah 40–55, or as though Jesus had created a "role" for himself out of a few texts taken out of context' (p. 603). For an account of how Luke's Gospel may be seen as shaped extensively by the narrative of the 'suffering servant', see David P. Moessner, 'Reading Luke's Gospel as Ancient Hellenistic Narrative: Luke's Narrative Plan of Israel's *Suffering* Messiah as God's Saving "Plan" for the World', in Craig Bartholomew, Joel B. Green and Anthony C. Thiselton (eds.), *Reading Luke: Interpretation, Reflection, Formation* (Milton Keynes: Paternoster; Grand Rapids, MI: Zondervan, forthcoming, 2005).

5   *Isaiah*, pp. 421–2. The most striking citations are in Lk. 22.37; Acts 8.32-35; 1 Pet. 2.21–25. But see also the direct quotations in Mt. 8.17; Jn 12.38; Rom. 10.13; 15.21; and the possible echoes in Mt. 20.28 / Mk 10.45; Acts 3.13, 26; Rom. 4.25; 5.18, 19; 1 Cor. 15.3; 2 Cor. 5.21; Phil. 2.5–11; Hebrews *passim*.

6   Childs, *Isaiah*, p. 422.

7   Sawyer documents such uses in *Fifth Gospel*, pp. 100–25. For some helpful comments on respecting the significance for Judaism, as well as Christianity, of Isaiah 53's portrayal of a God who brings life out of death, see Walter Brueggemann, *Isaiah 40–66* (Westminster Bible Companion; Louisville, KY: Westminster John Knox Press, 1998), pp. 149–50.

8   Cf. Clarke, 'Violence and the Cross', pp. 27f.

9   Childs writes of the analogy between the redemptive activity of the servant and the suffering of Christ as being an 'ontological' one: 'in the suffering and death of the servant of Second Isaiah, the self-same divine reality of Jesus Christ was made manifest' (*Isaiah*, p. 423).

10 Cf. Wright, *Jesus and the Victory of God, passim*.

11 Gunton, *Actuality*, pp. 145–9.

12 For brevity, throughout the rest of this chapter, reference will be made to verses in the song by verse number only – since, conveniently, it begins at v. 13 of chapter 52 and ends at v. 12 of chapter 53.

13 *Isaiah 40–66*, p. 146.

14 The poem contains various textual difficulties, which it is beyond the scope of this chapter to discuss: these are dealt with in the standard commentaries and reflected to some extent in the margins of the modern English versions.

15 Cf. the comment of Brueggemann (*Isaiah 40–66*, p. 146) that to ask who is the 'we' of the song 'from the outside is to miss the intimate, confessional tone of the pronouns. The lines of the poem are permitted on the lips of whoever it is who benefits from this indescribable transformation.'

16 Childs, *Isaiah*, p. 413.

17 The NIV makes this three by changing the Hebrew 'you' into 'the LORD' in the second clause: see further below.

18 The reading 'him' is supported in v. 14 by the Syriac and Targum versions, in v. 10 by the Vulgate; in both cases LXX has 'you'.

19 I italicize the 'our' not because of any linguistic indication in the Hebrew, but because it seems to bring out the thrust of the song's movement.

20 There are also verses where a more complex pattern is visible (see for instance the chiasms in vv. 3, 10 – when a key word of the opening line of the verse is echoed in the final line – 'despised', 'will of the LORD'; also the two balancing 'halves' of v. 7, each with three parallel terms).

21 In his own way, Handel brilliantly captured the weight of this statement in his *Messiah*: after the many playful repetitions of 'All we like sheep' comes the slow, solemn announcement: 'And the Lord has laid on him...'

22 The link between 'violence' and 'deceit' in the second half of v. 9 is also worth pondering.

23 However, Sawyer asserts that Isa. 53.11 clearly implies the servant's *literal* resurrection (*Fifth Gospel*, p. 187); Childs is not so sure (*Isaiah*, p. 419).

24 Cf. the portrayal of Christ in his passion by Vanstone, *Stature*, pp. 1–13, discussed in Clarke, 'Violence and the Cross', pp. 33–4. One can emphasize the passivity of Christ in his last hours while recognizing the strong sense of mission which had propelled him up to that point.

25 On the Hebrew word here,   , see Childs, *Isaiah*, pp. 417–18. He points out that though the word is used in cultic contexts in the Old Testament, it originally arose 'from a secular situation in which compensation for a misdeed was demanded' (p. 418). Thus the song does not depend on a cultic understanding of the servant's offering; rather, it is through a unique act of God that the servant's work is redemptive.

26 Cf. the discussion of the same problem in Ch. 1 above in respect of Genesis 22.

27 For a succinct rebuttal of those who deny that 'vicarious' suffering is to be seen here, see Childs, *Isaiah*, p. 415.

28 Something similar can be said of the statements in vv. 6, 10, 11, 12.

29 Anselm's understanding of the atonement laid itself open to such a reading, although, as Gunton shows, it is possible to read him in a more sympathetic light (*Actuality*, pp. 87–96).

30 See above: undoubtedly the death of Jesus was a judicial act in human terms, but this does not entail that it was 'divine punishment'.

31 On the servant as Israel see Brueggemann, *Isaiah 40–66*, p. 143.

32 One can hold this view and still agree with Childs that the figure portrayed here 'appears in every way to have been a historical personage' and that '[t]he language cannot be rendered metaphorically as the nation without straining the plain sense of the text in a tortuous fashion' (*Isaiah*, p. 414).

33 Cf. Moule, *Forgiveness and Reconciliation*, pp. 35f.

34 This contrasts with an interpretation of the 'song' in the Targums, in which the sufferings of the 'servant', far from being seen as those of the Messiah, are those *inflicted* by the Messiah on his people's oppressors: F. F. Bruce, *This is That: The New Testament Development of Some Old Testament Themes* (Exeter: Paternoster Press, 1968), p. 93.

35 By Kenton C. Anderson, Dean and Associate Professor of Homiletics, Northwest Baptist Seminary, Langley, British Columbia, Canada.

Chapter 4: The crucified God: Mark 15.25–39

[1] Larry W. Hurtado, *Mark* (NIBC, 2; Peabody: Hendrickson, 1989), p. 263.

[2] Craig A. Evans, *Mark 8:27–16:20* (WBC, 34B; Dallas: Word, 2002), p. 501.

[3] Hurtado, *Mark*, p. 276.

[4] Morna D. Hooker, *The Gospel according to Saint Mark* (BNTC; London: A & C Black, 1991), p. 376.

[5] James R. Edwards, *The Gospel according to Mark* (Grand Rapids, MI: Eerdmans, 2002), p. 475.

[6] Gunton, *Actuality*, pp. 165–6.

[7] John Calvin, *Institutes of the Christian Religion* (LCC, 20; ed. J. T. McNeill; Philadelphia: Westminster Press, 1960), II.xvi.11.

[8] Jürgen Moltmann, *The Crucified God* (London: SCM Press, 1974), p. 147.

[9] Moltmann, *Crucified God*, p. 152.

[10] Moltmann, *Crucified God*, p. 242.

[11] Leanne Van Dyk, *The Desire of Divine Love: John McLeod Campbell's Doctrine of the Atonement* (New York: P. Lang, 1995), p. 106.

[12] William C. Placher, *Jesus the Savior: The Meaning of Jesus Christ for Christian Faith* (Louisville, KY: Westminster John Knox Press, 2001), pp. 128–9.

[13] Anthony Clarke, *A Cry in the Darkness: The Forsakenness of Jesus in Scripture, Theology and Experience* (Oxford: Regents/Smith & Helwys, 2002), p. 229.

[14] Hooker, *Mark*, p. 378.

[15] Clarke, *Cry*, p. 28.

[16] Hooker, *Mark*, p. 379.

[17] Martin Luther, 'The Heidelberg Disputation', Thesis XX (LCC, 16; London: SCM Press, 1962), pp. 274–307 (278, 290).

[18] Martin Luther, 'De Servo Arbitrio' (LCC, 17; London: SCM Press, 1969), pp. 99–334 (201).

[19] Alister E. McGrath, *Luther's Theology of the Cross* (Oxford: Blackwell, 1985), p. 166.

[20] Moltmann, *Crucified God*, p. 214, original italics.

[21] Clarke, *Cry*, p. 216.

[22] Moltmann, *Crucified God*, p. 246.

[23] Preached by Peter Stevenson at Rochester Diocese Readers' Training Weekend, Aylesford Priory, Kent, 8 February 2003.

[24] Anna Carter Florence, 'Put Away Your Sword! Taking the Torture out of the Sermon', in M. Graves (ed.), *What's the Matter with Preaching Today?* (Louisville, KY: Westminster John Knox Press, 2004), pp. 93–108 (99).

[25] Eugene L. Lowry, *The Homiletical Plot: The Sermon as Narrative Art Form* (Louisville, KY: Westminster John Knox Press, 2nd edn, 2001).

Chapter 5: Forgiveness from the cross: Luke 23.32–43

[1] I am grateful for comments received on an earlier version of parts of this chapter from Arthur Rowe.

[2] On this subject see James D. G. Dunn, *Jesus and the Spirit: A Study of the Religious and Charismatic Experience of the First Christians as Reflected in the New Testament* (London: SCM Press, 1975).

3 This is not the place for detailed discussion of 'objective' and 'subjective' theories of atonement. For a helpful overview, see Gunton, *Actuality*, pp. 155–67.

4 For helpful discussion of Luke's narrative approach and theology see Joel B. Green, *The Gospel of Luke* (NICNT; Grand Rapids, MI: Eerdmans, 1997) and *The Theology of the Gospel of Luke* (New Testament Theology; Cambridge: Cambridge University Press, 1995). For an excellent summary of the distinctive portraits of Jesus in the Gospels see Richard A. Burridge, *Four Gospels, One Jesus* (London: SPCK, 1994).

5 On this see Wright, *Jesus and the Victory of God*, p. 271.

6 See Green, *Gospel of Luke*, pp. 133–5.

7 Christopher M. Tuckett, *Luke* (New Testament Guides; Sheffield: Sheffield Academic Press, 1996), pp. 61–2. But see also the exploration of the echoes in Luke of the story of King David, in Scott W. Hahn, 'Kingdom and Church in Luke–Acts: From Davidic Christology to Kingdom Ecclesiology', in Bartholomew *et al.* (eds.), *Reading Luke*.

8 See Wright, *Jesus and the Victory of God*, pp. 162–97.

9 ἀφίημι; BDAG sense 2.

10 ἄφεσις.

11 Cf. the helpful exposition of the meaning of forgiveness in L. Gregory Jones, 'Crafting Communities of Forgiveness', *Int* 54.2 (2000), pp. 121–34 (121–26).

12 It is significant that the second half of the petition means literally 'every one that is indebted to us'. Indebtedness is not wholly metaphorical here. Cf. the story of the shrewd manager in 16.1–8, in which the manager gives his master a lead in the cancellation of debt that was probably incurred through illegal interest, knowing instinctively (it seems) that this is the way of hope and renewed relationship in a time of crisis. See Stephen I. Wright, 'Parables on Poverty and Riches', in Richard N. Longenecker (ed.), *The Challenge of Jesus' Parables* (McMaster New Testament Studies, 4; Grand Rapids, MI: Eerdmans, 2000), pp. 217–39, and literature cited there. The steward experiences the dynamic of the petition in the Lord's Prayer: he discovers forgiveness for himself through his release of other 'debtors'. An interesting mirror of this parable is that of the unforgiving servant in Matthew (18.23–35), where the servant *fails* to catch on to the king's surprising spirit of forgiveness.

13 Note that Luke does not even mention Peter's objection to Jesus' talk of his death, and Jesus' rebuke (compare Lk. 9.18–27 with Mk 8.27-38 and Mt. 16.13–18). Tuckett points out that, according to Luke, disciples gave up 'all' in a quite literal sense (5.11, 28; 14.33; 18.22): *Luke*, pp. 96–7.

14 On the close connection between the kingdom established by Jesus in Luke and the identity of the early church as depicted in Acts, see Hahn, 'Kingdom and Church'.

15 The history and significance of these metaphors is explored in Gunton, *Actuality*, pp. 53–82, 83–113 and 115–42 respectively.

16 Jesus directly quotes Isa. 53.12 in Lk. 22.37: 'It is written, "And he was numbered with the transgressors", and I tell you that this must be fulfilled in me', but the echoes in the Gospel are pervasive. See Moessner, 'Reading Luke's Gospel'; Wright, *Jesus and the Victory of God*, pp. 588–91. Cf. Ch. 3 above.

17 It seems significant that the same word is used of this 'testing' as is used of the 'testing' of Jesus by Satan (πειράζω).

18 Many commentators have seen this as the significance of the word πειρασμός here and in the Lord's Prayer, but for a contrary view see Moule, *Forgiveness and Reconciliation*, p. 192.

[19] See Hans Urs von Balthasar, *Mysterium Paschale: The Theology of the Easter Mystery* (Edinburgh: T&T Clark, 1990), p. 100: 'Jesus prays *in* the *peirasmos*, whereas the disciples pray to be preserved *from* it' (original italics). In this scene, of course, the disciples do *not* pray, but the prayer Jesus teaches them here (as in Lk. 11.4, 'lead us not into temptation') is surely precisely the prayer every Christian *can* pray by way of casting ourselves upon the victory of Christ who alone was able to enter the *peirasmos*.

[20] Joel B. Green, 'Jesus on the Mount of Olives (Lk. 22:30–46): Tradition and Theology', *JSNT* 26 (1986), pp. 29–48 (32), alluding to a suggestion of Jerome Neyrey.

[21] 'If the first Passion predictions explicitly mention Resurrection on the third day, and so exaltation after abasement, on the Mount of Olives all such peep-holes into future glorification are walled off': von Balthasar, *Mysterium Paschale*, p. 106.

[22] Childs, *Isaiah*, p. 419.

[23] For more detailed exegesis of Lk. 23:33–43 see Stephen I. Wright, 'Christ the King, Year C', in Roger E. Van Harn (ed.), *The Lectionary Commentary: Theological Exegesis for Sunday's Texts*. III. *The Gospels* (3 vols., Grand Rapids, MI: Eerdmans; London: Continuum, 2001), pp. 455–8.

[24] Cf. Lev. 5.17–19; Num. 15.25–31; Green, *Gospel of Luke*, p. 820.

[25] On Luke–Acts as modelling the preacher's task, see Mary Donovan Turner, 'Disrupting a Ruptured World', in Jana Childers (ed.), *Purposes of Preaching* (St Louis, MI: Chalice Press, 2004), pp. 131–40.

[26] Preached by Stephen Wright at St John the Divine, Selsdon, Greater London, on the feast of Christ the King, 21 November 2004.

[27] Abbreviated from Patrick Murphy, 'Lessons in Love', *Church Times*, 15 October 2004, p. 18.

[28] I preferred the word 'blindfolded' to 'blind' in the sermon. The casual metaphorical use of words like 'blind' in preaching can be demeaning to those with a literal disability. See Kathy Black, *A Healing Homiletic: Preaching and Disability* (Nashville: Abingdon Press, 1996), pp. 57–87. Since preaching the sermon, I have learned from Arthur Rowe of Rembrandt's engraving of *Three Crosses* in which, though the picture is bathed in light, the hardened criminal is blindfolded.

Chapter 6: The Word became flesh: John 1.1–14

[1] A recent illustration of this tendency is J. Ramsey Michaels, 'Atonement in John's Gospel and Epistles', in Charles E. Hill and Frank A. James III (eds.), *The Glory of the Atonement* (Downers Grove: InterVarsity Press, 2004), pp. 106–18. His treatment of the atonement in John's Gospel begins at John 1.29; the Prologue is not taken into account in his exploration of the theme.

[2] Carson, *John*, p. 149.

[3] George R. Beasley-Murray, *John* (WBC, 36; Waco: Word, 1987), p. 16.

[4] Jürgen Moltmann, *The Way of Jesus Christ* (London: SCM Press, 1990), p. 44. Cf. Colin E. Gunton, *Yesterday and Today: A Study of Continuities in Christology* (London: SPCK, 2nd edn, 1997), p. 182: 'The content of Christianity as a gospel about human forgiveness, reconciliation and flourishing is bound up with its Christology. Soteriology cannot be divorced from Christology…'

[5] E.g. in the classic work of Anselm where the life and death of the God-man are of 'infinite value', so that He makes 'ample satisfaction for the sins of the whole world,

and infinitely more': *Cur Deus Homo*, II, xviii.

6 Von Balthasar, *Mysterium Paschale*, pp. 22–3.

7 Athanasius, *The Incarnation of the Word of God: De Incarnatione Verbi Dei* (trans. anon; London: Geoffrey Bles, 1944). See also Athanasius, *Contra Gentes and De Incarnatione* (trans. Robert W. Thomson; Oxford: Clarendon Press, 1971). Citations below are mostly from the 1944 edition.

8 Alasdair I. C. Heron, 'Homoousios with the Father', in Thomas F. Torrance (ed.), *The Incarnation: Ecumenical Studies in the Nicene-Constantinopolitan Creed A.D. 381* (Edinburgh: Handsel Press, 1981), pp. 58–87 (74).

9 Heron, 'Homoousios', p. 72.

10 Thomas F. Torrance, *The Trinitarian Faith: The Evangelical Theology of the Ancient Catholic Church* (Edinburgh: T&T Clark, 1988), p. 149.

11 Athanasius, *De Incarnatione Verbi Dei*, §1, p. 25.

12 Athanasius, *De Incarnatione Verbi Dei*, §1, p. 26.

13 Athanasius, *De Incarnatione Verbi Dei*, §3, p. 28.

14 Athanasius, *De Incarnatione Verbi Dei*, §4, p. 30.

15 Athanasius, *De Incarnatione Verbi Dei*, §5, pp. 30–31.

16 Athanasius, *De Incarnatione Verbi Dei*, §6, p. 32.

17 Athanasius, *De Incarnatione Verbi Dei*, §7, p. 33.

18 Athanasius, *De Incarnatione Verbi Dei*, §8, pp. 33–34.

19 Athanasius, *De Incarnatione Verbi Dei*, §9, p. 35.

20 Athanasius, *De Incarnatione Verbi Dei*, §13, p. 41.

21 George Bebawi, 'Atonement and Mercy: Islam between Athanasius and Anselm', in John Goldingay (ed.), *Atonement Today* (London: SPCK, 1995), pp. 185-202 (190).

22 Athanasius, *De Incarnatione Verbi Dei*, §54. p. 93.

23 Athanasius, *Contra Arianos* 3.19, in 'Four Discourses Against the Arians', in P. Schaff and H. Wace (eds.), *St. Athanasius: Select Works and Letters* (Nicene and Post-Nicene Fathers of the Christian Church, 2nd series, vol. 4; Edinburgh: T&T Clark, 1891), pp. 303–447 (404).

24 Beasley-Murray, *John*, p. 13.

25 See Richard J. Bauckham, *2 Peter, Jude* (WBC, 50; Dallas: Word, 1992), p. 181: '*In what sense* do Christians become "divine"? In view of the background sketched above, it is not very likely that participation in God's own essence is intended. Not participation in *God*, but in the nature of heavenly, immortal beings, is meant. Such beings, in the concepts of Hellenistic Judaism, are *like* God, in that, by his grace, they reflect his glorious, immortal being, but they are "divine" only in the loose sense, inherited from Hellenistic religion, of being god*like* and belonging to the eternal world of "the gods." To share in divine nature is to become immortal and incorruptible (original italics).'

26 Torrance, *Trinitarian Faith*, pp. 156–7.

27 Athanasius, *De Incarnatione Verbi Dei*, §56, p. 95.

28 In Howard Peskett and Vinoth Ramachandra, *The Message of Mission* (Leicester: InterVarsity Press, 2003), p. 86.

29 Stephen W. Sykes, 'Life after Death: The Christian Doctrine of Heaven', in Richard W. A. McKinney (ed.), *Creation, Christ and Culture: Studies in Honour of T.F. Torrance* (Edinburgh: T&T Clark, 1976), pp. 250–71 (262–63).

30 Athanasius, *De Incarnatione Verbi Dei*, §54, p. 93.

31 Athanasius, *De Incarnatione Verbi Dei*, §20, p. 49.

32 Athanasius, *De Incarnatione Verbi Dei*, §54, p. 93.

33 Heron, 'Homoousios', p. 74.

34 Preached by Peter Stevenson at Chatsworth Baptist Church, West Norwood, London, 17 August 2003.

35 Polly Toynbee, *Hard Work: Life in Low-Pay Britain* (London: Bloomsbury, 2003), p. 2.

36 Toynbee, *Hard Work*, p. 12.

37 The enquiry set up under Lord Hutton by the British Government into the circumstances surrounding the death of the Ministry of Defence scientist Dr David Kelly.

38 Von Balthasar, *Mysterium Paschale*, p. 22.

39 Gail O'Day, 'The Gospel of John', in Leander E. Keck (ed.), *The New Interpreter's Bible*, IX; Nashville: Abingdon Press, 1995), pp. 491–865 (525–6).

40 Toynbee, *Hard Work*, p. 239.

41 O'Day, 'John', p. 524.

42 From the hymn by J. Byrom, 'Christians, awake!'

Chapter 7: The achievement of God's justice: Romans 3.21–26

1 The notion of Romans as a 'compendium of Christian doctrine' goes back to the reformer Philipp Melanchthon. See A. Katherine Grieb, *The Story of Romans: A Narrative Defense of God's Righteousness* (Louisville, KY: Westminster John Knox Press, 2002), pp. xvii–xviii.

2 For this summary account, as well as the more detailed exegesis of 3.21–26, I am indebted especially to Grieb, *Story*; N. T. Wright, 'The Letter to the Romans', in Keck (ed.), *The New Interpreter's Bible*, X, pp. 393–770 (especially 395–408, 464–86); and to conversation with my colleague David Southall. None of these, however, should be held responsible for my formulation of the issues, which is my own.

3 Such a distinction was given force by the strong distinction drawn by C. H. Dodd in *The Apostolic Preaching and its Developments* (London: Hodder & Stoughton, 1936), pp. 7–8, between 'evangelism' (the proclamation of the good news to the world) and 'teaching' (the instruction of converts) in the New Testament period.

4 On this see especially Wright, *Romans*, pp. 700–702.

5 For enabling me to see clearly the strong element of theodicy in Paul's argument in Romans – i.e. the dominance of his defence of God's justice in the sense outlined here – I am indebted to David Southall, *The Meaning of δικαιοσύνη Θεοῦ in Paul's Epistle to the Romans* (MTh dissertation; London: Spurgeon's College, 2002).

6 'Faithfulness of Jesus Christ' rather than 'faith in Jesus Christ' is the translation preferred here, and in a number of other places, by various commentators. For this reading of Paul's language see Richard B. Hays, *The Faith of Jesus Christ: The Narrative Substructure of Galatians 3:1–4:11* (Grand Rapids, MI: Eerdmans, 2nd edn, 2002). On Rom. 3.22f. see Wright, *Romans*, p. 469. In this verse, this translation has the advantage of saving Paul from what would be a near-tautology: 'through faith in Jesus Christ for all who have faith'.

7 See further Ch. 5 above.

8 We should also note the likely background of Paul's thinking in the 'sacrifice' of the Maccabaean martyrs, bringing on themselves the wrath of God for his people's sins so that Israel as a whole may be spared (2 Macc. 6.12–16; 7.38; 4 Macc. 6.28–29). In this sense the word ἱλαστήριον is itself used in 4 Macc. 17.22. See Wright, *Romans*, pp. 474–7, where he argues also for Isaiah 40–55 (especially 53) as a key background text for both Maccabees and Romans.

9   Cf. Grieb, *Story*, p. 40.

10 On this see Gunton, *Actuality*, pp. 125–6.

11 See further my comments on Isa. 53.5 in Ch. 3: above. It is important here also in Romans to hold in tension the biblical convictions of divine sovereignty in all human affairs and of human responsibility. God in his sovereignty transfigures the injustice of Jesus' murderers and the faithfulness of Jesus himself so that his death becomes God's great act of atonement. This should not, of course, be taken as implying that God simply acts after the human event; but stating the matter as I have may help to avoid the opposite extreme of a deterministic view of divine sovereignty which allows no room for human freedom.

12 Cf. the summary reflections in Wright, *Romans*, pp. 477–8.

13 For a helpful brief summary of this perspective and the issues it raises see Michael B. Thompson, *The New Perspective on Paul* (Grove Biblical Series, 26; Cambridge: Grove Books, 2002).

14 *Actuality*.

15 By A. Katherine Grieb, Associate Professor of New Testament, Virginia Theological Seminary, Alexandria, Virginia, USA.

16 On Paul's use of 'sin' and 'death' in a personified sense in Romans, seeing them as active powers, see Grieb, *Story*, *passim*, especially pp. 64–6.

17 Robinson Jeffers, *Selected Poems* (New York: Random House, 1965), p. 59.

Chapter 8: The reconciliation of the world: 2 Corinthians 5.11–6.2

1   Here we cannot enter into the complex debates about the background and composition of the letter. C. K. Barrett, *A Commentary on the Second Epistle to the Corinthians* (BNTC; London: A & C Black, 1973), offers a lucid introductory guide (pp. 1–50), though his differentiation between the 'false apostles' and the 'super-apostles' remains controversial. For the larger hermeneutical issues related to our contemporary use of the letter, as opposed to the more narrowly historical ones, Frances M. Young and David F. Ford, *Meaning and Truth in 2 Corinthians* (London: SPCK, 1987) is a useful, perhaps unique, resource. See too the helpful treatment of the narrative dimensions of Paul's letter-writing, focusing especially on 2 Cor. 5.11–6.2, in James W. Thompson, 'Reading the Letters as Narrative', in Joel B. Green and Michael Pasquarello III (eds.), *Narrative Reading, Narrative Preaching: Reuniting New Testament Interpretation and Proclamation* (Grand Rapids, MI: Baker Academic, 2003), pp. 81–105.

2   On the meaning of this verse see further the end of section 3 below.

3   It is widely suggested that even the picture of the 'triumphal procession' may have an ironic twist; Paul may be picturing himself as one of the *captives* in God's train. Barrett, however, regards Paul as picturing himself as 'one of the victorious general's soldiers' (*Commentary*, p. 98). Whichever way the image is interpreted, it clearly fits with the paradoxical vision of his ministry which Paul is setting forth: God's purposes are advancing triumphantly, but through the most unlikely means.

4   Thompson points out that Paul's suffering is linked to that of Jesus and that of Isaiah's 'suffering servant' through the use of the verb παραδίδωμι, 'hand over': see, e.g., 2 Cor. 4.11; Mt. 20.18, 19; Rom. 8.32; Is. 53.6, 12 (LXX) (*Reading*, pp. 93–4). Thompson's chapter points to many illuminating parallels between Paul's message in 2 Corinthians and that of Isa. 40–66.

5   The 'fear of the LORD' is to be understood from its background in the Old Testament as the quality of reverence, adoration, submission and obedience which is the appropriate posture of the creature before the Creator, and from which springs all wisdom (Ps. 111.10, etc.).

6   There has been much debate about the meaning of the Greek preposition ὑπέρ, usually translated simply by the ambiguous English 'for'. BDAG indicates the range of usage of this word when followed by the genitive case. Although in general it indicates 'for the sake of', meaning 'in the interest of' someone or something or 'on account of' a prior cause, it can mean 'in place of' or 'instead of'. BDAG places the usages in 2 Cor. 5.14f. among those where this latter meaning merges with the broader sense of 'for the sake of'.

7   I use this word in preference to 'representative'. The latter, although often paired with 'substitutionary' in discussions of the atonement, seems inadequately to convey the sense of passages like this with their strong assertion that this was truly a 'corporate' death. In other words, the word 'representative' often nearly collapses into a synonym for 'substitute'. Moreover, the meaning 'in place of' for the preposition ὑπέρ (see n. 6 above) is put in the same category as 'in the name of' by BDAG, which states that the expression ὑπὲρ αὐτοῦ is often used in the papyri 'to explain that the writer is writing "as the representative of" an illiterate person'. Thus the major New Testament lexicon itself discourages us from drawing a sharp distinction between 'substitute' and 'representative', at least as far as the key word ὑπέρ is concerned.

8   A most eloquent exponent of the theory was John Owen in *The Death of Death in the Death of Christ* (Edinburgh: Banner of Truth Trust, reprint edn, 1983), which was first published in 1650. See especially his discussion of the biblical usage of the words 'world' and 'all' on pp. 191–247. On 2 Cor. 5.14, 15 see pp. 238–40; on v. 19 see pp. 227–8). There is undoubtedly a tension in Paul's thought and language in the present passage between his vision of the universality of what God has done, and is doing, and his perception that it is in the Church, those who are 'in Christ', that his new creation is visible (v. 17). Thompson resolves the tension by suggesting that when Paul writes 'world' (v. 19) he means not the cosmos but 'humanity that has been alienated by sin' (*Reading*, p. 102). But an ultimate cosmic purpose of God is surely in view, not least because of the language of 'new creation', and I believe we stay closer to Paul if the tension is maintained. Indeed, such a tension seems to be required by Thompson's very convincing account of the narrative dynamics of Paul's argument: Paul looks towards an 'end' of the story, assured by God's sovereignty and Christ's work, but is caught up in the middle of it, appealing to the Corinthians to be reconciled to God (v. 20) and unsure of the outcome.

9   A comparison with Jn 15.18–21 is suggestive here.

10 On the background in Isa. 40–66 of 'new creation' here, see Thompson, *Reading*, pp. 100-101.

11 Barrett, *Commentary*, p. 175. For an excellent study of reconciliation, which includes discussion of this passage, see Miroslav Volf, 'The Social Meaning of Reconciliation', *Int* 54.2 (2000), pp. 158–72.

12 Volf underlines both the need to see 'justice' as embraced by 'reconciliation', and the need for 'reconciliation' to be conceived in inter-human as well as divine–human terms ('Social Meaning'). He thus counters both socio-political movements which put 'liberation' on a higher plane than 'reconciliation', and some Christian tendencies to conceive 'reconciliation' in purely individualistic, 'vertical' terms. He points out how with Paul on the Damascus road, Jesus 'named the injustice and

resisted the behaviour' but 'did so in the very act of offering reconciliation'; and that through Jesus' identification of *himself* as the one being persecuted (Acts 9.4–5) it is clear that enmity against human beings is inseparably bound up with enmity against God, and thus reconciliation with God *entails* reconciliation with human beings (pp. 165–6).

13 The word again is ὑπέρ, and it carries again the same suggestive mixture of overtones: 'for the benefit of', 'in place of'. One might say that just as Christ died as both substitute for and representative of all, so now Paul, his fellow-apostles and by extension the whole Church act as substitutes for and representatives of Christ.

14 I am grateful for conversation on this point with Dr N. T. Wright.

15 P. T. Forsyth, *Positive Preaching and the Modern Mind* (Carlisle: Paternoster, 1998 [1907]), p. 51.

16 Cf. Thompson's comment: 'The task of the preacher is not to explain this dense argument in detail, but to provide the opportunity for the congregation to enter into this ancient story of selfless love, recognizing that our community listens to many alternative stories that shape our understanding of the church's identity and mission' (*Reading*, p. 105).

17 By David J. Schlafer, author and homiletics teacher, Washington, DC, USA.

18 Eugene L. Lowry, 'Surviving the Sermon Preparation Process', *Journal for Preachers* 24.3 (Easter 2001), pp. 28–32 (29).

Chapter 9: The decisive victory: Colossians 2.8–15

1 Robert Webber, *Ancient-Future Faith: Rethinking Evangelicalism for a Postmodern World* (Grand Rapids, MI: Baker Books, 1999), p. 43, original italics.

2 Aulén, *Christus Victor*.

3 Webber, *Ancient-Future Faith*, p. 67.

4 James D. G. Dunn, *The Epistles to the Colossians and to Philemon: A Commentary on the Greek Text* (Carlisle: Paternoster, 1996), p. 35.

5 Dunn, *Colossians and Philemon*, p. 150.

6 Peter T. O'Brien, *Colossians, Philemon* (WBC, 44; Milton Keynes: Word, 1987), p. 125.

7 O'Brien, *Colossians, Philemon*, p. 126.

8 Dunn, *Colossians and Philemon*, p. 170.

9 Webber, *Ancient-Future Faith*, p. 67.

10 Martin Luther, *Lectures on Galatians 1535* (Luther's Works, 26; St. Louis: Concordia, 1963), p. 280.

11 Luther, *Lectures on Galatians 1535*, p. 282.

12 Luther, *Lectures on Galatians 1535*, p. 310.

13 'The law humbles us, grace exalts us. The law works fear and wrath, grace works hope and mercy. Through the law comes knowledge of sin. Through the knowledge of sin comes humility, and through humility grace is acquired. In this way, when God makes a man a sinner that he may make him righteous, God is bringing in his strange work that he may in the end bring in his proper work' (Luther, 'Heidelberg Disputation', p. 289).

14 McGrath, *Luther's Theology*, p. 155.

15 We might reflect profitably on the way in which God's test of Abraham in Genesis 22 could be seen as an *Anfechtung* (see Ch. 1 above).

[16] Martin Luther, 'Lectures on the Epistle to the Hebrews 1517–18' (LCC, 16; London: SCM Press, 1962), pp. 19–250 (59).

[17] Gunton, *Actuality*, pp. 58–9. Cf. Ch. 5 above.

[18] Gunton, *Actuality*, pp. 71–2.

[19] Placher, *Jesus the Savior*, p. 147.

[20] Placher, *Jesus the Savior*, p. 149.

[21] Robert Sherman, *King, Priest, and Prophet: A Trinitarian Theology of Atonement* (New York and London: T&T Clark International, 2004). See also Geoffrey Wainwright, *For Our Salvation: Two Approaches to the Work of Christ* (Grand Rapids, MI: Eerdmans, 1997).

[22] Calvin, *Institutes*, II. xv.3.

[23] Calvin, *Institutes*, II. xvi.6.

[24] Calvin, *Institutes*, II. xv.3.

[25] Calvin, *Institutes*, II. xv.3.

[26] Calvin, *Institutes*, II. xv.4.

[27] Calvin, *Institutes*, II. xv.5.

[28] Webber, *Ancient-Future Faith*, p. 60.

[29] Preached by Peter Stevenson at Elm Road Baptist Church, Beckenham, Kent, 26 October 2003.

[30] Tidball, *Message*, p. 257.

[31] Afua Kuma, *Jesus of the Deep Forest: Prayers and Praises of Afua Kuma* (Accra: Asempa Press, 1981), pp. 6, 7, 9, 18.

[32] Article in *Baptist Times*, 21 August 2003.

[33] Cf. the emphasis of Mike Graves on catching the 'music' of a text in *The Sermon as Symphony: Preaching the Literary Forms of the New Testament* (Valley Forge: Judson Press, 1997).

Chapter 10: The final sacrifice: Hebrews 9.11–14

[1] Lowry, 'Surviving', p. 29.

[2] Thomas G. Long, *Hebrews* (Louisville: John Knox Press, 1997), p. 3.

[3] Commentary on Heb. 6.19. John Calvin, *The Epistle of Paul the Apostle to the Hebrews and the First and Second Epistles of St. Peter* (Grand Rapids, MI: Eerdmans, 1963), p. 87.

[4] Anselm, *Cur Deus Homo*, I, xi.

[5] Anselm, *Cur Deus Homo*, II, xiv.

[6] Anselm, *Cur Deus Homo*, II, xviii.

[7] John Owen, *The Works of John Owen*, III (ed. W. H. Goold; London: Banner of Truth, 1965), pp. 177–8.

[8] Owen, *Works*, p. 180.

[9] Calvin, *Institutes*, II.xvi.5. Cf. II.xvi.12. 'As if he could atone for our sins in any other way than by obeying the Father!' See also E. David Willis, *Calvin's Catholic Christology: The Function of the So-called Extra Calvinisticum in Calvin's Theology* (Leiden: E. J. Brill, 1966), p. 85: 'What is saving in Christ's teaching, miracles, and death is not simply that they occurred, but that they occurred voluntarily. The heart of the reconstituting act is the free obedience of the Second Adam which displaces the willful disobedience of the first Adam, and frees the members of the Second Adam for new obedience in place of their inherited disobedience.'

[10] William Lane, *Hebrews 9–13* (WBC, 47B; Dallas: Word, 1991), p. 238.

11 Lane, *Hebrews 9–13*, p. 240.

12 Robert Sherman, *King, Priest, and Prophet*, p. 209.

13 Paul Ellingworth, *The Epistle to the Hebrews: A Commentary on the Greek Text* (Carlisle: Paternoster, 1993), p. 453.

14 Fred B. Craddock, 'The Letter to the Hebrews' in Leander E. Keck (ed.), *The New Interpreter's Bible* (Nashville: Abingdon Press, 1998), XII, pp. 1–173 (107).

15 Hugh Montefiore, *A Commentary on the Epistle to the Hebrews* (BNTC; London: A & C Black, 1964), pp. 154–5.

16 Ellingworth, *Hebrews*, p. 457.

17 Owen, *Works*, III, pp. 176–80.

18 Jürgen Moltmann, *The Trinity and the Kingdom of God* (London: SCM Press, 1981), pp. 82–3.

19 Sherman, *King, Priest, and Prophet*, p. 217.

20 John McLeod Campbell, *The Nature of the Atonement* (London: Macmillan, 6th edn, 1906), p. 130.

21 N. T. Wright, *Following Jesus: Biblical Reflections on Discipleship* (London: SPCK, 1994), p. 8.

22 Craddock, 'Hebrews', p. 108.

23 Tidball, *Message*, p. 263.

24 James B. Torrance, *Worship, Community and the Triune God of Grace* (Downers Grove: InterVarsity Press, 1996), p. 59.

25 Preached by Peter Stevenson at Rochester Diocese Readers' Training Weekend, Aylesford Priory, Kent, 5 March 2005.

26 David J. Schlafer, *Surviving the Sermon: A Guide to Preaching for Those who Have to Listen* (Boston: Cowley Publications, 1992), p. 63.

27 Schlafer, *Surviving*, p. 65, original italics.

Indices

Index of Names

Index of Subjects

Some words and concepts are so pervasive in the theme of this book that it was felt little would be gained by indexing them. These include sacrifice, death, and grace.

201

Index of Biblical References

Old Testament

New Testament